Pro Single Page Application Development

Using Backbone.js and ASP.NET

Gil Fink

Ido Flatow

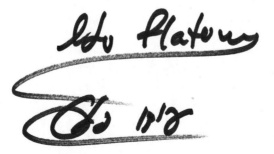

Apress·

Pro Single Page Application Development: Using Backbone.js and ASP.NET

ISBN-13 (pbk): 978-1-4302-6673-0

ISBN-13 (electronic): 978-1-4302-6674-7

President and Publisher: Paul Manning
Lead Editor: Gwenan Spearing
Technical Reviewers: Konstantin Tarkus and Fabio Claudio Ferracchiati
Development Editor: Anne Marie Walker
Editorial Board: Steve Anglin, Mark Beckner, Ewan Buckingham, Gary Cornell, Louise Corrigan, Jim DeWolf, Jonathan Gennick, Jonathan Hassell, Robert Hutchinson, Michelle Lowman, James Markham, Matthew Moodie, Jeff Olson, Jeffrey Pepper, Douglas Pundick, Ben Renow-Clarke, Dominic Shakeshaft, Gwenan Spearing, Matt Wade, Steve Weiss
Coordinating Editor: Christine Ricketts
Copy Editors: Michael G. Laraque and Christine Dahlin
Compositor: SPi Global
Indexer: SPi Global
Artist: SPi Global
Cover Designer: Anna Ishchenko

Distributed to the book trade worldwide by Springer Science+Business Media New York, 233 Spring Street, 6th Floor, New York, NY 10013. Phone 1-800-SPRINGER, fax (201) 348-4505, e-mail orders-ny@springer-sbm.com, or visit www.springeronline.com. Apress Media, LLC is a California LLC and the sole member (owner) is Springer Science + Business Media Finance Inc (SSBM Finance Inc). SSBM Finance Inc is a Delaware corporation.

For information on translations, please e-mail rights@apress.com, or visit www.apress.com.

Apress and friends of ED books may be purchased in bulk for academic, corporate, or promotional use. eBook versions and licenses are also available for most titles. For more information, reference our Special Bulk Sales–eBook Licensing web page at www.apress.com/bulk-sales.

Any source code or other supplementary material referenced by the author in this text is available to readers at www.apress.com. For detailed information about how to locate your book's source code, go to www.apress.com/source-code/.

*Dedicated to my lovely wife, Liora, and my wonderful kids,
Oron, Eyal, and Noya*

— Gil Fink

*To Rotem, my baby boy, may your joy know no bounds as you grow up,
just as it now fills your day*

— Ido Flatow

In memory of Noam Sheffer, a polymath, a colleague, and a dear friend

Contents at a Glance

Contents

About the Authors

Gil Fink is a web development expert and Microsoft ASP.NET/IIS MVP. He works as a senior consultant and architect at SELA Group. He is currently consulting for various enterprises and companies, where he helps to develop web and RIA-based solutions. He conducts lectures and workshops for individuals and enterprises that want to specialize in infrastructure and web development. He is also a coauthor of several Microsoft Official Courses (MOCs) and training kits and the founder of Front-End.IL Meetup. You can read his publications on his blog at `http://blogs.microsoft.co.il/gilf`.

Ido Flatow is a senior architect and trainer at SELA Group, a Microsoft ASP.NET/IIS MVP, and an expert on Microsoft Azure and web technologies such as WCF, ASP.NET, and IIS. Ido is a coauthor of Microsoft Official Courses for WCF 4 (10263A) and Building Web Services for Windows Azure (20487B), coauthor of the book *Pro .NET Performance*, and the manager of the Israeli Web Developers User Group. You can follow Ido's work on his blog at `http://blogs.microsoft.co.il/blogs/idof` and on Twitter: @IdoFlatow.

About the Technical Reviewers

Konstantin Tarkus runs a small software consulting company, and over the last 10 years, he has helped multiple companies and tech startups to design their custom web and cloud applications on top of the Microsoft Web Platform. He is a strong proponent of the single page application (SPA) model and thinks that this book will be a valuable reference for web application developers interested in developing SPAs.

Fabio Claudio Ferracchiati is a senior consultant and a senior analyst/developer using Microsoft technologies. He works for Brain Force (`www.brainforce.com`) in its Italian branch (`www.brainforce.it`). He is a Microsoft Certified Solution Developer for .NET, a Microsoft Certified Application Developer for .NET, a Microsoft Certified Professional, and a prolific author and technical reviewer. Over the past ten years, he's written articles for Italian and international magazines and coauthored more than ten books on a variety of computer topics.

Acknowledgments

We would like to thank our reviewers, **Konstantin Tarkus** and **Fabio Claudio Ferracchiati**, who provided a lot of valuable feedback for each chapter in the book. They also helped to make the text very accurate, and we thank them for that.

Thanks to our colleagues and coworkers at SELA Group who took the time to review our early drafts and provide notes and corrections. Special thanks to Sasha Goldstein, SELA CTO, who was responsible for a lot of valuable feedback that improved the book's content.

Thanks to our family and friends, who waited patiently for us to finish writing and supported us in the process. Your support kept us going and helped us finish the book on time.

And last, we both wish to give our sincerest thanks to the people at Apress who made this book a reality. We would like to thank Gwenan Spearing for her guidance and help, Christine Ricketts for coordination and support, Christine Dahlin and Michael G. Laraque for copyediting, and Dhaneesh Kumar for helping the book get into production.

Introduction

One of the most important and exciting trends in web development in recent years is the move toward single page applications, or SPAs. Instead of clicking through hyperlinks and waiting for each page to load, the user loads a site once, and all the interactivity is handled fluidly by a rich JavaScript front end.

Most single page application development is done on the front end, as opposed to traditional web applications, which use server-side interactions and server-side render engines to do the same. This transition helps to create a more fluid user experience (UX) and makes web applications resemble desktop applications. Major web applications such as Gmail and Google Docs are implemented as SPAs, demonstrating that SPAs are the way to write your future web applications and not merely a transient trend.

As SPAs become the *de facto* standard of web application development, this book will be your one-stop shop for creating fluid, modern applications on the Web.

About This Book

This book will suit professional web developers familiar with HTML and JavaScript who wish to learn more. Readers will require experience with .NET and C# in order to follow along with Part III, which covers back-end development with ASP.NET Web API, but most of the content covers JavaScript.

What Do You Need to Know Before You Read This Book?

You need to have a good understanding of HTML and JavaScript, ideally from creating rich web apps. You need to understand the DOM API, know how events work, and have a solid grasp of the HTML elements and their DOM object counterparts. We will explain a lot about techniques to create object-oriented JavaScript and modular JavaScript, but we are not covering basic JavaScript.

How This Book Is Structured

This book is divided into four parts. Part I lays the groundwork for SPA development. You'll master some JavaScript techniques that will be useful later on and get to know the building blocks of a single page application, including modules, routing, and MV* frameworks.

In Part II, you'll build the client for your application. This is where the magic happens, as we take you through the process step by step. Backbone.js is the ideal library for demonstrating SPA development in practice, but in your future applications, you can apply the same principles with other frameworks.

Part III takes you through the process of building the server side of your application, using ASP.NET Web API, and hooking up the two parts of your application to create a working whole.

SPA development also comes with its own particular challenges, including tracking history, user interface performance, and how to handle search engine optimization. In Part IV, we guide you through some of these issues and advanced techniques and conclude by showing you how to deploy your application.

Part I: The Road to Single Page Application Development

Chapter 1: Introducing Single Page Applications (SPAs)

The book starts with an introduction to single page applications in which we explain the history and how we got to develop SPAs in the first place. In this chapter, you will learn how it all started and what the milestones were that led to contemporary web development.

Chapter 2: JavaScript for SPAs

This chapter explains in detail numerous critical JavaScript techniques that are essential for building SPAs. You will mainly learn how to create object oriented JavaScript and how to use it professionally. At the end of the chapter, we cover ECMAScript and explore future developments in ECMAScript 6.

Chapter 3: Modular JavaScript Development

Modular JavaScript is crucial for dividing your SPA into smaller parts that are maintainable and reusable. In this chapter, you will get to know a lot of patterns to create modular JavaScript. You will also learn about RequireJS library and how it can help you to create modular JavaScript.

Chapter 4: SPA Concepts and Architecture

In this chapter, you will learn about the building blocks of an SPA. You will be exposed to MV* and its influence on today's JavaScript writing. You will learn about routing, template engines, and crucial HTML5 JavaScript APIs that will help you to create your SPA. At the end of the chapter, we will also explain SPA architecture concepts.

Part II: Building the Front End

Chapter 5: Getting Started with Backbone.js

Backbone.js is the library that we use in this book. It is very small, and it is mostly used to impose structure in your code. In this chapter, you will get to know Backbone.js, and you will learn how to use its API to enforce structure and to create a more modular and reusable front end.

Chapter 6: Creating a Single Page Application Step by Step

Once you have the set of tools to create an SPA, you will create an SPA step by step. In this chapter, you will combine all the knowledge that you learned in the first five chapters and will build TheAgency, an SPA. You will create an SPA that works without a back end, and later in the book, you will see how to refactor it to work against a back end.

Part III: Building the Back End

Chapter 7: Creating a Back-End Service with ASP.NET Web API

Most SPAs are powered by a back-end service, which is usually developed as an HTTP-based service. In this chapter, you will learn how to create an SPA back-end service using ASP.NET Web API, a framework for developing HTTP-based services. This chapter will cover the basics of ASP.NET Web API and will take you through the steps of creating a set of services for the TheAgency SPA you created in Chapter 6.

Chapter 8: Implementing HTTP Concepts with ASP.NET Web API

When creating HTTP-based services, there are many features of HTTP that you can take advantage of, such as content negotiation and caching. In this chapter, you will learn some of the not-so-basic features of HTTP—content negotiation, caching, versioning, and streaming—and how to implement them with ASP.NET Web API. You will then use what you learned to extend the TheAgency SPA, to add more functionality to its back-end services.

Chapter 9: Communication Between Front and Back End

Once you've learned how to create a back-end service using ASP.NET Web API, you will learn how the front end can communicate with the back end. In this chapter, you will be shown both how to use Ajax and how to use it with the Backbone.js library. Later, you will refactor TheAgency to work with the back end you built in Chapters 7 and 8. At the end of the chapter, we discuss other communication options, such as Web Sockets, Server-Sent Events, and more.

Part IV: Advanced SPA Topics

Chapter 10: JavaScript Unit Testing

This chapter explains in details how to unit test JavaScript. We start by explaining what Behavior Driven Development (BDD) is. Later, you will get to know the Jasmine library, which is a BDD JavaScript library that will help you to create tests for your JavaScript code. At the end of the chapter, we create tests for TheAgency application.

Chapter 11: SPA Performance Tuning

Performance tuning is a crucial process when you create a web application. It helps you provide a better experience for your users, who won't need to wait for things to happen. In this chapter, you will have an opportunity to learn a lot of techniques to improve your performance, both in the front end and the back end.

Chapter 12: Search Engine Optimization for SPAs

SPAs are mostly created in the front end, using JavaScript. JavaScript itself is very difficult to optimize for search engines. In this chapter, you will learn what a search engine crawler is and how to use techniques to make an SPA optimal for search engines.

Chapter 13: SPA Deployment

In this, the last chapter of the book, you will learn the last step of SPA—deploying the application and its back-end service. You will also learn some of the familiar techniques used to deploy web applications and services to remote servers, whether they are hosted on-premises, in private, or in the public cloud.

PART I

The Road to Single Page Application Development

CHAPTER 1

■ ■ ■

Introducing Single Page Applications

A single page application (SPA) is a web application that uses only one HTML web page as a shell for all the application's web pages and whose end-user interactions are implemented by using JavaScript, HTML, and CSS. Most of the SPA development is done on the front end as opposed to traditional web applications that rely heavily on web server interactions and that reload new web pages whenever navigation occurs. SPAs resemble native applications in their behavior and development but they run inside a browser process as opposed to native applications, which run in their own process. In order to understand why SPA development is so trendy today, we need to understand the changes that happened in the web environment that led to today's SPAs. In this chapter you will learn a little bit about web development history and reasons to build SPAs in the first place.

How the Web Has Evolved

In 1990, Tim Berners-Lee successfully implemented HTML and HTTP, creating the world wide web (WWW) as we know it today. At first, web sites were just a bunch of HTML web pages presented in a browser. The content presented in the web pages was static and included mainly text and images. The web pages were connected through links, and navigation from one page to another resulted in full-page refreshes. Later on, server-side scripting languages like PHP and Active Server Pages (ASP) were invented to enable the creation of dynamic web pages. The dynamic web pages were created on the server side and then sent in the response to the client. This ability enabled web developers to develop more sophisticated web applications that could react to user interactions.

Around 1996 JavaScript was introduced as a client-side scripting language. JavaScript could help to create client-side logic, and it introduced a new option to create dynamic web pages. But most of the web developers in those days developed server-centric web sites and couldn't see the full potential of JavaScript as a programming language. JavaScript was used only to dynamically change the user interface (UI) of a web page. The user experience in those days was horrible, due to factors like slow browsers and slow Internet connections, mainly because every operation in a page resulted in posting back to the server and refreshing the whole page.

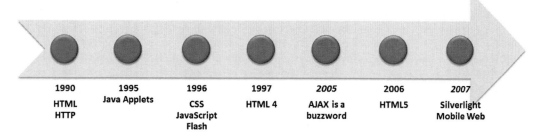

Figure 1-1. *A rough timeline of web evolution*

The shift came around the year 2000 when Flash and Java applets started to gain a lot of attention. You could (and still can) host an embedded Flash or Java object inside a single web page and it can give you a hosting environment for all the user interaction. Working with Flash or Java resembles working on a native application and helps to create a richer user experience. On the other hand, Flash and Java have major flaws–they are third-party browser plug-ins that need stand-alone installation and security consideration. Moreover, it doesn't feel natural to build web applications with plug-ins. Around 2007, Silverlight, another browser plug-in, was introduced by Microsoft to offer yet another option to create rich Internet applications (RIAs). This time you could write a RIA using a .NET environment, which is hosted in the browser. Silverlight didn't get a lot of adoption because of the same Flash and Java plug-in flaw.

Another way of creating an application within a single web page was to create a web page with an embedded iframe HTML element. In that option, the web page wasn't refreshing all the time when server interaction occurred on the iframe surface, and refreshes happened only in the iframe surface. This solution imposed security problems (cross-domain issues, for example), and it wasn't good enough since you still had the same refresh problem but this time only in one section of your web page. Moreover, as a developer you had to maintain both the hosting application and the hosted application and had to find ways to communicate between the hosting and hosted applications. That and other problems made the iframe solution very problematic and developers preferred to avoid it if they could.

JavaScript, as opposed to the plug-ins discussed previously, is part of the browser. It doesn't require additional runtime like Flash, Java, and .NET and that is one of its huge advantages. You don't need to embed JavaScript in the web page. Also, JavaScript can change the whole look and feel of a web page without the need to refresh a section in the web page like in the iframe option. JavaScript doesn't introduce extra security concerns like browser plug-ins. But JavaScript wasn't mature enough, and the browser render and JavaScript engines weren't fast enough in those days. These facts helped plug-ins like Flash to be widely adopted and created a bad name for JavaScript.

The Ajax Revolution

One of the turning points for the evolution of JavaScript happened around 2005 when Asynchronous JavaScript and XML (in short, Ajax) started to emerge as a standard for web application creation. Ajax wasn't a new technology or a revolutionary product; it was just a combination of development techniques and the XMLHttpRequest object. What made Ajax so attractive was the ability to make asynchronous requests to a remote server and then render only one section of the web page. Doing asynchronous operations resulted in better responsiveness. Asynchronous operations don't block the UI, which stays responsive for other user interactions, and when the operation ends a callback can refresh the relevant part of the web page.

Google was one of the first companies to understand the full potential of Ajax and used it in Gmail and Google Maps. Gmail and Google Maps made such an impact that the development techniques used in them became the standard to develop web applications and the World Wide Web Consortium (W3C) turned the XMLHttpRequest object, the main Ajax object, into a web standard.

Later on, JavaScript Document Object Model (DOM) libraries like jQuery and Prototype were created, and creating JavaScript-driven applications became easier. Those libraries included abstraction on top of JavaScript and the DOM and also had utility functions that helped to create Ajax operations in fewer lines of code. Those reasons helped developers to increase their productivity and made front-end development much faster and less prone to common pitfalls. I do remember the days that I wrote raw Ajax functionality, and, trust me, that wasn't a nice experience at all. When I first used jQuery I remember thinking that my development life just became so easy.

The combination of libraries and Ajax helped to reduce the barrier of writing JavaScript. Companies like Microsoft or Yahoo, for example, started to be involved in some of the major libraries, and that helped the libraries to be accepted by the developers' community. Today, a lot of integrated development environments (IDEs) offer web application starter templates that include some of the major libraries like jQuery in Visual Studio, for example.

HTML5 and JavaScript

Another turning point that helped JavaScript to become the language it is today was the next version of the HTML standard, HTML5, which started being developed around 2006. The first public working draft of the HTML5 specification was published in 2008. HTML5 included a lot of new additions to the modern web that are more specific to the JavaScript language. HTML5 includes ways to handle communication, graphics, multimedia, and more, and JavaScript takes a big role in those specifications. HTML5 helped to drive the browser vendors to improve their JavaScript engines. Due to that, today we have faster and hardware-accelerated browsers. Moreover, JavaScript engines can run server technologies like NodeJS and Meteor, which make JavaScript more valuable for developers.

Around 2006 two different groups, W3C and Web Hypertext Application Technology Working Group (WHATWG), cooperated to create a new HTML standard based on HTML4. HTML4 hadn't had a revision since 1997 and it didn't fit with the evolving modern web. The new standard, HTML5, included many new HTML elements like video and audio in order to minimize the dependency on browser plug-ins. Also, the standard included more than 50 (and still counting) new application programming interfaces (APIs) to enable a lot of missing functionality that the modern web needed. For example, you can create pixel graphics by embedding a canvas element in your web page and drawing on it using JavaScript code. You can incorporate multimedia as part of the web page without the need for plug-ins like Flash. You can create bidirectional communication channel with servers by using Web Sockets. All of these new features and more helped to shape today's modern applications.

Another important feature included in HTML5 is the ability to use the device APIs to access hardware devices with JavaScript. For example, with the geolocation JavaScript API you can use the underlying GPS (if available in your device) or the `navigator.getUserMedia` JavaScript function can get data from webcams or microphones in your device. The option to use devices helped the adoption of JavaScript as a platform for creating mobile applications.

The Mobile Web and JavaScript

The last turning point in favor of JavaScript was the mobile web evolution. In the last few years, smartphones and tablets became the main devices that we use in our daily life. Those devices run different operating systems like Android and iOS, which require different application development skills and knowledge. One of the ways to create real cross-platform applications is to create a web application. Web applications are platform agnostic because they are hosted in a browser. You can find browsers in any platform and this is why web applications can help application vendors to reach more users.

With HTML5 and the new JavaScript APIs it is simpler to develop mobile-oriented web applications. You can use responsive web design to change the application look and feel, according to the device resolution or screen width and height. You can use JavaScript APIs to understand orientation, location, and touch events. You can use development platforms, such as PhoneGap, to wrap your web application in an app container and deploy it to app stores.

Moreover, it became very common for vendors to create operating systems that are based on JavaScript or that use JavaScript as one of the main development languages. Windows 8, for example, incorporated JavaScript as a language to develop Windows Store apps. Firefox OS and Chrome OS also use JavaScript as a language to develop against the operating system. The change is happening today and JavaScript is becoming much more powerful than ever.

On the other hand, JavaScript is still not mature enough as a development language and it misses a lot of abilities that developers expect. Changes to the language itself are on the way with ECMAScript 6, which is the next specification version of JavaScript. Until ECMAScript 6 is released, there are two options: writing hardcore JavaScript or using JavaScript preprocessors to generate your JavaScript code.

JavaScript Preprocessors

JavaScript currently doesn't include a lot of language features that developers expect like modules, classes, and interfaces. In order to mimic those language features you have to structure your JavaScript code very well. Lacking to do that often results in unmaintainable JavaScript applications that include very elusive bugs.

One way to avoid the JavaScript maturity problem is to use JavaScript preprocessors. JavaScript preprocessors are languages and a set of tools that compile what you write into JavaScript. The preprocessors use industrial JavaScript good practices to generate the JavaScript for you from your language of choice. Once you go down the preprocessors path, you write code in another language, which includes features like modules and classes and then compiless it into JavaScript.

There are a lot of JavaScript preprocessors and some of them are very popular. The following are some examples:

- CoffeeScript: `http://coffeescript.org/`
  A custom language that has Ruby-like syntax and could be a natural fit for Ruby developers. CoffeeScript was released in 2009 and is very popular. The CoffeeScript author, Jeremy Ashkenas, is also the author of Backbone.js, which is used in this book as an MV* framework.

- Dart: `https://www.dartlang.org/`
  Another less popular custom language that compiles into JavaScript. Dart was released in 2011 and it is currently developed by Google.

- Google Web Toolkit (GWT): `http://www.gwtproject.org/`
  Google released GWT in 2006. It is a set of tools that enables you to write Java code and then generate JavaScript from that code. Google used GWT to develop Gmail and other known Google products.

- TypeScript: `http://www.typescriptlang.org/`
  A JavaScript superset language that adds to JavaScript missing language features and generates JavaScript code from the written TypeScript code. TypeScript was created by Microsoft and was released at the end of 2012.

Once you decide to create an SPA and your developers aren't familiar with JavaScript, you can take the JavaScript preprocessors path in order to create the front end. In our opinion, writing native JavaScript is preferable to using JavaScript preprocessors. The main reason is that once you are a JavaScript novice and you are aware of the language pitfalls JavaScript preprocessors don't add a real value. Even so, JavaScript preprocessors are very popular today and they are an alternative that you need to be aware of.

Now that we covered a little bit of history and you learned about major milestones in JavaScript, our next step will be to compare different application types.

Comparing Application Types

The combination of Ajax, HTML5, and the mobile web helped to lead to the evolution of JavaScript and made JavaScript a more popular language today. They also helped to create new techniques to build modern web applications, of which SPAs are one. Before we explore SPA characteristics, we will first explore traditional web applications and native applications. Later on, we will be able to make a comparison among all three options.

Traditional Web Applications

Since the creation of web servers and server-side scripting languages like PHP and ASP, developers have been able to write web applications that are server-centric. Server-centric web applications/traditional web applications are browser-based applications that don't need any client installation. Traditional web application version updates are published to web servers and are seamless to the application clients. That helps to solve the problem of high-maintenance costs that are a creation flaw of native applications. A native application version release might include a lot of considerations like different operating system versions or different hardware components, for example.

A traditional web application renders web pages when it receives an HTTP request from the browser. The rendered pages are sent back as an HTTP response and that triggers a web-page refresh in the browser. In a web-page refresh, the whole web page is replaced by a new page. Figure 1-2 shows a web-page life cycle in a traditional web application.

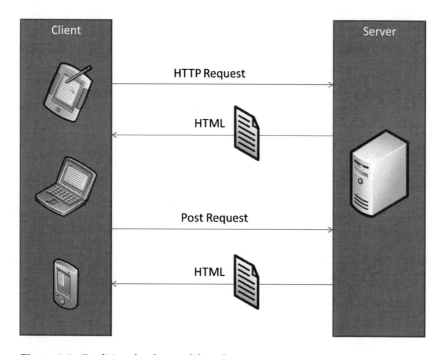

Figure 1-2. *Traditional web-page life cycle*

As you can see in the figure, a request for a page is sent to the server and a response is returned as HTML. Later on, the user might submit a form (triggering a post request) and the results again are sent as HTML. Once that HTML arrives to the client, a full web-page refresh occurs.

As a result of the server-centric approach, the weight on client development is small and JavaScript is mainly used for making simple UI changes or for animations. Figure 1-3 is a traditional web application architecture suggestion written by the Microsoft Pattern and Practices team, and it shows the small weight the client had in the past.

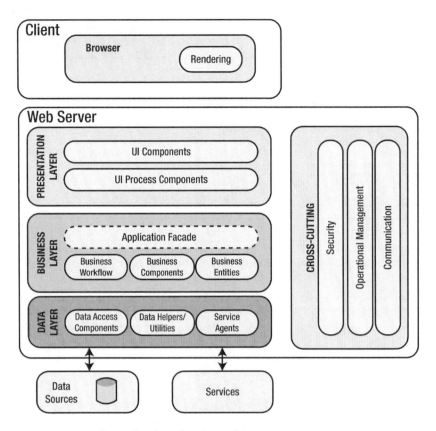

Figure 1-3. *Traditional web application architecture*

As you can see in the figure, most of the application logic sits on the server side and the client is only used to render the web pages it receives.

In a traditional web application, when a user interacts with web pages, he or she can trigger an HTTP request, which is handled by the server. For example, if a user clicks a button on a web page, the click will trigger an HTTP request, which is handled by the server. Later on, the user will get a web-page refresh in the browser and the result of the button interaction is shown. Handling events on the server can be very long and up until a result comes back the user waits and the web application isn't responsive. That is, of course, a bad user experience. Moreover, if there is no Internet connection the application won't work.

Another aspect of creating traditional web applications is state persisting and data management. The user state and application state are persisted mainly on the server side, using mechanisms like session or application states, and data are also stored on the server side. That poses another problem, which is the need to query the server any time states or data are needed. Again, each request will result in a browser web-page refresh. Moreover, state or data changes need to be updated in the server and each server action might take some time, which means that the user sits and wait for a response. This is why the responsiveness of traditional web applications wasn't so good.

In the past I built a lot of traditional web applications using ASP.NET Web Forms and, later on, ASP.NET MVC. As a junior developer, I didn't see the problems mentioned before with web-page refreshes and state management. In 2006, I was involved in the creation of an Ajax-oriented web page. It was the first time I'd built a client-oriented web page and it was only then that I started to understand the difference between server- and client-centric web pages. What we did was to create a dictionary page that changed the terms in the page according to the selected letter.

We could write the whole web page in a server-centric approach but our team leader decided that it should be created using Ajax. It took me and another team member some time until we finished the task but the gain for us was huge. Since then, every time I create a traditional web application I try to figure out how to improve the user experience and to minimize the dependency on the server.

The same change happened for a lot of other web developers at the same time. The result was a new hybrid approach to developing web applications. These were called RIAs. With RIAs the weight of development was divided between the client and server sides. Web pages used Ajax to communicate with the server and to request states or data. In the RIA approach you still had web-page refreshes when navigating from one page to another or for doing some business logic. On the other hand, you used Ajax and JavaScript to perform a lot of presentation logic without full-page refreshes. RIA development became very popular, and users began to expect that functionality from web applications and sites. Figure 1-4 shows what an RIA architecture might look like.

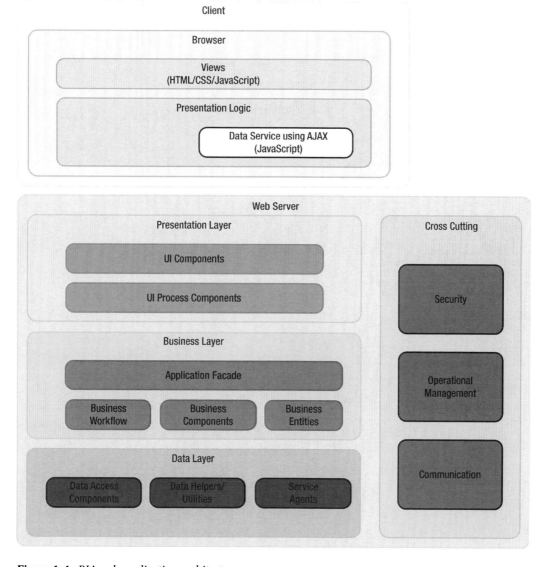

Figure 1-4. *RIA web application architecture*

As you can see, the weight on the client side has grown in comparison to the architecture in Figure 1-3, which showed that traditional web applications used a browser only for HTML rendering. Here you can see that some business logic is performed on the client side.

Native Applications

Native applications are stand-alone executable applications that need to be installed first. They can run on only one platform—the platform that they were created for—and this is their strength and also their main weakness. Native applications are designed to take advantage of the local hardware and operating system. Because there is a dependency on the hardware and operating system, native application deployments can be very complicated. In each application version you need to take into consideration operating system versions, driver versions, and even device architecture (32 bits or 64 bits). That makes the development of native applications harder and their deployment phase a main issue in the application development process. Figure 1-5 shows a native application architecture suggestion written by the Microsoft Pattern and Practices team.

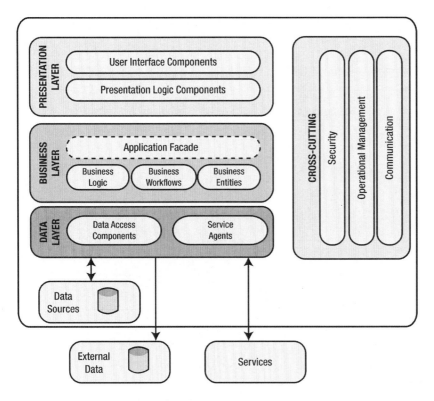

Figure 1-5. *Native application architecture*

In the figure you can see that all the application is created as one piece of software that includes all the logic. Sometimes you will use external services in native applications but the main processing occurs in the application itself.

As written previously, the dependency on the operating system is a main issue in native application development. There are a lot of different operating systems like Windows, UNIX, OS X, Android, and more. If you want to reach clients in all the operating systems you have to make a version of your application for each of them or else you just narrow the application distribution. That means that you need developers who know how to create an application for every platform and the time you spend on creating an application can be multiplied by the number of operating systems that you want to support.

On the other hand, as opposed to traditional web applications, native applications can keep their local state by using local databases or files. This possibility enables developers to create a rich user experience because interaction with local resources is faster than using remote resources on remote servers. Moreover, the option to use local resources enables the application to be available and responsive when there is no Internet connection. Responsiveness and availability are huge advantages over traditional web applications.

In this section we explained the differences between traditional, modern web applications and native applications. Now that you have a toolset for comparison between the application types, we can explain what SPAs are.

So What Is an SPA?

As mentioned in the first paragraph of this chapter, an SPA is a full web application that has only one page, which is used as a shell for all the other application web pages and uses JavaScript, HTML5, and CSS for all front-end interaction. In SPAs there are no full post back to the server, no full refreshes of a single web page, and no embedded objects. On the other hand, you use an HTML element in which its content is replaced from one view to the other by a front-end routing and templating mechanism. Table 1-1 includes a comparison of key application features among traditional web applications, native applications, and SPAs.

Table 1-1. *Traditional, Native, and Single-Page Applications Comparison*

Features	Traditional	Native	SPA
Cross-platform functionality	√	X	√
Client-state management	X	√	√
No installation required	√	X	√

As you can see in the table, the SPA is the intersection between traditional web applications and native applications, and it includes all of their main characteristics. That knowledge can help you when you go to decision makers to convince them to implement an SPA.

The main difference between an SPA and a traditional application or RIA is the web-page life cycle. Figure 1-6 shows the SPA web-page life cycle.

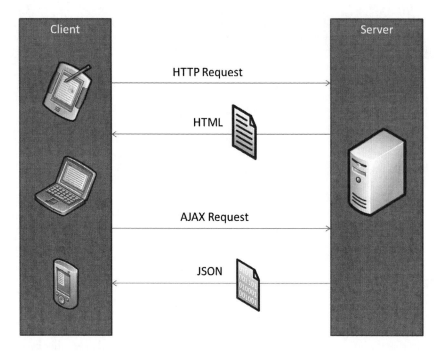

Figure 1-6. *SPA web-page life cycle*

If you compare this to the traditional web application page life cycle shown in Figure 1-2, the main change is the nature of the requests and responses that follow the initial HTTP request. With an SPA you use Ajax to request data and you get as a response data in JavaScript Object Notation (JSON) format or prerendered pieces of HTML. Once the data arrive for the client, the client will partially render the HTML to represent the changes. Also, moving from one page to another in an SPA occurs on the client side, which is different to what happens in traditional applications and RIAs.

Another change between an SPA and traditional web application is state management. In an SPA, because you aren't leaving or refreshing the main web page you can persist your state in the browser memory. Also, if you want to persist the application state in offline scenarios or when users close the browser, you can use HTML5 storage types to keep the state. Later on when the user gets back online, you can return him or her to the last state of the application without involving the server.

The main SPA building blocks include the following:

- JavaScript libraries and frameworks: You will use MV* frameworks and many other JavaScript libraries in order to build your front end.

- Routing: Front-end routing is the way to navigate between views in an SPA. All the views are created in the front end inside a main HTML element, and a front-end router manages the navigation from page to page.

- Template engines: A template engine is used on the client side in order to render or rerender the parts that are used in the single page.

- HTML5: HTML5 is used to create the main SPA web page and to interact with it. You will use a lot of new JavaScript APIs for communication, multimedia, storage, and more.

- Backend API and Representation State Transfer (REST): The server acts as a web API that the app is consuming and doesn't have a server-side rendering option for web pages.

- Ajax: All interactions with the server are asynchronous calls using Ajax. When a response arrives from the server, the web page is partially rendered using JavaScript (if needed).

In Chapter 4, "SPA Concepts and Architecture", those main building blocks will be explained more thoroughly. While these are the main SPA building blocks there are other essential building blocks that can help develop an SPA (for example, real-time communication, data management on the client side, etc.). Now that we know what an SPA is, let's understand the benefits of creating an SPA.

Why SPA Development?

SPAs integrate the best of two worlds: the native application and the traditional web application. When you develop an SPA you get the portability and cross-platform functionality of a web application as well as the client-state management and responsiveness of a native application.

SPAs are web applications and therefore their deployment is seamless to their users. Users don't need to install SPAs because they are online as opposed to native applications, which are installed once and later on need continuous updates for new versions. SPAs can be updated more occasionally by their developers, which creates more flexibility for the developers.

In SPAs most of the business logic is implemented in the client and the server is used as an API for things like authentication, validation, or persistency to databases. Because the logic is performed on the client, SPAs are super responsive and they make users feel like they are using native applications. There is no need to wait for server logic to occur and for page refreshes because everything is being done on the client.

SPAs are also very responsive in terms of server interaction. All the operations that go to the server are performed using Ajax and therefore the UI can still receive events and won't be stuck. Also, if the server operation is very long, you can notify the user that something is occurring by using notifications or animated images. Again, this is something the users expect from native applications but get from SPAs.

All of these factors make an SPA the perfect tool for creating next-generation web applications.

Summary

SPAs have been part of web development for a long time. You can create SPAs with plug-ins like Flash, Java, and Silverlight, but those plug-ins impose a lot of development considerations such as security or user plug-in adoption, for example. Since 2005, with the combination of Ajax, HTML5, and the mobile web, JavaScript became more attractive for developers. With benefits like seamless deployment, cross-platform functionality, and more, JavaScript gained a lot of attention from developers. Moreover, a lot of patterns for building native applications have shifted to the JavaScript world.

Today, you can't build a web site or application without investing a lot of your time in writing JavaScript code. Users expect web sites and applications to run fast and to be fluid. If you don't give them their desired experiences they won't come back to your site or app.

In the next chapter you will learn a lot of good practices for writing JavaScript applications. Understanding these practices will help you to move forward with the rest of the book.

CHAPTER 2

■ ■ ■

JavaScript for SPAs

In Chapter 1 you learned about the history of web development and how we ended up with single page applications (SPAs). The major part of an SPA is its front end and the main language for writing SPAs is JavaScript. In order to write maintainable and reusable JavaScript code it is not enough just to learn JavaScript basics. In this chapter and in Chapter 3 as well, you will delve into techniques and patterns for writing better JavaScript code. In this chapter, you will get to know how to create and use JavaScript objects, how to create namespaces, and how to mimic encapsulation in your code. You will also get to know some JavaScript pitfalls and hopefully learn to avoid them.

In Chapter 3, "Modular JavaScript Development", you will learn about how to create JavaScript modules, what the Asynchronous Module Definition (AMD) is and how to use the RequireJS library. It is very crucial to understand the concepts that are described in Chapters 2 and 3 in order to create more successful SPAs.

■ **Note**   We assume that you know basic JavaScript syntax and that you have some experience with the language. This chapter tries to be very practical and to show how to write professional JavaScript code.

A Little JavaScript History

JavaScript was created by Brendan Eich around 1995. Brendan developed a language called LiveScript for Netscape Navigator 2 in order to enable simple processing on the front end. It is said that it took him around 10 days to come out with the main features of the language. Very close to the Netscape Navigator 2 release, Netscape changed the LiveScript name to JavaScript and the rest is known. JavaScript adoption was very fast and later on when plug-ins like Java applets didn't succeed JavaScript blossomed. Today, JavaScript is the de facto language of the web and some call it the assembly language of the web.

Around 1997, because of its huge adoption, JavaScript started to be standardized by the ECMA International standards organization. JavaScript's first standard edition was released in the same year as the ECMA-262 specification, which is also referred to as ECMAScript. Since ECMA-262 was released the browser vendors are trying to implement their JavaScript engine according to the specification. The last version of ECMAScript, ECMAScript 5.1, was released around 2011.

JavaScript was developed as a functional, dynamic, and prototype-based language. It includes good language features like functions, closures, loosely typed language, dynamic objects, and more. JavaScript also includes a lot of problematic features like global variables, the `with` statement, and the `continue` statement. These features can lead you into a lot of JavaScript pitfalls so you might want to avoid using them. There is a recommended book by Douglas Crockford, *JavaScript: The Good Parts*, that explains all those language features in details.

Now that we have had a little bit of history, our first task is to understand JavaScript functions.

JSFIDDLE

In this chapter and also in Chapters 3, 4 and 5 most of the code examples include links to their fiddle versions in jsFiddle. If you are not familiar with jsFiddle, it is a web site that includes an online playground for JavaScript, HTML, and CSS (see Figure 2-1).

Figure 2-1. *jsFiddle web site*

The web site includes a script pane for your JavaScript code, an HTML pane for your HTML, a CSS pane for CSS, and a result pane to show you the resulting functionality. jsFiddle also includes options for configuring the environment and the libraries that you want to use. We use jsFiddle to test all the code snippets in this chapter and you are encouraged to do the same. You can paste the code snippets in this chapter into the JavaScript pane and the templates into the HTML pane. Later you can run the JavaScript and see the output in the developer tools console that you use.

Functions in JavaScript

JavaScript is a functional language, and functions are its first-class citizens. A function in JavaScript is a sequence of JavaScript statements that represents a single named operation. You can pass values to a function; the function executes some logic and when it finishes it returns a value. This behavior isn't different from other programming languages. Listing 2-1 shows a simple function declaration.

Listing 2-1. Simple Function Declaration http://jsfiddle.net/gilf/3JbSd/

```
function hello(arg1, arg2) {
    console.log(arg1 + " function");
}
```

In JavaScript, as opposed to many other languages, a function is an object. That means that you can pass functions as parameters to other functions and you can manipulate functions during runtime. When you declare a function, like in Listing 2-1, a function is created from the global `Function` object and it inherits the functionality included in its `Function.prototype`.

▨ **Note**   We will discuss prototype and JavaScript inheritance later in the chapter.

Listing 2-2 is equivalent to the code in Listing 2-1 but it instantiates a `Function` object instead of declaring a function.

Listing 2-2. Declaring a Function Using the Function Object `http://jsfiddle.net/gilf/z6bez/`

```
var hello = new Function("arg1", "arg2", "console.log(arg1 + ' function');");
hello("hello"); // outputs 'hello function'
```

As you can see, the `Function` object constructor receives a list of arguments and the function body in string representation. The returned function is set into a hello variable, which is accessible to use later in your code. The second line in the code runs the `hello` function with an argument.

Every JavaScript function, even functions without a `return` statement, returns a value. If you want to return something from a function, use the `return` statement. If you omit the `return` statement, by default functions will return the undefined type.

Functions receive function parameters, which in JavaScript are called arguments. The evaluation strategy in JavaScript is the call-by value, which means that any argument that is passed to a function is passed by value. If you change an argument inside a function block, the change isn't reflected outside the function. On the other hand, when you pass JavaScript objects to a function the JavaScript runtime will copy the original reference of the object and pass it by value to the function. That means that if you change an object property, the change will be reflected outside the function scope. JavaScript is not a call-by-reference language like object-oriented languages such as C# or Java.

The arguments Object

The dynamic nature of JavaScript enables you to pass to functions any number of arguments. That means that if a function receives two arguments, you can pass it only one argument or even three arguments. This behavior is enabled because every JavaScript function includes an `arguments` object, which is an array-like object, inside its function body. As its name implies, the `arguments object` stores the arguments that the function receives and you can change the stored arguments. When you call a function with fewer parameters than it expects, every omitted parameter will get the undefined type. If you pass a function more parameters than it expects, you can use the `arguments` object with the index of a parameter in order to use it. Listing 2-3 shows how to use the `arguments` object to output the arguments to the console, and how you can change an argument without using its parameter name.

Listing 2-3. Using the arguments Object `http://jsfiddle.net/gilf/d4PKF/`

```
function funcName(arg1, arg2) {
    console.log(arguments[0]) // outputs to the console arg1 or undefined if nothing was passed
    console.log(arguments[1]) // outputs to the console arg2 or undefined if nothing was passed
    console.log(arguments[2]) // outputs to the console undefined

    arguments[1] = "changed"; // will change arg2 to the "changed" value
}
```

The previous example is very simple. You can use the knowledge of the `arguments` object to create very useful and powerful functionality. For example, the function in Listing 2-4 will calculate the sum of any given number of arguments.

Listing 2-4. Using the arguments Object to Create a sum Function `http://jsfiddle.net/gilf/64vtT/`

```
function sum() {
        var x = 0,
            i = 0;
        for (; i < arguments.length; i++) {
                x += arguments[i];
        }
        return x;
}
```

Anonymous Functions

Another JavaScript language feature that is related to functions is the ability to create anonymous functions. Functions can be declared and assigned to a variable. This option is called function declaration. A function can also be declared as a callback parameter to another function. This option is called function expressions. When you create functions in these ways, they are created as anonymous functions and are unnamed (unless you specify a name in the function expression). Listing 2-5 shows how to declare an anonymous function.

Listing 2-5. Declaring an Anonymous Function `http://jsfiddle.net/gilf/u8Mkw/`

```
Var unnamed = function(arg1) {
        console.log(arg1);
}
unnamed('hi there'); // outputs 'hi there' to the console
```

In Listing 2-5, the declared function has no name and the function is set to the unnamed variable. The name property of the unnamed variable in Listing 2-5 will contain an empty string since the function has no name. Another usage scenario for creating anonymous functions is for callbacks. For example, Listing 2-6 shows how to use an anonymous function as a callback inside another anonymous function.

Listing 2-6. Passing an Anonymous Function as a Callback to a Function `http://jsfiddle.net/gilf/wkryN/`

```
// declare the first function that uses another function reference inside
var funcWithCallback = function(funcReference) {
  console.log(funcReference());
}

// calling the previous declared function with an anonymous function
funcWithCallback(function() {
        return "Hello";
}); // outputs "Hello" to the console
```

Nested Functions

The last JavaScript language feature that is related to functions is the nested function. In JavaScript you have the ability to create functions inside other functions, which are then called nested functions. Nested functions are not available outside their parent function. This knowledge can help us to encapsulate functionality inside nested functions.

■ **Note**   We will discuss encapsulation later in the chapter.

Nested functions can access their parent variables or parent other nested functions, which are in the same scope. That means that any function declared inside a parent function is a nested function that will be accessible to use by any other nested function which exists at the same nesting level under the same parent. On the other hand, parent functions can't use nested function variables or inner functions. Listing 2-7 shows how to declare a nested function.

Listing 2-7. Declaring a Nested Function `http://jsfiddle.net/gilf/JpmyH/`

```
// declare the first function that uses another function reference inside
function parent() {
        var variable = "variable data";
        console.log("parent"); // outputs "parent"
        function nested() {
                console.log("nested"); // outputs "nested"
                console.log(variable); // outputs "variable data"
        }
        nested();
}
parent();
```

In the code the output will be "parent," "nested," and then "variable data." Now that you understand more about JavaScript functions, we can talk about JavaScript scope.

JavaScript Scope

Scope refers to language rules regarding when a variable can be referenced or assigned. Scope is also used to determine accessibility of variables and functions to other callers. In JavaScript, you have two scopes that we will describe: the global scope and function scope. There are other JavaScript scopes, like the catch scope in the `try..catch` block and the `with` scope, which should be avoided and are not used regularly.

The Global Scope

The global scope is a scope that includes JavaScript language features, and it is accessible by any JavaScript code that you write. The window, document, or console objects are examples for objects that exist in the global scope. Any time you write code outside a function your code resides in the global scope. Listing 2-8 shows how you can create a variable and function in the global scope.

Listing 2-8. Global Variable and Function `http://jsfiddle.net/gilf/A6HB9/`

```
// a global variable
var global = "I'm global";

function globalFunc() {
        console.log("I'm a global function");
}
```

■ **Note**   Putting variables or functions in the global scope is bad practice and later on we will learn how to avoid it.

Function Scope

The function scope is a scope that is created inside a function. Other language features like loops don't create a scope in JavaScript and that might confuse developers who come from other programming languages. Listing 2-9 shows how to create a function scope.

Listing 2-9. Function Scope http://jsfiddle.net/gilf/fnU2V/

```
var global = "I'm global";

// a global variable
function globalFunc() {
        var local = "local";
        console.log(global);
}
globalFunc(); // outputs "I'm global"
console.log(local); // throws an error because local is scoped inside globalFunc
```

In the example, a variable is created inside the globalFunc, which can be only used inside the globalFunc scope and in nested functions inside globalFunc. The local variable is not accessible from the higher-level scope and this is why you will get an error if you try to use it outside globalFunc. Later in the chapter, we will discuss closures and the this keyword, which are also related to JavaScript scope.

Immediate Function Execution Expressions

JavaScript enables you to declare a function and run it as soon as you have finished declaring it. That behavior is called an immediate function execution expression (IFEE). In some JavaScript books and articles you may find it under the names "self-invoking" or "self-executing" functions. Listing 2-10 shows how to create an IFEE.

Listing 2-10. Immediate Function Execution Expression http://jsfiddle.net/gilf/93Xr3/

```
(function () {
    console.log('IFEE');
}());

// another option to do the same thing
(function () {
    console.log('IFEE');
})();
```

IFEEs are used to create a function scope around code initialization or for executing some functionality once. In such situations, creating a named function is a waste of memory and you want to dispose of the function as soon as you can. Using IFEEs helps to create a scope that doesn't "pollute" the global scope and this is another advantage of using this pattern. Immediate functions can get parameters and can return values. Listing 2-11 shows how you use an IFEE with parameters and how to return a value from an IFEE.

Listing 2-11. An IFEE with Parameters and Returned Value `http://jsfiddle.net/gilf/eE7wC/`

```
var returnedValue = (function (msg) {
    return msg;
}("Hello"));
console.log(returnedValue); // outputs "Hello"
```

In the example the IFEE receives an `msg` argument, which is just returned from the IFEE. When we talk about JavaScript namespaces later on we will return to IFEEs and you will see how they can help you. Until then, keep in mind that a lot of libraries and frameworks use IFEEs in their code base. Now that we understand what functions are and what JavaScript scope is, we can continue to learn about JavaScript objects and common JavaScript object patterns.

Working with Object-Oriented JavaScript

JavaScript is not a pure object-oriented language. The concept of objects in JavaScript is a little different to in object-oriented languages. Objects in JavaScript are a dynamic collection of properties and functions. A property is just a relation between a key (property name) and its value. The value can be simple type, object, or function. Because of the dynamic nature of JavaScript, you can change objects during runtime by adding and removing their properties.

Another key issue in JavaScript is that functions are objects. This relation doesn't exist in many object-oriented languages, so it is critical to understand it.

There are four main ways to create an instance of an object:

- Using literal object notation/object initializers
- Using the new notation with a constructor function
- Using the new notation with the Object object
- Using the Object.create function

Literal Object Notation

Literal object notation/object initializers use curly brackets to instantiate an object. It is easy to write {} to instantiate an empty JavaScript object. If you want to add properties during initialization, you write properties as follows in Listing 2-12.

Listing 2-12. Literal Object Notation Initialization `http://jsfiddle.net/gilf/C7dpA/`

```
var obj = {
    prop1: value1,
    prop2: value2
};
```

In the example, each property is an identifier and each value can be any type in JavaScript even functions. When you create an object with literal object notation, you get a singleton representation with no known type. If literal object notation looks familiar, it is because JavaScript Object Notation (JSON) is a subset of literal object notation. We will talk about JSON at the end of the chapter.

The new Notation and Constructor Functions

Another way to create an object is to use the new notation. In order to use the new notation, you need to create a constructor function that will be used as the blueprint to create instances. A constructor function is a regular function but with one major difference, which is that you can refer to an instance by using the this keyword. In order to differentiate constructor functions from other JavaScript functions it is common to use uppercase at the beginning of the function name. Listing 2-13 shows a constructor function for a Car.

Listing 2-13. Constructor Function http://jsfiddle.net/gilf/5e7U6/

```
function Car(type) {
        this.speed = 0;
        this.type = type || "No type";
        this.drive = function(newSpeed) {
                this.speed = newSpeed;
        }
}

var bmw = new Car("BMW");
console.log(bmw.speed); // outputs 0
console.log(bmw.type); // outputs "BMW"
bmw.drive(80);
console.log(bmw.speed); // outputs 80
```

Each instance will have two properties, speed and type, and a function called drive. The type property is received during the initialization and if it is not supplied a default value is supplied. You can see the use of logic in the code to check whether the car type was supplied. One thing to notice is the use of the this keyword to create instance properties for each instance. Another thing to understand is that each instance of a car will have its own instance of the drive function. If you want to create a "static" function you use a prototype. Later on, we will discuss the this keyword and some of its pitfalls and also prototypes.

After you create a constructor function, all you have to do is to use the name of the constructor with the new notation and you get an instance of an object. Currently, JavaScript doesn't include the class keyword to create classes like other object-oriented languages, and constructor functions can help us to mimic class functionality.

The Object Base Type

The third way to create a JavaScript object is to use the Object object with the new notation. Once you create a new instance, you can dynamically add properties to it like in Listing 2-14.

Listing 2-14. Using the Object Object to Instantiate an Object http://jsfiddle.net/gilf/7yTSh/

```
var obj = new Object();
obj.a = "property a";
obj.b = "property b";

console.log(obj.a) // outputs property a
console.log(obj.b) // outputs property b
```

The `Object.create` Function

The last option when creating an instance of an object is to use the `Object.create` function. The `Object.create` function was presented in ECMAScript 5 and is implemented on all major modern browsers. If you are using legacy browsers like Internet Explorer 6 or 8, the function is not supported. `Object.create` receives two arguments: the `object` prototype and a `properties` object. The `properties` object is a literal object that includes all the object instance properties and their descriptors. One of the property descriptors is the value descriptor that is used to set the property value. Listing 2-15 shows some examples that use the `Object.create` function.

Listing 2-15. Object.create Function http://jsfiddle.net/gilf/jfYgL/

```javascript
var a = Object.create(null, { a: { value: 1 }, b: { value: 2 }}); // no prototype
var b = Object.create({}, { a: { value: "a" }, b: { value: "b" }}); // prototype is an empty obj
var c = Object.create({}, { a: { value: true }, b: { value: false }}); // prototype is an empty obj

console.log(a.a); // outputs 1
console.log(a.b); // outputs 2
console.log(b.a); // outputs a
console.log(b.b); // outputs b
console.log(c.a); // outputs true
console.log(c.b); // outputs false
```

■ **Note** To explain all the options included in `Object.create` would be out of the scope of this book. The Mozilla Developers Network (MDN) includes a very thorough explanation about the `Object.create` function and you are encouraged to go and read about it at the following link: `http://mzl.la/1ioPTnC`.

JavaScript Prototype Inheritance

We mentioned the `prototype` property with regard to the `Object.create` function and that brings us to inheritance in JavaScript. JavaScript, as opposed to many object-oriented languages, uses a prototype-based inheritance. In prototype-based inheritance, every object can have a prototype that is a template that the object is based on. That means that if an object has a prototype, it includes all the prototype's properties and functions.

Every constructor function has a prototype property that links it to its parent object. By default that property is `undefined`. When you assign an object to the prototype property, each instance created by the constructor function will have the same behavior and structure like its prototype. Listing 2-16 shows how to add a prototype to the Car constructor function that we created previously in Listing 2-13.

Listing 2-16. Using a Prototype Property http://jsfiddle.net/gilf/h8jGy/

```javascript
function Car(type) {
        this.speed = 0;
        this.type = type || "No type";
}
Car.prototype = {
        drive: function(newSpeed) {
                this.speed = newSpeed;
        }
}
```

```
var bmw = new Car("BMW");
console.log(bmw.speed); // outputs 0
console.log(bmw.type); // outputs "BMW"
bmw.drive(80);
console.log(bmw.speed); // outputs 80
```

As opposed to the previous constructor function in Listing 2-13, now we have only one instance of the drive function, which is shared by all the Car instances. This, of course, can minimize the memory consumption when we have many Car instances in memory.

When you change the prototype during runtime, all the instances are updated with the change. Moreover, if you want to change only one instance-inherited functionality, you can set the function reference on the instance. When you do that, it overrides the functionality only on the instance and not on all the other instances. Listing 2-17 shows how it works.

Listing 2-17. Changing an Instance of Prototype Functionality http://jsfiddle.net/gilf/4FJcX/

```
function Car(type) {
        this.speed = 0;
        this.type = type || "No type";
}
Car.prototype.drive = function(newSpeed) {
                this.speed = newSpeed;
}

var bmw = new Car("BMW");
var honda = new Car("Honda");
honda.drive = function(newSpeed) {
        this.speed = newSpeed + 10;
}

console.log(honda.speed); // outputs 0
console.log(honda.type); // outputs "BMW"
honda.drive(80);
console.log(honda.speed); // outputs 90
console.log(bmw.speed); // outputs 0
console.log(bmw.type); // outputs "BMW"
bmw.drive(80);
console.log(bmw.speed); // outputs 80
```

You can create prototype chains and therefore deeper inheritance hierarchies by adding prototypes to your constructor functions. That enables the creation of a complex inheritance tree but it also imposes a small problem. Once you use an instance property or a function and it doesn't exist on the object, the behavior is to check its existence on all the prototypes up until it is found or not. If the property or function isn't found, an error occurs. Going down the prototype chain can cause some performance issues and you are encouraged not to create very deep inheritance trees.

The this Keyword

Another aspect of mastering objects in JavaScript is the this keyword. In JavaScript the this keyword doesn't resemble the this keyword in other object-oriented programming languages and it is a source of many bugs or future bugs if it is used incorrectly.

The this keyword exists only in a function scope and it is determined by how the function was called. It can be different each time a function is called because it refers to the calling object. If there is no calling object, JavaScript runtime assigns the global scope (in the browser it is the window object) to the this keyword. The following code will output to the console as true if we call it outside a function scope or the function was called in the global scope: console.log(this === window);.

A function can be called as an object function and this will be set to the object itself. For example, the code in Listing 2-18 declares an object with a property and a function. In the function we return the property using the this keyword, which is the object itself. This is why calling the function later on will result in printing 1 in the console.

Listing 2-18. Calling an Object's Function http://jsfiddle.net/gilf/2ZJj3/

```
var obj = {
        property: 1,
        func: function () {
                return this.property;
        }
};
console.log(obj.func()); // outputs 1
```

The same behavior will happen in functions that were declared on an object's prototype chain. If you use the this keyword in a prototype function and later on you call the function on the object itself, the this keyword will be set to the object. In Listing 2-19 you can see that behavior in action.

Listing 2-19. Calling an Object's Prototype Function http://jsfiddle.net/gilf/RASLR/

```
var o = {
        func: function () {
                return this.property;
        }
};
var obj = Object.create(o, { property: { value: 1}});
console.log(obj.func()); // outputs 1
```

In the example, we created an object that will react as a prototype. In that object we are declaring a function that uses the this keyword to return an object property. Later on, we create a new object with the previous object as its prototype and we call the prototype function. That will result in returning the property of the object as expected.

When using constructor functions, the this keyword is bound to the new constructed object. In Listing 2-20, we use the this keyword in the constructor function to create properties on the instantiated object.

Listing 2-20. Using the this Keyword in a Constructor Function http://jsfiddle.net/gilf/RASLR/

```
function Car(type) {
        this.type = type;
        this.speed = 0;
}
var bmw = new Car("BMW");
console.log(bmw.type); // outputs "BMW"
```

The this keyword can be deceiving. Up until now you might think that it functions like in other object-oriented languages. But that is not true. Listing 2-21 includes a bug that we can cause with the this keyword.

Listing 2-21. this Keyword Pitfall http://jsfiddle.net/gilf/8pHJM/

```
function Car(type) {
        this.type = type;
        this.speed = 0;
        this.func = function() {
                return this.type;
        }
}
var bmw = new Car("BMW");
var func = bmw.func;
console.log(func()); // outputs undefined
```

In the code, we declare a function inside our object that references the instance of the object by using the this keyword. Later on, we store the func function and call it in the next line. The execution context to the stored function is not a Car instance and it returns undefined.

Once you understand that the this keyword is set to the execution context of the function, you won't encounter pitfalls like in the previous example. There are ways to save the instance of the object and avoid those pitfalls.

The way to be really sure that the this keyword is the relevant object is by using call, apply, and bind functions. The call and apply functions are part of Function.prototype and therefore exist for any function. Both of the functions do the same thing: call the function with an object as context. The difference between the functions is their arguments. Listing 2-22 shows how to use both call and apply to give context to the code from Listing 2-21.

Listing 2-22. call and apply Functions http://jsfiddle.net/gilf/UqLrt/

```
function Car(type) {
        this.type = type;
        this.speed = 0;
        this.func = function() {
                return this.type;
        }
}
var bmw = new Car("BMW");
var func = bmw.func;
console.log(func.call(bmw)); // outputs BMW
console.log(func.apply(bmw)); // outputs BMW
```

The first argument that call and apply have received is the context object. After the first argument, call receives a sequence of arguments as parameters to pass to the function call while apply receives an array of arguments.

The third function, the bind function, was introduced in ECMAScript 5 and isn't supported in legacy browsers. Once you use the bind function on a function and give it a context it returns a new function that is bound to the context. Every time you call the bound function it will have the same context, regardless of how you use it. Listing 2-23 shows an example of the bind function.

Listing 2-23. bind Function http://jsfiddle.net/gilf/JaA7L/

```
function Car(type) {
        this.type = type;
        this.speed = 0;
        this.func = function() {
                return this.type;
        }
}
```

```
var bmw = new Car("BMW");
var func = bmw.func.bind(bmw);
console.log(func()); // outputs BMW
```

Now that you know how to create objects in JavaScript, it is time to learn how to mimic namespaces.

Creating JavaScript Namespaces

Namespaces, or named scopes, are a feature that you expect to see in object-oriented languages. Namespaces help to group a set of identifiers into a container that has some logical meaning. An identifier can be a named class, named interface, or any other language element that is contained inside a namespace. Because the same identifier can be used in more than one namespace but with a different meaning, using namespaces can help reduce name collisions.

JavaScript wasn't created with namespaces. On the other hand, you learned that JavaScript includes function scopes. With this information in mind, we can mimic namespace scope by creating a function scope. Doing so will help to reduce the number of objects that is associated with the global scope. It will also help to avoid collisions between identifiers created for an application when using external libraries, for example. Listing 2-24 shows how you create a namespace using a function scope.

Listing 2-24. Creating a Namespace http://jsfiddle.net/gilf/nsZ79/

```
var ns = ns || {};
```

What you see in Listing 2-24 is a simple check on whether the namespace was declared previously. If the namespace was declared, the left side of the statement is evaluated and the ns variable will include the previously defined namespace. If the namespace wasn't declared previously, a new object literal (which is another way to create an object in JavaScript) will be created and be set to the ns variable. That is it: you have a namespace.

Once you have namespaces, you can group functionality with related logic under namespaces and arrange your code. Listing 2-25 shows how to make the Car constructor function from Listing 2-24 into the previously declared namespace.

Listing 2-25. Adding a Car Constructor Function to a Namespace http://jsfiddle.net/gilf/7nZXb/

```
var ns = ns || {};
ns.Car = function (type) {
        this.speed = 0;
        this.type = type || "No type";
}
ns.Car.prototype = {
        drive: function(newSpeed) {
                this.speed = newSpeed;
        }
}

var bmw = new ns.Car("BMW");
console.log(bmw.speed); // outputs 0
console.log(bmw.type); // outputs "BMW"
bmw.drive(80);
console.log(bmw.speed); // outputs 80
```

Now we can combine another language feature that will help us to create a more robust solution to a namespace: IFEEs. We can use IFEEs to initialize a namespace once with its relevant functionality. Listing 2-26 wraps the code from Listing 2-25 inside an IFEE.

Listing 2-26. Creating a Namespace Using an IFEE http://jsfiddle.net/gilf/H7DB9/

```
var ns;
(function (ns){
        ns.Car = function (type) {
                this.speed = 0;
                this.type = type || "No type";
        }
        ns.Car.prototype = {
                drive: function(newSpeed) {
                        this.speed = newSpeed;
                }
        }
}(ns = ns || {}));

var bmw = new ns.Car("BMW");
console.log(bmw.speed); // outputs 0
console.log(bmw.type); // outputs "BMW"
bmw.drive(80);
console.log(bmw.speed); // outputs 80
```

If you open JavaScript library code, like jQuery for example, you will probably see the same code structure. Most of the known libraries create their functionality inside a namespace in order to avoid name collisions. jQuery's $ sign is a namespace that includes all jQuery functionality.

Right now you might be puzzled by the code structure you saw in Listing 2-26. You might not understand why or where to use it but this will be clearer when we introduce the ability to add encapsulation to your JavaScript code.

Closures and Encapsulation

Before we move to encapsulation in JavaScript, we need to understand closures.

> *What [closure] means is that an inner function always has access to the vars and parameters of its outer function, even after the outer function has returned. (Douglas Crockford, Private Members in JavaScript,* http://javascript.crockford.com/private.html)

When a function returns another function, which references any variable defined on the first function, JavaScript creates a closure. A closure keeps the variables alive even after the original function has returned.

In Listing 2-27, the outer/parent function returns a function that contains functions that, once called, will output the exact date. The returned function will keep the date variable alive up until it is not referenced anymore.

Listing 2-27. Creating a Closure http://jsfiddle.net/gilf/L6SAn/

```
function closureFunc() {
        var date = new Date();
        return function () {
                return date.getMilliseconds();
        };
}
var func = closureFunc();
console.log(func()); // outputs the current milliseconds
```

Because functions are objects, we could change the previous example and return an object with functions that access the date variable. Listing 2-28 shows how to do that.

Listing 2-28. Creating a Closure That Returns an Object http://jsfiddle.net/gilf/L4hmd/

```
function closureObj() {
        var date = new Date();
        return {
                getCurrentMilliseconds: function() {
                        return date.getMilliseconds();

                }
        };
}
var obj = closureObj();
console.log(obj.getCurrentMilliseconds()); // outputs the current milliseconds
```

The date variable won't be accessible outside of the function and the closure and that helps to create privacy.

There is no native way to create privacy and encapsulation in JavaScript. JavaScript doesn't include language features like accessors, private members, or the private keyword, which are very important for encapsulation in object-oriented languages. On the other hand, we can emulate privacy in JavaScript by using closures. Having private functions and variables will enable you to encapsulate your code and to create more meaningful constructs.

Once you create a closure, variables defined in the outer function are only available inside the closure. On the other hand, variables defined within the returning object/function are available to everybody as an API. The code from Listing 2-28 shows exactly that. The date variable can be considered a private member of the returned object. It is accessible only by the getCurrentMilliseconds API function.

Listing 2-29 shows how we can emulate accessors by using closures.

Listing 2-29. Emulating Accessors by Using Closures http://jsfiddle.net/gilf/S5SNS/

```
var obj = (function () {
        var privateMember;
        return {
                setMember: function (value) {
                        privateMember = value;
                },
                getMember: function () {
                        return privateMember;
                }
        };
}());
obj.setMember('hello');
console.log(obj.getMember()); // outputs hello
```

In the example, we create a singleton object by using an IFEE. The object exposes two functions to get and to set its private member. This code structure is very common and in Chapter 3, we will learn more about how this code can help us to write modules.

■ **Caution**   Closures keep variables and functions in memory as long as the closures exist. That can lead to high memory consumption and might affect performance if you are not careful. In order to avoid this problem, use closures only for particular tasks.

JSON

JSON is a data format that is widely used in development. JSON is a lightweight format, as opposed to XML, which is designed for sending data to web servers and back. You use JSON with Ajax in order to send requests to servers and get back responses that can be parsed easily into JavaScript objects. The JSON format relates to JavaScript literal object notation and is considered its subset that was specially designed for transport.

Unlike literal object notation, JSON doesn't support functions, and property names are enclosed in double quotes. The following example shows how a Car object can look in JSON format:

Listing 2-30. Car in JSON http://jsfiddle.net/gilf/GQYZv/

```
var car = {
        "type": "BMW",
        "speed": 0,
        "color": ["white", "blue"]
};
```

JSON objects can also store JavaScript array objects, which helps to represent "one to many" relations. The color property in the previous example is an array of colors.

Developers don't usually create or manipulate JSON objects but rather create objects in their own language and convert them into JSON representation. You can use JavaScript's JSON.stringify and JSON.parse functions to serialize and deserialize JavaScript objects into JSON format. In Listing 2-31 you can see the use of JSON.stringify and JSON.parse functions.

Listing 2-31. Using JSON.stringify and JSON.parse Functions http://jsfiddle.net/gilf/XLV9u/

```
var car = {
        "type": "BMW",
        "speed": 0,
        "color": ["white", "blue"]
};
var carSerializedVersion = JSON.stringify(car);
console.log(carSerializedVersion); // outputs {"type":"BMW","speed":0,"color":["white","blue"]}

var carParsedVersion = JSON.parse(carSerializedVersion);
console.log(carParsedVersion.type); // outputs BMW
```

■ **Note**   This is a short description about JSON, which is a huge topic. If you like to learn more about the format you can go to the json.org web site and you will find everything that you need.

ECMAScript and Its Impact on Future Code

As written at the beginning of this chapter, ECMAScript is the standard for JavaScript. The current version of ECMAScript is 5.1 and it was published as a recommendation in 2011. New versions, ECMAScript 6 and 7, are currently at the development stage; ECMAScript 6 was about to be released at the time we wrote this book.

■ **Note** You can find ECMAScript documentation on the ecmascript.org web site.

ECMAScript 5 brought a small number of changes, mainly in the area of working with objects. On the other hand, ECMAScript 6, which is called Harmony, adds significant changes to the language to support complex applications. In this part we will review some of the changes that you need to be aware of in ECMAScript 5 and 6.

■ **Note** While most of the modern browsers support ECMAScript 5, ECMAScript 6 is not a recommendation yet and its support in modern browsers is minimal. We do hope that browsers will add ECMAScript 6 features as soon as the standard is out because it will make it easier to write modular JavaScript code.

ECMAScript 5 Highlighted Features

- Native JSON serializer support. You learned about the JSON.parse and JSON.stringify functions. Up until ECMAScript 5's release, JSON serialization wasn't supported natively by the browsers and you had to use JavaScript libraries in order to serialize and deserialize JSON objects.

- Changes to the Object object. Many new functions were added to the Object object, including defineProperty, create, and getOwnPropertyDescriptor. You got to know a little bit about the create function. The functions that were added enable objects to be created more easily or to enable a reflection-like mechanism to investigate objects and understand them.

- Changes to the Function object. The Function object got the bind function that we explained in this chapter.

- Changes to the Array object. The Array object includes a lot of new utility functions like forEach, map, and filter. The new functions help reduce the dependency on JavaScript utility libraries that added this functionality.

- Strict mode. Using the "use strict"; string tells the JavaScript runtime that you want to use a restricted variant of JavaScript. When running in strict mode, there are several changes to normal JavaScript semantics. Strict mode also enforces thorough error checking on your code and helps you avoid error-prone JavaScript constructs.

ECMAScript 6

While ECMAScript 5 is implemented in most modern browsers, ECMAScript 6 is still in development and therefore it is advised not to use it currently. On the other hand, it is essential to understand ECMAScript 6's new features because we use JavaScript patterns like constructor functions to emulate some of the missing JavaScript features from ECMAScript 6.

New Language Syntax

We will start with new language syntax:

- Arrow functions/lambda expressions support. ECMAScript 6 includes support of arrow functions/lambda expressions. That means that you can pass lambda as callback code instead of a function and the runtime will know how to use it.

  For example, this code

  [1, 2].map(function(x) {return x + x; }); can become
  `[1, 2].map(x => x + x);` which is shorter and less confusing.

- Default parameters support. You can use default parameters instead of writing logical or statements to fill some default value in function execution.

  For example, the following code

  `function echo(msg) { return msg || "hello"; }` can become
  `function echo(msg = "hello") { return msg; }` which is more expressive than the first line of code.

- Constant values. JavaScript is dynamic by nature and it has no constants. ECMAScript 6 adds the ability to create constants by using the const keyword. Trying to assign a value to a constant will result in a runtime error. The following code shows how to create a constant value using ECMAScript 6 syntax:

  `const someValue = 5;`

- `for..of` loop. This is a new kind of loop that enables the script to iterate over iterable objects like arrays. The following code shows an example of the `for..of` loop:

  ```
  var arr = [1, 2];
  for (var i of arr) { console.log(i); // outputs "1", "2" }
  ```

Classes, Modules, and More

ECMAScript 6 also includes runtime changes. These include the addition of classes and modules, which are long-time expected JavaScript language features. With the introduction of classes and modules it will be less difficult to create scalable JavaScript applications. Listing 2-32 shows you the difference between using a constructor function and using the class keyword in ECMAScript 6.

Listing 2-32. ECMASCript 6 Classes

```
// ES 6
class Car {
        constructor(type = "No type") {
                this.speed = 0;
                this.type = type;
        }
        drive(newSpeed) {
                this.speed = newSpeed;
        }
};
```

```
// ES 5
function Car(type) {
        this.speed = 0;
        this.type = type || "No type";
}
Car.prototype = {
        drive: function(newSpeed) {
                this.speed = newSpeed;
        }
}
```

The same code is equivalent between ECMAScript 6 and the constructor function. On the other hand, the ECMAScript 6 version is more readable and concise. You can see the use of the constructor keyword, which is another ECMAScript 6 language feature.

If you want to inherit from the Car object, ECMAScript 6 includes the extends keyword, which lets you define the inheritance chain. Listing 2-33 shows how to extend the Car class with a BMW class both in ECMAScript 6 and in a previous version of JavaScript.

Listing 2-33. ECMASCript 6 Inheritance

```
// ES 6
class BMW extends Car {
        constructor(color = "black") {
                super("BMW");
                this.color = color;
        }
};

// ES 5
function BMW(color) {
        Car.call(this, "BMW");
        this.color = color;
}
BMW.prototype = Object.create(Car.prototype);
BMW.prototype.constructor = BMW;
```

Again, you can see the difference between the versions and how you can use ECMAScript 6 to write less code.

ECMAScript 6 module syntax isn't finalized yet as we write the book, but it is supposed to add at least three new keywords to the JavaScript language: module, export, and import. The module keyword will create a module to wrap and encapsulate code into logical groups. Modules are equivalent to namespaces. The export keyword will enable you to declare code the modules expose. The import keyword will enable you to ask the runtime to fetch a dependent module to the current module and later on will enable you to use the imported module.

ECMAScript 6 is going to bring a lot of positive changes to the JavaScript language and it will help us to create beautiful JavaScript code with a lot of new syntactic sugar. Until it is a recommendation, you will need to use the patterns that you learn in this chapter and the next.

Summary

JavaScript is not an easy language to learn. It includes a lot of good language features and, of course, pitfalls. In order to create more reusable and maintainable JavaScript code this chapter drilled down into a lot of JavaScript development aspects.

You learned about functions and JavaScript scope. This knowledge will help you avoid scope problems later on when you code. You learned how to create objects and constructor functions to emulate classes, which are a missing JavaScript language feature. This knowledge will help you when we discuss more about modular JavaScript. You learned about closures and how to mimic privacy in JavaScript. This tool helps to create encapsulation and to hide the internals of what you are doing.

In the next chapter we will continue with JavaScript and you will be exposed to ways to create modular JavaScript and to one of the useful libraries to achieve that: RequireJS.

CHAPTER 3

Modular JavaScript Development

Modularity is a quality that you expect applications to have whether they are single page applications (SPAs) or just modern web applications. Modular code helps to create big and scalable applications. It also enables reusability and extensibility of your application's parts. The lack of modular code can be the difference between a successful application and an unsuccessful one.

In the last part of Chapter 2, "JavaScript for SPAs," you learned that ECMAScript 6 will include the option to create modules. Until modules are a part of JavaScript, we need ways to emulate modular behavior. That is where this chapter comes in.

The Façade Pattern in JavaScript

Before we start to explain modules, you need to understand the façade pattern, which is one of the building blocks for writing JavaScript modules. A façade is a high-level interface to a larger code base that hides the underlying code complexity. The façade exposes an application programming interface (API), which limits the available functionality that we can use and helps to encapsulate a lot of the inner code behavior. That means that façade differs greatly from the reality of the implementation. Listing 3-1 shows how to create a façade structure in JavaScript.

Listing 3-1. Façade Pattern Structure in JavaScript http://jsfiddle.net/gilf/n7TVH/

```
var obj = (function () {
        // object inner implementation

        return {
                // exposed façade API
        };
}());
```

As you can see, once a function returns an object, the object acts as a façade to the inner implementation, which is encapsulated. The inner implementation is encapsulated by the function scope created by the outer function.

Note   The immediate function execution expression (IFEE) in the example is used to create the instance of the object.

Now let's see some code that uses this pattern.

In Listing 3-2 you can see that the car implementation is concealed and it includes the speed private member and two functions, driveFaster and printSpeed. The façade itself includes only the drive function, which includes some logic to drive the car.

Listing 3-2. Façade Pattern in JavaScript http://jsfiddle.net/gilf/8T23n/

```javascript
var car = (function () {
        // object inner implementation
        var speed = 0;

        function driveFaster() {
                speed += 10;
        }

        function printSpeed() {
                console.log(speed);
        }

        return {
                // exposed façade API
                drive: function(newSpeed) {
                        while (speed < newSpeed) {
                                driveFaster();
                                printSpeed();
                        }
                }
        };
}());

car.drive(80); // output to the console 10, 20, …80
```

Now that you know how you can create a façade in JavaScript, it is time to learn what modules are.

Modules to the Rescue

Modules are pieces of code that enclose some logic implementation details and follow the Single Responsibility Principle (SRP). That means that modules should have only one responsibility that is exposed through the API in a façade. Modules can also help you to separate the concerns in your application and organize the application with more meaningful structure. Another good outcome of using modules is the ability to test your application with unit tests that test each module independent of other modules.

The problem is that JavaScript doesn't include the option to create modules currently. You saw in the previous chapter that modules are going to be a part of the language in the future but we want to enjoy separation of concerns and the SRP in current applications. The only way to do it is following proven patterns that enable us to structure our JavaScript code into the emulation of modules.

The patterns that are discussed in the following part are not the only patterns to create modules but they are the common ones.

Different Options to Create JavaScript Modules

There are four common JavaScript patterns for creating modules in JavaScript:

- Prototype pattern

- Module pattern

- Revealing module pattern

- Revealing prototype pattern

During this section we will describe each pattern, how to implement it, and its pros and cons. We will start with the first pattern: the prototype pattern.

Prototype Pattern

We met the prototype pattern in Chapter 2. The pattern created a constructor function and added a prototype to it. Each object that is constructed from the constructor will act as a module that encapsulates its functionality. Listing 3-3 shows a template for writing the prototype pattern.

Listing 3-3. The Prototype Pattern Template

```
function ObjectName(<put here parameters>) {
        // create instance functionality
}
ObjectName.prototype = {
        // create prototype functionality
}
```

Listing 3-4 shows the pattern in action.

Listing 3-4. The Prototype Pattern http://jsfiddle.net/gilf/a7Ak2/

```
var Car = function (type) {
        this.speed = 0;
        this.type = type || "no type";
};
Car.prototype = {
        drive: function(newSpeed) {
                this.speed = newSpeed;
        }
}

// Later in code
var car = new Car("bmw");
car.drive(60);
```

The prototype pattern includes pros and cons, and they are summarized in Table 3-1.

Table 3-1. *Pros and Cons for the Prototype Pattern*

	Pros	Cons
Prototype Pattern	It uses JavaScript's built-in features.	Handling the `this` keyword inside the prototype is a little tricky.
	Functions and variables aren't a part of the global scope.	You define the prototype separately from the constructor function.
	Functions are loaded into memory only once and not for every instance.	
	You can override the parent (prototype) implementation in specific instances.	

Module Pattern

The module pattern is probably the most common pattern from the four options. It uses the façade pattern in order to expose its API. Listing 3-5 shows a template for writing the module pattern.

Listing 3-5. The Module Pattern Template

```
var Module = function () {
        // private variables
        // private functions

        return {
                // public members and functions
        };
};
```

■ **Note**   This is our suggestion for a module pattern template. There are other ways to create the template. For a good resource about the module pattern, you may want to read Ben Cherry's article at `http://bit.ly/ZlsyRI`.

Listing 3-6 shows the module pattern in action.

Listing 3-6. The Module Pattern `http://jsfiddle.net/gilf/gf9k5/`

```
var Car = function(type) {
        // private variables
        var speed = 0;
        var type = type || "No type";

        // private functions
         function printSpeed() {
                console.log(speed);
        }
```

```
        return {
                // public members and functions
                drive: function(newSpeed) {
                        speed = newSpeed;
                        printSpeed();
                }
        };
}

// Later in code
var car = new Car("bmw");
car.drive(60);
```

The module pattern includes pros and cons, and they are summarized in Table 3-2.

Table 3-2. *Pros and Cons for the Module Pattern*

	Pros	**Cons**
Module Pattern	It hides implementation and exposes only the API.	It can cause in-memory function duplication for each instance.
	Functions and variables aren't a part of the global scope.	The ability to extend modules is much harder.
		Debugging might be a little difficult.

Revealing Module Pattern

The revealing module pattern is very close to the module pattern by its implementation but the only difference between them is that you create a singleton module. In order to do that you declare the module and wrap it inside an IFEE. Listing 3-7 shows a template for writing the revealing module pattern.

Listing 3-7. The Revealing Module Pattern Template

```
var Module = (function () {
        // private variables
        // private functions

        return {
                // public members and functions
        };
}());
```

Listing 3-8 shows the pattern in action.

Listing 3-8. The Revealing Module Pattern http://jsfiddle.net/gilf/bbAWq/

```
var car = (function(type) {
        // private variables
        var speed = 0;
        var type = type || "No type";
```

```
        // private functions
        function printSpeed() {
                console.log(speed);
        }

        return {
                // public members and functions
                drive: function(newSpeed) {
                        speed = newSpeed;
                        printSpeed();
                },
                print: printSpeed
        };
}("bmw"));

// Later in code
car.drive(60);
```

In the code you can see that the module exposes two API functions: drive and print. The exposed function names don't need to have the same names as the inner function implementation. Also, you can see that the IFEE here creates a singleton implementation of the module.

The revealing module pattern includes the same pros and cons like the module pattern but it adds its own pros and cons. The pros and cons are summarized in Table 3-3.

Table 3-3. *Pros and Cons for the Revealing Module Pattern*

	Pros	Cons
Revealing Module Pattern	It hides implementation and exposes only the API.	The ability to extend modules is much harder.
	Functions and variables aren't a part of the global scope.	Debugging might be a little difficult.
	It is a cleaner way to expose the public interface.	
	You have only a single instance of the module.	

Revealing Prototype Pattern

The revealing prototype pattern is a combination of the revealing module pattern and the prototype pattern. In the revealing prototype pattern, you use the same structure that we used in the revealing module pattern but on the prototype. That means that there is a singleton prototype that exposes some functionality and there is a constructor function that this singleton uses as its prototype. Listing 3-9 shows a template for writing the revealing prototype pattern.

Listing 3-9. The Revealing Prototype Pattern Template

```
var Module = function () {
        // private/public variables
        // private/public functions
};
```

```
Module.prototype = (function() {
        // private implementation

        return {
                // public API
        };
}());
```

Listing 3-10 shows the pattern in action.

Listing 3-10. The Revealing Prototype Pattern http://jsfiddle.net/gilf/TukSx/

```
var Car = function(type) {
        this.speed = 0;
        this.type = type || "no type";
}
Car.prototype = (function() {
        // private functions
        var printSpeed = function() {
                console.log(this.speed);
         }

        var drive = function(newSpeed) {
                this.speed = newSpeed;
                printSpeed.call(this);
        }

        return {
                // public members and functions
                drive: drive
        };
}());

var car = new Car("bmw");
car.drive(60);
```

In the code you can see that the main, interesting part of the revealing prototype pattern is, of course, the prototype. You create a single instance of a prototype and you use the same structure that you used in the revealing module pattern.

The revealing prototype pattern includes pros and cons, and they are summarized in Table 3-4.

Table 3-4. *Pros and Cons for the Revealing Prototype Pattern*

	Pros	Cons
Revealing Prototype Pattern	It hides implementation and exposes only the API.	Handling the this keyword inside the prototype is a little tricky.
	Functions and variables aren't a part of the global scope.	You define the prototype separately from the constructor function.
	Functions are loaded into memory only once and not for every instance.	
	It is extensible.	

What Is the Asynchronous Module Definition?

You learned how to create JavaScript modules in the previous section. In JavaScript development, you encapsulate your functionality inside modules, and in most projects each module exists in its own file. Having modules reside in their own stand-alone files complicates development a little because JavaScript developers need to constantly watch and be aware of dependencies among modules. Moreover, we need to load the modules in a specific order to avoid errors at runtime.

The way to load JavaScript files, and therefore modules, is to use script tags. In order to load module dependencies, you need to load the dependency first and then the dependent. When using script tags, you need to arrange their loading in that specific order and the scripts will be loaded synchronously. If you have many JavaScript files with a lot of dependencies, maintaining the order of the files can become a nontrivial task.

The async and defer Attributes

You can use the `async` and `defer` attributes in your script tags to make their load asynchronous. The `async` attribute was introduced in HTML5. When the attribute exists in a script tag, it signals the browser to download the script asynchronously and not to block the rendering process. At the first opportunity after the script finished downloading and before the window's `load` event the browser will execute the script. Listing 3-11 is an example of how to use the `async` attribute.

Listing 3-11. The async Attribute

```
<script src="jsFileName.js" async></script>
```

As you can see, the use of the attribute is very simple. One problem with the `async` attribute is that you can't know the execution order of scripts that use it. That means that if you have a dependency in one module on another module, using the `async` attribute might not load the modules in the exact order and that might cause errors. The `async` attribute is supported by all modern browsers and in Internet Explorer from version 9 onward.

The `defer` attribute is an old attribute that is supported in a lot of legacy browsers. The `defer` attribute signals the browser that a script should be executed in parallel to other scripts and without stopping the page rendering. Scripts that use the `defer` attribute are guaranteed to run in the sequence that they are written in the code. Deferred scripts run before the `DOMContentLoaded` page event.

Listing 3-12. The defer Attribute

```
<script src="jsFileName.js" defer></script>
```

Using the `async` and `defer` attributes can help you to load your modules in an asynchronous way but it introduces problems with dependencies, order of loading, and the exact point of executing. This is where the Asynchronous Module Definition (AMD) enters the picture.

AMD

The AMD is all about defining modules in a way so that the module and its dependencies can be asynchronously loaded and in the right order. Figure 3-1 shows an example of loading modules synchronously.

Figure 3-1. *Synchronous module loading*

Loading modules synchronously may cause a small performance penalty on your application loading. Figure 3-2 shows what the AMD looks like.

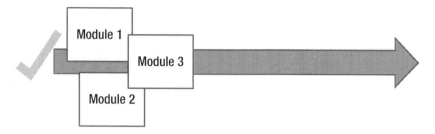

Figure 3-2. *Asynchronous module loading*

The AMD has no specification or standard in ECMAScript but definitions can be found in CommonJS. CommonJS is an attempt to standardize common JavaScript patterns.

■ **Note** If you would like to find out more about CommonJS, you can go to its online specification wiki: `http://wiki.commonjs.org/`.

In the CommonJS AMD part you can find the proposal for a mechanism for defining modules that are then loaded asynchronously with all their dependencies. The proposal includes a definition for a `define` function that will define a module with its ID, dependencies array, and module implementation. One of the common libraries that implements AMD is RequireJS, which is our next topic.

■ **Note** If you want more details about the CommonJS AMD proposal, you can go to the following link: `http://bit.ly/aqsM8d`.

The RequireJS Library

■ **Note** You can download RequireJS from its website: `http://requirejs.org`.

RequireJS is a JavaScript file loader and module definer library. It is one of the libraries that we used in each project that we worked on in the last year. RequireJS is supported both in browsers and in server environments like NodeJS. RequireJS enables you to define modules and to load modules and the relevant module dependencies in their right order.

■ **Note** During this book we use RequireJS as a module loader. There are other good libraries that expose the same functionality, like Almond, for example, but RequireJS is probably the most commonly used.

When you use RequireJS, it creates script tags for each dependency you defined and loads those dependencies on the fly during runtime by using the `head.appendChild` function. After the dependencies are loaded into memory, RequireJS figures the right order in which to define modules and calls each module definition in that right order. That means that when you use RequireJS you need only one root script to load the entire application. RequireJS will handle all the loading for you. In order to use RequireJS functionality appropriately, you need to define each of your modules with the RequireJS API or you can expect errors during runtime.

The RequireJS API is very small and it exists inside the `requirejs` namespace. RequireJS includes three main API functions:

- `define`: The function used to define modules
- `require`: The function used to load required module dependencies
- `config`: The function used to configure RequireJS runtime

The first two functions are global functions that will exist once you load RequireJS, and the config function exists on the `requirejs` namespace. Later on, you will learn how to use the API functions, but first we will explain how to start the RequireJS loading process.

The data-main Attribute

Once RequireJS is loaded into memory, it searches for a script tag that includes the `data-main` attribute. That script should be the same script that you will use to load RequireJS. The `data-main` should be set to the base URL for all the other scripts that you want to load. From the base URL, RequireJS starts loading all the modules in your application. Listing 3-13 shows a script tag with the `data-main` attribute.

Listing 3-13. Using the data-main Attribute

```
<script src="scripts/require.js" data-main="scripts/app.js"></script>
```

In the previous example, the base URL is set to a script named `app.js` that exists in the `scripts` folder. Also the `src` attribute points to the place where you will find the RequireJS library.

■ **Note** HTML5 introduced the `data-*` attributes. The specification enables developers to add their own custom attributes into Document Object Model (DOM) elements, as long as the custom attribute names are prefixed with `data-`. The `data-main` attribute is a `data-*` attributes usage example.

Another way to define the RequireJS base URL is by configuring it with the `config` function. RequireJS assumes that all the dependencies reside in scripts files and this is the reason you can declare a dependency without the use of the .js suffix.

The config Function

RequireJS exposes the option to configure its runtime and to change the default runtime settings. In order to do that you will use the requirejs.config function. The config function receives an options object that can include many configuration options. Table 3-5 summarizes the main RequireJS configuration options.

Table 3-5. *RequireJS Main Configuration Options*

Option	Description
baseURL	The root path to start the loading of modules
paths	Path mapping for modules that don't exist under the base URL
shim	Configuration for dependencies, exports, and initialization function to wrap scripts that don't use the RequireJS define function
waitSeconds	The timeout, in seconds, for loading a script; by default, it is set to 7 seconds
deps	Array of dependencies to load

■ **Note**   There are more configuration options, and you can find more about them at the RequireJS website: http://requirejs.org/docs/api.html#config.

Listing 3-14 shows the usage of the config function.

Listing 3-14. The config Function

```
requirejs.config({
    //By default load any module IDs from scripts/app
    baseUrl: 'scripts/app',

    //except, if the module ID starts with "lib"
    paths: {
        lib: '../lib'
    },

    // load backbone as a shim
    shim: {
        'backbone': {
            //The underscore script dependency should be loaded before loading backbone.js
            deps: ['underscore'],

            // use the global 'Backbone' as the module name.
            exports: 'Backbone'
        }
    }
});
```

In the example, you can see that a few things are configured. First of all, the base URL is set to scripts/app. RequireJS will process all the scripts it is loading from that root. We will take a look more deeply into the paths and shim options.

Paths

In Listing 3-14, we used the paths option. The paths option enables you to map module files that don't exist under the base URL. The configured path is used with base URL relative paths. In Listing 3-14, you probably noticed the use of paths to define that if a module ID starts with lib then it should be loaded from a lib folder. The lib folder exists in the filesystem at the same level as the scripts folder.

Shim

The shim option is a very crucial option to configure in RequireJS. A shim is a library or module that wasn't created by using the RequireJS define function. In order to use such a library or module as if it were created using the define function, use the shim option.

The shim option enables you to set the dependencies' names, using the deps array, and how the library or module is exported to the JavaScript runtime, using the exports option. In the main application that we will build later on in this book, we use the Backbone.js library, which isn't defined with the define function.

Listing 3-14's example shows how you can load Backbone.js as a shim. Backbone.js has a dependency on a library called Underscore.js and in the deps array we declare the dependency on Underscore.js. Also, you can see that we use the exports option to export Backbone.js as a module named Backbone. That module will exist in the global scope and will be available as if it were defined by RequireJS.

Now that you understand how to configure RequireJS, it is time to learn how to define a module.

Defining Modules Using RequireJS

You learned how to define modules using common module design patterns. RequireJS enables you to define modules using the define function. By convention, each module should exist in its own file and there should be only one define call in each JavaScript file.

Listing 3-15. The define Function Signature

```
define(
    moduleID, // optional string argument
    [dependencies], // optional array of dependencies
    definition function // the definition of the module
);
```

The define function receives a module ID, an array of dependencies, and a definition function. By convention, the module definition function receives as arguments all the previous dependencies you supplied and in the order you supplied them.

If you don't supply a module ID, by default RequireJS will use the file name of the module as its module name. This is very crucial to understand because most of the time you won't use an module ID. On the other hand, when you have the same file name for different modules that is where the module ID comes in handy.

There are some options to define a module using RequireJS:

- As a property bag of name/value pairs
- As a function
- As a function with dependencies

The easiest way to define a module is to create it as a property bag of name/value pairs. In this option you get a singleton object. Listing 3-16 shows how to define a property bag module with RequireJS.

Listing 3-16. Defining a Property Bag Module

```
define({
        firstName: "John",
        lastName: "Black"
});
```

The second option is to define a module as a function without any dependencies. That function might do some work but it must return an instance or a constructor function. If a constructor function is returned, you can create more than one instance of your module. Listing 3-17 shows how to define a function without dependencies by using RequireJS.

Listing 3-17. Defining a Function Without Dependencies

```
define(function () {
        // do something inside of the module if necessary

        return {
                firstName: "John",
                lastName: "Black"
        }
});
```

Because functions are objects in JavaScript, both of the previous examples are very close. The only difference between the previous two examples is that in a function you can do something while in a literal object you can't.

The third option is to define a module to use a function with dependencies. When you use dependencies, you add an array with dependency names as a first argument and the module definition function afterward. The order of the dependency names in the array should match the order of the arguments that the module definition function receives. Listing 3-18 provides an example of a simple module definition.

Listing 3-18. Defining a Module with Dependencies

```
define(["logger"], function(logger) {

        return {
              firstName: "John",
              lastName: "Black",
              sayHello: function () {
                  logger.log("hello");
              }
        }
});
```

As you can see, we pass an array to the define function with a logger dependency. RequireJS will load the logger module before it executes the module definition function. You can also see that in the module definition function there is an argument called logger. That argument will be set to the logger module once it is loaded by RequireJS. In the example you can see that the defined module uses the logger dependency to log "hello" if the sayHello function is called. Now that you understand how to use RequireJS to define modules, it is time to learn about the require function.

Using the require Function

Another useful function in RequireJS is the `require` function. The `require` function is used to load dependencies without the creation of a module. The `require` function receives an array of dependencies to load and a callback function that gets as arguments the loaded dependencies. For example, Listing 3-19 uses the `require` function, which defines a function that requires jQuery to work.

Listing 3-19. Using the require Function

```
require(['jquery'], function ($) {
    //jQuery was loaded and can be used now
});
```

■ **Caution** Pay careful attention to the fact that the `require` function will load the file called `jquery.js` and it doesn't deal with version numbers. If you have version numbers in the file name, you should add the versions to the name of the file or use the `paths` option in the `config` function.

The `require` function can also be used to load a module into a variable. When you want to use the `require` function to load a module, you supply the module name and use a variable to get the output of the `require` function. Listing 3-20 shows how to load a jQuery library into a variable.

Listing 3-20. Using the require Function to Load Only One Dependency

```
var $ = require('jquery');
```

The RequireJS library will be used later in the book but for now this is all you have to know in order to use it to define and load modules.

Summary

Modules are not a part of JavaScript, but there are proven patterns that you can use to emulate them. It is very necessary to create modules in order to separate application concerns and to make the application more composable. The RequireJS library can be very useful both to define modules and as a module loader. We will use the library later on when we create our SPA.

In the future, when ECMAScript 6 is a recommendation, modules will be a part of JavaScript, and we will be less dependent on the patterns that you learned. But who knows when that will happen. Now that you have mastered JavaScript and you know how to use patterns to create modular JavaScript, you are ready to start creating SPAs.

CHAPTER 4

■ ■ ■

SPA Concepts and Architecture

In Chapter 1 we discussed the main events that led to today's JavaScript single-page application (SPA) development. We also introduced the main building blocks of SPAs and talked a little about them. In this chapter we will drill down into these building blocks and explain them in more detail. You will get to know the difference between MVC (**M**odel/**V**iew/**C**ontroller) and MVVM (**M**odel/**V**iew/**V**iew**M**odel), the main communication tools that you use in SPAs, the main HTML5 features that are useful in SPAs, and a little about representational state transfer (REST). Later on we will discuss SPA architecture considerations, like where the MVC or MVVM patterns fit in the whole architecture picture or where to use the different building blocks.

The first thing we will discuss is the main SPA building blocks.

Main SPA Building Blocks

SPAs are based on single pages and JavaScript interactions. But what makes an SPA isn't only the single page but the building blocks that help to create it.

The main SPA building blocks include the following:

- JavaScript libraries and frameworks

- Routing

- HTML5 JavaScript application programming interfaces (APIs)

- Client-side template engine

- Server back end API and REST

What distinguishes an SPA from any other web application or site is the front end routing mechanism. Before we talk about routing, let's first talk about JavaScript libraries and frameworks.

JavaScript Libraries

One of the great things about JavaScript is the JavaScript libraries ecosystem. If you need a JavaScript feature in your web application or site, somebody has probably published a library that implements that feature. On the other hand, with the flood of so many libraries, developers find themselves in major dilemmas regarding which library to use and in which situation. There is no rule of thumb for how to choose JavaScript libraries and that leads to a lot of confusion.

GUIDELINES FOR CHOOSING JAVASCRIPT LIBRARIES

Here are some guidelines, from experience, for choosing JavaScript libraries:

- The library supports the functionality that you need. It is an obvious guideline but sometimes we pick libraries because they have a buzz right now or they look great. If the framework doesn't supply the need functionality, don't use it.

- The library has good performance. You should make sure that a library that you pick is fast. Users expect that web applications or sites will be fast and if a library slows you down, you should think twice whether to use it.

- The library has a supportive community. We prefer libraries that have a community that support them. A supportive community shows the value of the library in the eyes of many developers. Moreover, it might indicate that other developers can help you, whether in online content or code examples. Last but not least, if a lot of developers are using the library it might indicate that the library is of good quality.

- Do known web applications or sites use the library? This is a question that we often ask ourselves before picking a library. If you don't find proof that known web applications or sites use the library, this might indicate that it isn't being used in production environments.

- The library has good documentation. One of the frustrating things about JavaScript libraries is the lack of documentation. Without documentation you are walking in the dark and you can't really be sure that you are using the library in the right way. We always prefer documented.

- There is library code modularity. You most likely won't use all the features that a library exposes. It is considered a good practice to create a modular library. A modular library can help you adopt only the features that you need and by doing that you will decrease the size of the files that your users download.

SPAs heavily use JavaScript and therefore you will need some JavaScript libraries in order to create them. There are an enormous number of JavaScript libraries, and most of them can be categorized into the following groups:

- Document Object Model (DOM) manipulation: Libraries, like jQuery, Prototype, MooTools, and more, that enable the selection of DOM elements and ways to manipulate those elements.

- Utilities: Libraries like Underscore and jQuery that can add missing useful JavaScript functionality.

- MV*: Libraries and frameworks like Backbone.js, AngularJS, Ember.js and Knockout.js that implement user interface (UI) design patterns like MVC and MVVM. Lately, these libraries/frameworks are a must-have in order to develop rich front ends.

- Routing: Libraries like Sammy.js, History.js and Crossroads.js that are used for routing and browser history management.

- Templating and rendering: Libraries like JsRender, Underscore and Handlebars that are used as front-end render engines.

- Data manipulation: Libraries like Breeze.js that are used for data manipulation and that help to support data-driven scenarios.

- Asynchronous Module Definition (AMD): Libraries like RequireJS and Almond that are used as module loaders and module definers.

- Plug-ins: Any library that adds more features to the previous categories.

■ **Note**   There are other categories that can be used but these are the main ones.

In this book we use some of the libraries mentioned here. The most important library/framework that you are going to choose is your MV* library/framework.

MV* in the Front End

In most of the modern web applications that you are going to build, you will probably use some sort of MV* framework/library. These frameworks/libraries are based on the MVC or MVVM design patterns and this is why everybody uses the * sign. MV* frameworks/libraries can help you to separate your application front end concerns into maintainable parts and to help you to structure your code. Before we talk about the frameworks/libraries, let's first understand their patterns and how they are implemented.

MVC

MVC is one of the famous UI patterns. It has been used in applications for more than four decades and it is very suitable to web development, both in server-centric applications and client-centric applications. Each of the MVC parts has its own purpose:

- The *model* represents the application domain and is mostly used as a data structure.

- The *view* is the display of the model or the model projection in the UI. Another responsibility of views is to observe the models that they represent and respond to any changes.

- The *controller* handles input and is responsible for passing the model to the view or updating the model when it is being changed in the view.

Figure 4-1 shows the MVC parts and how they relate to each other.

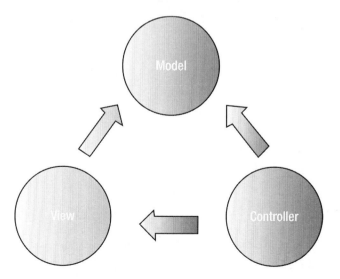

Figure 4-1. *MVC pattern diagram*

MVC helps to separate different concerns like handling inputs, UI, and data structures.

MVVM

MVVM is another known UI pattern that was developed in the last decade. Each of the MVVM parts has its own purpose:

- The *model* represents the application domain and is mostly used as the data structure.

- The *view* is the display of the model or the model projection.

- The *view model* handles UI input and is responsible for one- or two-way binding between the view and the model. It can also pass commands from the view to the model.

The difference between MVC and MVVM is the view model's responsibility. While controllers can serve more than one view, the view model is coupled only to one view. Moreover, the view model is used as a container for data and commands that the view can use and not as an orchestrator like controllers in MVC. Figure 4-2 shows the MVVM parts and how they relate to each other.

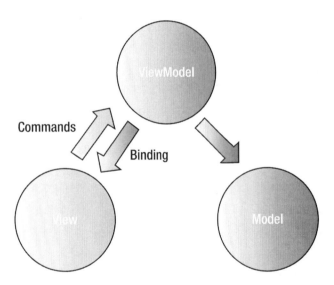

Figure 4-2. *MVVM pattern diagram*

MVVM helps to separate different concerns like handling inputs, UI, and data like MVC does, but MVVM is a derivative of MVC where the view model acts as a very specific controller.

The Roles of MV* Frameworks in SPAs

One thing you might ask yourself is why you would bother to use an MV* framework/library in your application. If you are coming from server-centric web applications or from native application development, you probably used MVC or MVVM patterns. Using MV* frameworks/libraries on the client side is the same as in other applications. You separate your application concerns into reusable and testable parts. You create more meaningful structures, and later on maintenance can become easier.

In SPAs, MV* frameworks/libraries act as the main foundation. Most of those frameworks/libraries supply features for routing, communication, templating, and more. This is why choosing the right MV* in your application is so crucial. There are many MV* frameworks and libraries and these are the most interesting ones in our opinion:

- **Backbone.js**: An MV* library that includes only basic five core components. It was written by Jeremy Ashkenas, the author of CoffeeScript. It helps to structure your code and gives only the small subset of needed features to create SPAs. Backbone.js was one of the first MV* libraries and it influenced most of the new frameworks and libraries. In the book we use Backbone.js because it includes the smallest set of tools for creating an SPA. Another reason for Backbone. js usage is that it is not opinionated like most of the other major frameworks.

- **AngularJS**: This very popular MV* framework is maintained by Google. AngularJS includes component-based architecture and is very opinionated. It also includes a lot of conventions that you have to know and use (or else nothing will work as expected). AngularJS includes many features that help to build SPAs and is considered a "one-stop shop" for creating SPAs.

- **Ember.js**: This is another popular MV* framework, which was written by Yehuda Katz and Tom Dale. It incorporates common JavaScript idioms and best practices to provide its features. Like AngularJS, it is considered a "one-stop shop" for creating SPAs.

- **Knockout.js**: This popular MVVM library was originally written by Steve Sanderson. As opposed to the previous three frameworks/libraries, Knockout.js only includes MVVM features like bindings, dependency tracking, and templating. In order to create an SPA, Knockout.js isn't enough and you will have to use other libraries to close the gaps.

- **Durandal**: A popular framework (mainly used by .NET developers) that was written by Rob Eisenberg. It is based on popular libraries like Knockout.js, RequireJS, and jQuery. Durandal combines these libraries and supports client-side routing, simple application life cycle, and state management, making it an interesting MV* framework to consider.

■ **Note**   In the book we use Backbone.js as the foundation for the application we build. Chapter 5 will introduce this library. The book doesn't include a comparison between the frameworks, but there is a good framework comparison in Addy Osmani's "Journey Through The JavaScript MVC Jungle" article (`http://bit.ly/MOSsut`).

Once you know about MV* frameworks and libraries and their role on the client side, it is time to move to the most important building block: routing.

Routing in an SPA

Routing is the main feature that differentiates SPAs from other modern web applications. In an SPA you have only a single page. In order to navigate from one page to another, you need a mechanism that will intercept navigation events, change the look and feel of the single page, and also save the history of the navigation. This is where routing comes in.

In SPAs you stay always on the same page and that can be challenging in these ways:

- How do you save navigation history?

- How do you align with the browser back button?

- How do you do deep linking?

- How do you keep the navigation state available?

- How can you be search engine optimized (SEO)?

Most challenges are solved by the new HTML5 History API. The HTML5 History API includes a set of new APIs that provides access and manipulation options for the browser's navigation history. On the other hand, the History API is not supported by legacy browsers like Internet Explorer 6-9. You might think this means that we are in trouble when we want to write applications that need to support legacy browsers, but that is not the case. You can use routing libraries that include fallbacks that handle routing in legacy browsers. This can help you create SPAs that work in legacy browsers.

■ **Tip** All the libraries that implement routing have something in common. Underneath, they use the HTML5 History API. The `window` object includes a `history` property that holds a `history` object. The `history` object, which is implemented as a stack, provides access to the browser's navigation history and exposes an API to manipulate the history stack. You can use APIs like `back` and `forward` to go back and forward; you can use the `pushState` function to add your own state into the history stack; and you even have a `popstate` event to wire handlers to respond to changes in the history state.

The History API isn't supported by legacy browsers, and this is why you should use libraries that include fallback behaviors if the API is not supported.

There are three main options for solving the challenges mentioned. First, you can choose an MV* framework/library that provides routing and navigation. All the MV* frameworks/libraries that I mentioned earlier include routing and navigation support, except Knockout.js. (Backbone.js does include built-in routing. You will get to know the Backbone.js router in the next chapter.) Second, you can use a routing library that will handle all the routing and navigation for you. Libraries like Sammy.js, History.js, and Crossroads.js can help with that. A last option, which is not recommended, is to tailor your own implementation. The last two options won't be discussed in this book.

The # Sign Role in Routing

One last thing about routing on the client side is the use of the # sign. In regular HTML development, the # sign is used for bookmarks. You create a hyperlink element with a `name` attribute set to some name. That hyperlink will act as a bookmark. Later on, you use another hyperlink and this time you use the `href` attribute to point to the bookmark by using the # sign. Clicking the second hyperlink will move the browser context to the first link and also change the URL by adding to it a # and the name to go to. Listing 4-1 shows how to do that.

Listing 4-1. Using Hyperlinks Bookmark Behavior http://jsfiddle.net/gilf/xTtGv/

```
<a name="link"></a>

<!-- Later on in the web page -->
<a href="#link">Move to link</a>
```

A lot of SPA routers use the # sign to indicate a new route, whether it is in dedicated routing libraries or in an MV* framework that implements routing. The # sign is attached at the end of the application URL, and all the routing that appears after it is used to navigate inside an SPA. This is why in an SPA you might see routes like http://MyWebSite/#about or http://MyWebSite/#comments/1.

▨ **Note**   The use of the # sign is not mandatory for routing engines but you will find it implemented in many frameworks and libraries.

Now that you know a little bit about routing, we will proceed to a new topic that is not related to routing: the HTML5 JavaScript APIs.

Leveraging HTML5 JavaScript APIs

We have already learned about the HTML5 History API. The History API is just one API in HTML5 that helps to create SPAs. There are a lot of other new HTML5 JavaScript APIs that also help to implement SPAs but the most relevant APIs are in these categories:

- Offline and storage
- Connectivity
- Performance

▨ **Note**   There are many other HTML5 APIs that can help to implement SPA features but the previous categories have the most relevant APIs in our humble opinion.

Offline Web Applications and Storages

The offline and storage APIs enable you to persist local data in the browser and to support application availability in offline scenarios. These options can help you create functionality that resembles native/smart clients, which save their states locally on a client's device.

These are the offline and storage APIs:

- Web Storage
- IndexedDB
- Application Cache

Web Storage

Web Storage is a simple key/value pair dictionary that is stored in the web browser. All the data in Web Storage are stored in string format so if you want to save objects you need to serialize them into a string representation. The data stored in Web Storage are local and are not sent to the server and the server has no knowledge about the stored data. Web Storage is divided into two different storage objects that are different only by their lifetime management:

- `sessionStorage`: The lifetime of the data is accessible to any page from the same site opened in that window.

- `localStorage`: The lifetime of the data spans multiple windows and lasts beyond the current session. Also, the data are persisted when the browser is closed.

The browser allocates a `sessionStorage` and a `localStorage` for every domain. This means that every domain can use a dedicated storage. Each browser's Web Storage implementation is different, so if you browse a web application with both Internet Explorer and Chrome you won't get the same `local/sessionStorage`. Also, the capacities of each storage mechanism differ between browsers.

Both `sessionStorage` and `localStorage` include the same API:

- `length`: A property that holds the number of key/value pairs in the storage.

- `key(index)`: Returns the key in the storage that is related to the given index.

- `getItem(key)`: Returns the related value for the provided key. If the item doesn't exist, the function returns null. You will need to parse the returned value if you saved something that is not in string format.

- `setItem(key, value)`: Inserts or updates the given key/value pair.

- `removeItem(key)`: Removes the item that has the given key.

- `clear`: Empties the storage.

In Listing 4-2, you can see the Web Storage API in action.

Listing 4-2. Web Storage API Usage `http://jsfiddle.net/gilf/VpYbw/`

```
localStorage.setItem("key", "value"); // will add a new item to the storage
var val = localStorage.getItem("key"); // will retrieve the item that coresponds to the "key"
localStorage.removeItem("key"); // will remove the item that corresponds to the "key"
localStorage.clear(); // will clear all the local storage data
```

IndexedDB

As opposed to Web Storage, which is a dictionary, IndexedDB is a real in-browser database. IndexedDB holds object stores that persist records. Each record has a key path and a corresponding value, which can be simple types or JavaScript objects and arrays. The object stores can include indexes for fast retrieval of records and can store a large number of objects.

IndexedDB is mostly asynchronous and it is exposed through the `window.indexedDB` object. Legacy browsers, like Internet Explorer 6-9, don't support IndexedDB, and if you need to support specific browsers you should check if IndexedDB is supported.

■ **Tip** The "Can I Use…" web site includes updated information about the support of HTML5 APIs in browsers. Go to the web site to check if a feature is supported in the browsers you target: `http://caniuse.com/`.

In order to start working with IndexedDB, you first need to open the database. Because the IndexedDB API is asynchronous, send an open request with the database name by using the `indexedDB` object's open function and add event listeners to the `success` and `error` of the request. Listing 4-3 shows how to use the open function.

Listing 4-3. Opening an IndexedDB

```
var db;
var request = indexedDB.open("MyDatabase");
request.onerror = function(evt) {
  console.log("An error occurred with error code: " + evt.target.errorCode);
};
```

```
request.onsuccess = function(evt) {
  db = request.result;
};
```

The open function receives an additional version number argument. When the database version is smaller than the provided version, the upgradeneeded event will be triggered and you will be able to change the database's structure in its event handler. Changing the version of the database is the only way to change the structure of the database.

The IndexedDB can include zero or more objectStores. objectStores are like tables in relational databases. objectStores hold the key/value records and can have key paths, key generators, and indexes. In order to create an objectStore use the IndexedDB's createObjectStore function. The function receives the name of the objectStore and an options literal object, which configures aspects like key paths and key generators.

Listing 4-4. Creating an objectStore

```
var db;
var request = indexedDB.open("CarDB", 1);
request.onsuccess = function (evt) {
        db = request.result;
};

request.onerror = function (evt) {
        console.log("An error occurred with error code: " + evt.target.errorCode);
};

request.onupgradeneeded = function (evt) {
        var objectStore = evt.target.result.createObjectStore("cars",
                                { keyPath: "id", autoIncrement: true });

        objectStore.createIndex("type", "type", { unique: false });

        objectStore.add({ type: "bmw", speed: 0 }); // insert a dummy object to the store
};
```

In the previous code the only interesting part is the upgradeneeded event handler. In the handler, the first line creates an objectStore with a key path on an id object property. The key path is the main index of the stored value and if it doesn't exist in the object you need to supply a key generator, which in the example is set to autoIncrement.

In the previous code you can also see the creation of an index in the objectStore. You use the createIndex function and supply the index name, the object's property name to be indexed, and an options literal object to define whether the index enforces a unique constraint.

Once you have an objectStore you can start manipulating it. The only way to create CRUD (create/read/update/delete) operations is by using IndexedDB transactions. There are two transaction options: read-only and read/write. In order to create a transaction, you need to request a transaction on an objectStore from the opened IndexedDB database. Listing 4-5 shows how to create a transaction.

Listing 4-5. Creating an IndexedDB Transaction

```
var transaction = db.transaction("[cars]", "readwrite");
```

Once you have the transaction, you can use it to retrieve the objectStore and to request to perform an operation on the store. You can add event listeners to the request, success, and error events. Listing 4-6 shows how to add a new car into the cars' objectStore.

Listing 4-6. Adding a Car Object into the objectStore

```
var transaction = db.transaction("[cars]", "readwrite");
var objectStore = transaction.objectStore("cars");
var request = objectStore.add({ type: "honda", speed: 0 });
request.onsuccess = function (evt) {
    // do something when the add succeeded
};
```

In order to delete a record from the objectStore, use the delete function with the key path of the object. In order to update a record, use the put function with the updated object.

In order to read a record from the objectStore, use a read-only transaction and use one of these three options:

1. Use the get function with the key of the record.

2. Use an index with an index name.

3. Use a cursor to iterate over the objectStore.

Listing 4-7 shows an example of using the get function.

Listing 4-7. Simple Object Retrival Using the get Function

```
var transaction = db.transaction(["cars"], "readonly");
var objectStore = transaction.objectStore("cars");
var request = objectStore.get(1);
request.onsuccess = function(event) {
        // Do something with the request.result!
        Console.log(request.result.type);
};
```

You will use IndexedDB in client-side data-drive scenarios and it can be helpful to decrease the dependency on the server database for things like lookup tables or profile data. In this book, we don't use IndexedDB but it is very crucial to know about it from a developer's point of view. We had the opportunity, for example, to use IndexedDB in a very interesting PhoneGap application. In the application, we needed a database on the client side that could handle a lot of queries quickly. IndexedDB was the best choice and it succeeded in handling the amount of data that we needed to store.

■ **Note** IndexedDB is a huge subject and a lot of its aspects are out of the scope for this book, which covers basic functionality. If you wish to learn more about the database, start by reading "Using IndexedDB" on the Mozilla Developer Network web site: http://mzl.la/I6tzeQ.

Application Cache

The Application Cache API enables interactions with web applications even when there is no network connectivity. The server provides an endpoint with a cache manifest file that includes a list of URLs to cache. When the client receives that manifest and includes support to Application Cache, it will read the list of URLs from the manifest file and download the resources and cache them locally. Once you try to access the application after the resources are downloaded, you will get them from the cache.

In order to let the client know that there is a cache manifest file in the server, the html tag includes a new manifest attribute. Listing 4-8 shows how to use this attribute.

Listing 4-8. html Tag with Manifest Attribute

```
<!DOCTYPE html>
<html manifest="/appCache.manifest">
<body>

</body>
</html>
```

The Content-Type of the manifest file in the server must be set to text/cache-manifest and it must be encoded as UTF-8.

The manifest file requires a CACHE MANIFEST header and is built with three sections: explicit, network, and fallback sections. The explicit section defines all the resources that the browsers need to cache. The explicit section is used with the CACHE header, which can also be omitted. The network section indicates the resources that need the network to function. The fallback section defines what to do if some file is not successfully cached. Listing 4-9 includes an example of a manifest file.

Listing 4-9. Cache Manifest File

```
CACHE MANIFEST
CACHE:
/site.css
/scripts.js
/image1.jpg
/image2.jpg

FALLBACK:
/offline.html

NETWORK:
/login.html
```

Application Cache also includes JavaScript APIs that can be found in the windows.applicationCache object. The applicationCache object contains functions for cache status, cache update, and cache event handlers. Another feature of Application Cache is a new Boolean property called online on the navigator object and two new global JavaScript event handlers for the offline and online events. Listing 4-10 shows the use of these features.

Listing 4-10. Using the Application Cache API

```
// the online event is triggered when the environment returns from offline to online
window.addEventListener("online", function(e) {
   console.log(navigator.online); // will output true
}, true);

// the offline event is triggered when the environment returns from online to offline
window.addEventListener("offline", function(e) {
   console.log(navigator.online); // will output false
}, true);
```

With the combination of the Application Cache API and one of the storage APIs, you can create offline web applications much more easily than before.

Connectivity

The regular way to communicate with servers in SPAs is by using Ajax and the XMLHttpRequest object. The HTML5 connectivity APIs add new ways that enable web applications to communicate with servers. The connectivity APIs include WebSockets, Server-Sent Events, and CORS (cross-origin resource sharing). While connectivity is very important, we will learn more about these APIs in Chapter 9.

Performance

There are a lot of new improvements to JavaScript that increase its performance. In Chapter 3 you got to know the async attribute, which adds a way to load scripts asynchronously. One of the interesting APIs in the performance area is Web Workers.

JavaScript runs only in the UI thread. In the past we used the setTimeout and setInterval functions to mimic concurrency but those solutions can create a lot of mess in your application. Web Workers can help to change that situation. If you have a long-running task and you wish to do it in JavaScript without blocking the UI thread you can use Web Workers.

A Web Worker is a background worker that runs scripts in parallel to the UI thread. The worker itself is independent of any UI scripts and has its own execution environment. A Web Worker includes a message-passing mechanism for data coordination or data retrieval.

In order to run a Web Worker, you need to create a Web Worker object and pass to it an execution script URL. Once the worker is created it includes events that you can wire into, like the message and error events. In the running script you can pass data to the UI thread message event listener by using the postMessage function. You can also terminate the running of a worker by using the terminate function.

Listing 4-11 shows how to create a new Web Worker.

Listing 4-11. Creating a Web Worker

```
var wb = new Worker("script.js");
wb.onmessage = function (evt) {
    console.log(evt.data); // will print to the console the data returned by the Web Worker
}
wb.postMessage(20); // will send to the Web Worker a message
```

In the example, a new Web Worker is created and it will run the script.js file. You can also see how to wire the message event and how to retrieve the message data by using the evt event argument. Listing 4-12 shows the script.js file.

Listing 4-12. The Web Worker Script

```
function f(n) {
    var s = 0;
    if (n == 0) return (s);
    if (n == 1) {
        s += 1;
        return (s);
    }
    else {
        return (f(n - 1) + f(n - 2));
    }
}
```

```
self.addEventListener("message", function (n) {
    var value = "";
    for (var i = 0; i <= n.data; i++) {
        value += "  " + f(i);
    }

    postMessage(value);
}, false);
```

In the `script.js` implementation, you run the Fibonacci number algorithm. The most interesting thing to notice here is the use of `self`. In a Web Worker there is no `this` keyword. If you need to relate to the worker itself, for example, to wire the message event listener, you need to use the `self` keyword.

Web Workers can be very handy when you need to do some long calculations or to run heavy JavaScript algorithms.

Client-Side Template Engines

An SPA is built on only a single page. That means that you will have to partially render that single page very often as a result of user interaction. This is where client-side template engines come into the picture.

There are many client-side template engines that you can use: for example, Underscore or Handlebars. The main purpose is to get a model object, a template written in the engine convention and to output HTML that can be attached to the DOM. When you use client-side render engines, you separate the view markup from the view logic and that helps to create a more maintainable code.

The syntax of the template you create depends on the template engine you use. The engine responsibility is to take care of template parsing. It is also responsible for replacing template placeholders with the actual data from the model.

Underscore as a Template Engine Example

In this book we use the Underscore library as a template engine. Underscore is a utilities library that adds a lot of missing JavaScript functionality. Underscore exposes its API by using the underscore sign. One of these utilities is a template engine with its own syntax.

In order to create a template that can be used to render a model, you first need to compile the template. Use the `_.template` function to compile a template. The `_.template` **function receives three arguments: a template string, an** `optional data` **object to render, and an** `options literal` **object for settings. If the** `_.template` **function receives the template string only, it will return a compiled template as a function that can be run. If the** `_.template` **function receives the template string and the data object, it will compile and run the template and return the HTML itself. Listing 4-13 shows how to use a simple template to render the car type.**

Listing 4-13. Simple Template Rendering http://jsfiddle.net/gilf/K6qw7/

```
var executedTemplate = _.template("<div><%= type %></div>", { type: "bmw", speed: 0 });
console.log(executedTemplate); // outputs <div>bmw</div>
```

In the previous code you can see the use of a placeholder with the `<% %>` syntax. In Underscore there are three placeholder options:

- Interpolate placeholder using the `<%= %>` syntax: In this option, Underscore inserts the result of the given expression. The properties of the data object are available to use in the placeholder.

- Evaluate placeholder using the `<% %>` syntax: In this option, Underscore evaluates the given code. This syntax enables you to use loops and conditions in Underscore.

- HTML-escaped placeholder using the <%- %> syntax: In this option, Underscore inserts the result of the given expression but if the data include special characters, it will escape them. The following characters will be escaped: - & < > " ' /.

Listing 4-14 is a template that can be used on an array of cars to create an unordered list of cars.

Listing 4-14. A Template with a Loop http://jsfiddle.net/gilf/vJ9T3/

```
var templateString = "<div>Cars:</div>"
        + "<ul><% _.forEach(cars, function (car, i) { %>"
        + "<li><%= car.type %></li>"
        + "<% }) %>"
        + "</ul>";
var cars = { cars : [{ type: "bmw", speed: 0 }, { type: "honda", speed: 0 }] };
var executedTemplate = _.template(templateString, cars);
console.log(executedTemplate); // outputs <div>Cars:</div><ul><li>bmw</li><li>honda</li></ul>
```

In the example you can see another Underscore function, forEach, which is used to iterate over the cars array and add a list item for each car type.

Once you understand how to use a template engine, it might raise new questions, like how to manage the templates or where to put them. There are a few options that you can use:

- Use script tags in the single page, which will hold the templates.

- Load the templates from the server.

The use of script tags to hold templates is very common. In order to use this technique the script tag should have an ID and its type should be set to text/template. You will use the ID to find the script and to use it. Listing 4-15 shows a script tag with a template.

Listing 4-15. A Template in a Script Tag http://jsfiddle.net/gilf/vJ9T3/

```
<script type="text/template" id="cars-template">
        <div>Cars:</div>
        <ul>
        <% _.forEach(cars, function (car, i) { %>
                <li><%= car.type %></li>
        <% }) %>
        </ul>
</script>
```

Putting the templates in as scripts eliminates the need to load them from the server and decrease the network traffic. On the other hand, the single-page HTML becomes very big and it includes a lot of template script tags. You should find the balance between loading templates and hosting them inside the HTML.

Once you want to use a template in the script tag you need to get its HTML and that is easy when you use libraries like jQuery. Listing 4-16 shows you how to use jQuery to get the template and pass it to Underscore.

Listing 4-16. Runtime Usage of Template Script Tag http://jsfiddle.net/gilf/25CjK/

```
var cars = { cars : [{ type: "bmw", speed: 0 }, { type: "honda", speed: 0 }] };
var executedTemplate = _.template($('#cars-template').html(), cars);
console.log(executedTemplate); // outputs <div>Cars:</div><ul><li>bmw</li><li>honda</li></ul>
```

The second way to manage templates is to load them from the server. With this option you store the templates as HTML files on the server and load them by using Ajax when they are needed.

One of the interesting things about RequireJS is the text.js plug-in that allows you to specify text-based dependencies. Because templates are text-based, using text.js can be a very convenient way to load templates.

■ **Note** You can download the text.js plug-in from the RequireJS web site: http://bit.ly/wlSsmi.

---

text.js is automatically loaded into memory once you put the text! prefix for a dependency in the RequireJS require or define functions. Pay attention to the fact that it will happen only if the RequireJS library file and text.js file are placed in the same folder. Imagine that you have a template called cars-template.html, which exists in the templates folder in the server; Listing 4-17 shows you how to load the template.

Listing 4-17. Loading a Template Using the text.js Plug-in

```
define(["text!templates/cars-template.html"],
    function(html) {
        var cars = { cars : [{ type: "bmw", speed: 0 }, { type: "honda", speed: 0 }] };
        var executedTemplate = _.template(html, cars);
        console.log(executedTemplate); // outputs <div>Cars:</div><ul><li>bmw</li><li>honda</li></ul>
    }
);
```

■ **Note** The template file is an HTML file that includes the same template in Listing 4-15 but without the script tag that wraps the template.

---

text.js includes one restriction that you must know about. It uses the XMLHttpRequest object, which is restricted to cross-domain policies. This means you should use the plug-in with a web server. If you load files using file:// access you might have cross-domain issues.

Server Back End API and REST

SPAs include a lot of logic that is implemented in the client side, but that doesn't mean you should stop using web servers. It means that the web server's role is changing.

The web server role in an SPA is to help deliver the single web page to the client and to expose the relevant resources that the client needs, like templates, for example. Another role of the web server is to expose the web API that the SPA can use to do common server logic like authentication, authorization, back-end database manipulation, and more.

Most web servers today enable you to create a rich web API over HTTP. A web API is an API that exposes endpoints to enable CRUD operations. Those endpoints can also expose resources like video and audio streams and more. Most web API platforms try to align to the REST architecture style and this is why it is important to know what REST is.

REST was defined around the year 2000 by Roy Fielding in his doctoral dissertation. REST describes an architectural style that takes advantage of the resource-based nature of HTTP, for the purpose of creating scalable and extendable applications. Not every HTTP-based service can be considered a RESTful service. To be considered a RESTful service, your service needs to comply with several architectural guidelines:

- Each resource exposed by the service needs to be represented by a meaningful uniform resource identifier (URI). There is no single endpoint for a RESTful service.

- You need to use the matching HTTP verb, such as GET, POST, PUT, and DELETE, when you interact with a resource. In addition, the service is required to return a meaningful HTTP response code according to the result of the service action.

- The resource returned from the service needs to use a self-documenting schema, describing its state, the actions you can perform on the resource (sort of a resource state machine), and the interactions it has with other resources in the system. This type of service is also referred to as a hypermedia service.

■ **Note**   In this book we do not preach about the accurate use of the REST architectural style. Most parts of the HTTP-based services demonstrated here will not use all the parts of the REST architectural style due to the need to keep the demonstrated code and output simple and to-the-point.

There are a lot of frameworks that can help you create your own web API. Here are some examples:

- ASP.NET Web API: A web API built into the ASP.NET framework. In this book we will build our back end with this technology.

- WCF HTTP Services: You can use Windows Communication Foundation with HTTP binding to create a service that exposes the web API. This is another framework inside the .NET framework that enables you to create your web API. On the other hand, WCF isn't dedicated to a web API and you should favour ASP.NET Web API if you are building a .NET back end.

- Express framework: A web application framework for node.js that includes the ability to create web APIs very easily.

■ **Note**   Each development environment, like PHP, Java, and .NET, has its own web API framework. In this book we use the ASP.NET Web API.

SPA Architecture

When building SPAs, you will combine both modular JavaScript and an MV* framework. You will also use a back end with some technology to expose your application server API. In Figure 4-3 you can see a diagram of the suggested SPA architecture.

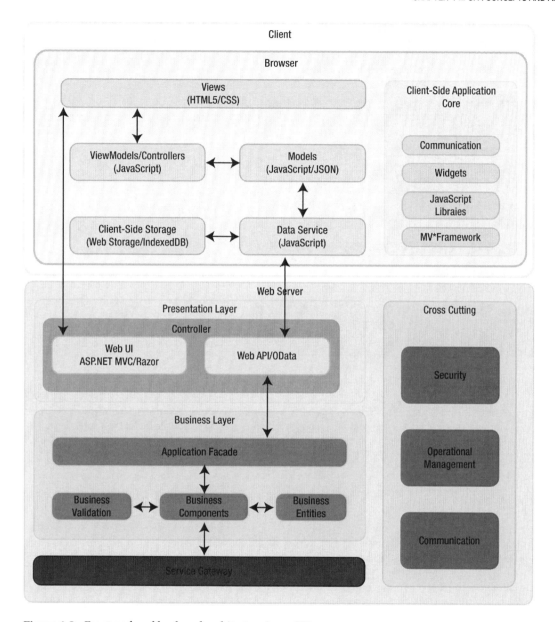

***Figure 4-3.** Front-end and back-end architecture in an SPA*

In the browser area what you see is how a logical module in the application is created. The module has views, controller/ViewModel, and model and data service to interact with the server or with client-side storage options like IndexedDB or Web Storage. Each module interacts with the application core that is built on JavaScript/CSS libraries.

You can also see the use of the ASP.NET Web API as a back end to the application. Once the application starts the part that is the web UI in the server returns the first view and later on any other interaction with the server is handled by the exposed API.

The previous figure is not enough because it shows only how a logical module in the application would look. In scalable JavaScript application architecture, you have more than one module. Once you have a lot of modules the way they interact is through a mediator or an event aggregator. In Figure 4-4 you can see a high-level diagram of the front end architecture of a scalable JavaScript application.

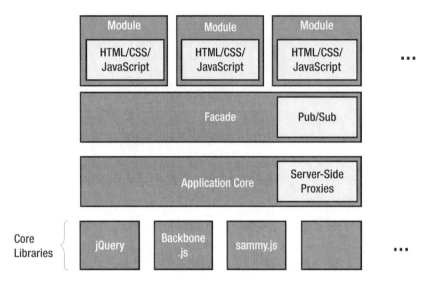

Figure 4-4. *Front-end scalable architecture in an SPA*

In the figure you can see that the application core is constructed from the core JavaScript/CSS libraries (like in Figure 4-3). The only missing part is the Pub/Sub section, which is used to decouple logical modules from one another. Each module is still constructed from view, controller/ViewModel, model, and a data service, but you can't see them in this figure.

Summary

SPAs are just web applications with routing mechanisms that differentiate them from other modern web applications. Most of the SPAs that you build today will include an MV* framework/library that will help you to structure your code. SPAs also include new HTML5 JavaScript APIs that help to add to the SPAs' abilities, such as storage or offline support, which were related only to native applications.

This chapter concludes the first part of the book, which included basic JavaScript and SPA concepts that you need to know before you start writing an SPA. In the next part you will learn about Backbone.js and we will build an SPA front end with it.

PART II

Building the Front End

■ ■ ■

CHAPTER 5

Getting Started with Backbone.js

In the previous part of this book, you were introduced to single page application (SPA) concepts. You also learned how to make best use of JavaScript language features in order to create a more modular and maintainable JavaScript application. At the end of the part, you learned about the building blocks of an SPA. In this part, we will construct an SPA front end by using these tools and building blocks.

First, we'll learn more about Backbone.js, the MV* library that is used here. Once you understand Backbone.js basics, in the next chapter, "Creating an SPA Step by Step," we will build an SPA front end for an application called TheAgency. The application will enable us to manage a secret service agency's agents and their tasks. But first things first, let's get to know the Backbone.js library.

■ **Note**   We chose Backbone.js because it is simple, nonopinionated, and doesn't enforce any conventions. Also, Backbone.js has a large community and it is part of many production web sites and web applications like the following:

- Trello

- Code School challenge page

- Khan Academy

- Airbnb

- Walmart Mobile

You can find a list of more web sites and applications that use Backbone.js at http://backbonejs.org/#examples.

Because we won't cover all Backbone.js application programming interfaces (APIs), you can find more Backbone.js documentation on the Backbone.js web site: http://backbonejs.org.

What Is Backbone.js?

Backbone.js is an MV* library (not a framework) that provides structure for your application's front end. Backbone.js consists of five main objects that you can extend and add your own functionality to:

- Models: Data structures that include data and the ability to create custom events.

- Views: View objects that include the view logic, templating option using Underscore.js, and declarative event handling.

- Collections: A collection of models that includes an API for handling and manipulating the collection.

- Events: An inner Backbone.js module that enables you to extend any object with the ability to bind and trigger custom events.

- Routers: A router module that is used to create the front-end routing functionality in a Backbone.js-based application.

We will explore each of the five main objects and their main APIs. We will also learn how to combine those objects in order to create the structure for your front-end code.

While other frameworks include many features, Backbone.js includes the smallest set of objects that you need for enforcing structure. It doesn't decide for you how to create a user interface (UI), how to write your application logic, or even how to organize your folders. The freedom Backbone.js gives you is one of its strengths. On the other hand, there are a lot of features that you will need to write by yourself and therefore there are a lot of Backbone.js plug-ins that add more abilities to the library.

In order to get started with Backbone.js you need to download its latest version and also to download Underscore.js. Backbone.js has a hard dependency on Underscore.js, which it uses as a utility library for its collection objects and as a template engine. If you are going to use the Backbone.js history support, which is part of the Backbone.js router object or view Document Object Model (DOM) manipulation, you should also include jQuery in your project.

■ **Note**   Here are the sites for downloads:

- Backbone.js: `http://backbonejs.org`

- Underscore.js: `http://underscorejs.org/` (You should pay attention to the download version, which is >= 1.5.0.)

- jQuery: `http://jquery.com/`

Once you put the libraries in your project, you can start writing your front end. Listing 5-1 shows a boilerplate for a web page that includes Backbone.js and all its dependencies.

Listing 5-1. Backbone.js Web-Page Boilerplate `http://jsfiddle.net/jnf8B/`

```
<!DOCTYPE HTML>
<html>
<head>
    <meta charset="UTF-8">
    <title>SPA Title</title>
</head>
<body>
        <!-- Your HTML goes here -->
        <script src="/scripts/lib/jquery.min.js"></script>
        <script src="/scripts/lib/underscore-min.js"></script>
        <script src="/scripts/lib/backbone-min.js"></script>
        <!-- Your scripts go here -->
</body>
</html>
```

In the example you can see that by convention we use all the libraries from a folder called `lib`, which exists in the `scripts` folder. After running these scripts, you can access Backbone.js functionality through the `Backbone` object, Underscore.js through the `_` sign, and jQuery through the `$` sign.

Now that the environment is set up, our first step is understanding how to work with Backbone.js models.

Models

Models are data structures that are used to express domain objects and also incorporate the domain object's logic. In their basic form they are just objects like any other object and even a simple literal object can be a model if it expresses a part in your domain model. While a model could only have properties to hold data, it can also include some business logic for validation or serialization options. A model can have relationships with other models; it can include collections of other models or just single instances of other models. By nesting models inside other models, developers can create their domain model.

Defining a Model

Backbone.js includes a `Backbone.Model` object. The `Backbone.Model` object is used to create models and to expose the model logic. `Backbone.Model` will wrap a simple JavaScript Object Notation (JSON) data structure with more functionality like validation and computed properties. Once you create your model object using Backbone.js, it will also support functionality for managing model changes.

In order to create a new model in your application, you need to extend the `Model` object. See Listing 5-2 for an example.

Listing 5-2. Extending a Model

```
var Car = Backbone.Model.extend({});
```

You can see that we are passing an empty literal object to the extend function. The object can get configuration options for the model and we will explore these soon.

Once you extend the model, you can start using it as a front-end domain model in your application. Listing 5-3 shows how to use the previous model in your code.

Listing 5-3. Creating and Using a Model `http://jsfiddle.net/gilf/jwFtQ/`

```
var Car = Backbone.Model.extend({});
var bmw = new Car();
var honda = new Car({
        type: "honda",
        speed: 0
});
console.log(JSON.stringify(bmw));  // prints {}
console.log(JSON.stringify(honda)) // prints {"type":"honda","speed":0}
```

As you can see in the example, we create two instances of the `Car` model, which are then logged to the console. We use the `JSON.stringify` function to serialize the cars into string representations in order to log them. If you try to log the objects themselves, you will get `[object Object]` printed twice in the console. Another thing that you might notice is that the model constructor can get an object with properties and it will use it as the model initial data and properties.

As mentioned earlier, you can configure the model initializer by providing an options object. The following aspects of the model can be configured by the options object:

- initialize: Called whenever a new model is created. The function doesn't receive arguments.

- defaults: Sets default values to the model properties.

- idAttribute: Indicates the ID of the model. By default it is set to id, which is an identifier that is created by Backbone.js.

- validate: Validates the model. This function will be called by model API functions like save and set. We will explore model validation later in the topic.

- You can also add any function that you want each instance to have.

Listing 5-4 shows how to extend a Car model with some of the previous options.

Listing 5-4. Creating a Model with an Options Object http://jsfiddle.net/gilf/4d4DT/

```
var Car = Backbone.Model.extend({
        initialize: function() {
                console.log("initialized");
        },
        defaults: {
                speed: 0,
                type: "no type"
        },
        print: function() {
                console.log(JSON.stringify(this));
        }
});

var bmw = new Car(); // prints "initialized"

var honda = new Car({
        type: "honda",
        speed: 0
}); // print "initialized"

bmw.print(); // prints {"speed":0,"type":"no type"}
honda.print() // prints {"type":"honda","speed":0}
```

Model APIs

When you extend objects and transform them into models, you have rich API functions and properties at your disposal. The main API functions and properties are the following:

- get: Retrieves the current value of a model property. The function receives as an argument the name of the property. Pay attention that model properties aren't exposed by the model instance. This is why you have to use the get function to get the property value.

- set: Sets a new value to a model property. The function has two forms–setting only one property and setting several properties. In the first form, you pass two arguments–the property name and the new value. In the second form, you pass a literal object with the property names and their new values. Setting a value triggers the change event of the model.

- **toJSON**: Returns the JSON shallow copy representation of the current model. Pay attention that you get a JSON object and not the string representation of the JSON object.

- **clone**: Returns a new instance of the model with all the current model attributes.

- **attributes** property: Holds all the current values of the model's properties. If you need direct access to the properties, use the **attributes** property. You should always prefer to access the properties using the **get** function instead.

- **cid** property: Holds a string that represents the ID of the model on the client side. The ID is generated by Backbone.js when a model is created. The **cid** is very helpful for when you create new models, which should be saved to the server later, and therefore don't have a real identifier.

- **validationError** property and **isValid** function: **validationError** indicates that there was a validation error and holds it. The **isValid** function checks whether the model is in a valid state.

▪ **Note**   There are four more main API functions—**fetch**, **save**, **destroy**, and **sync**—which will be explained in more detail in Chapter 9, when we create the whole SPA and integrate the client and the server.

Listing 5-5. Using Model API Functions and Properties http://jsfiddle.net/gilf/ZSXkL/

```
var Car = Backbone.Model.extend({
        defaults: {
                speed: 0,
                type: "no type"
        }
});

var bmw = new Car();
console.log(bmw.get("speed")); // prints 0

bmw.set("speed", 80);
console.log(bmw.attributes.speed); // prints 80

console.log(bmw.toJSON()); // prints [object Object]
console.log(bmw.cid); // prints c1
```

As you can see in the code we use the **get** function to retrieve the speed of a car object, we use the **set** function to set the speed to 80, and then we use the **attributes toJSON** and **cid** to print to the console a few details about the car.

Model Validation

Another aspect that is included in the model is the ability to write custom validations. Every model has a **validate** function, which is left undefined if you don't pass a validation function when you extend the **Backbone.Model** object. Once you override the **validate** function, you get the ability to write your own custom validation and then you can impose business validation logic on the front end.

The **validate** function is called when you try to persist your model to the server by using the **save** function. You can also indicate that you want validation to occur when you use the **set** function by passing to the **set** function a {validate:true} options object. Another option for running the **validate** function is to use the **isValid** model function, which calls the **validate** function if it wasn't called on the model.

The validate function receives two arguments: a copy of the current model attributes, and an options object, which is the option object that was passed to the save or set functions. You can use the attributes to validate your model current state. If the current state is valid, the validate function shouldn't return anything. If the current state is invalid, the validate function should return an error.

If the state is invalid, a few things will occur:

- The save function won't continue and persist the model data to the server.

- The invalid event will be triggered on the model.

- The model validationError property will be set to the value that validate returned.

Listing 5-6 shows how to use the validate function.

Listing 5-6. Using the validate Function http://jsfiddle.net/gilf/9pph8/

```
var Car = Backbone.Model.extend({
        defaults: {
                speed: 0,
                type: "no type"
        } ,
        validate: function(attrs, options) {
                if (!attrs.type) {
                        return "A car must have a type!";
                }
        }
});

var bmw = new Car();
bmw.set("type", "", {validate: true});

console.log(bmw.validationError); // prints "A car must have a type!"
console.log(bmw.get("type"));     // prints "no type" which is the previous type
```

In the previous example, we validate that the car must have a type by checking if the type is "falsy." You can see that since the validation didn't pass the bmw object still has its type set to "no type."

One last thing about model validation is that the invalid event will be triggered if the validation failed. You can add an event handler to the invalid event, which receives two arguments: the model before the state change and the error. Listing 5-7 shows how to wire the invalid event handler on the model by using the on model function.

Listing 5-7. Adding an Event Handler to the invalid Event http://jsfiddle.net/gilf/Tx8sm/

```
var Car = Backbone.Model.extend({
        defaults: {
                speed: 0,
                type: "no type"
        } ,
        validate: function(attrs, options) {
                if (!attrs.type) {
                        return "A car must have a type!";
                }
        }
});
```

```
var bmw = new Car();
bmw.on("invalid", function(model, error) {
        console.log(model.get("type") + " " + error);
});
bmw.set("type", "", {validate: true});  // prints "no type A car must have a type!"

console.log(bmw.validationError); // prints "A car must have a type!"
console.log(bmw.get("type"));     // prints "no type" which is the previous type
```

In the example you can see how to add the invalid event handler to the model by using the on function. The event will be triggered when you try to set or save a property and the validation fails. The invalid event and how to add an event handler brings us to how to use model events.

Model Events

In Listing 5-7 you saw how to add an event handler to a model instance by using the on function. The on function is part of the Events API that belongs to the Events object.

■ **Note**   The Events object is explained later in the chapter. For now, you just need to know that it includes API functions for adding and removing event handlers.

The Backbone.Model has some events that you can add handlers to. The most interesting one is the change event. The change event is triggered whenever the model state changes. You can add a handler to listen to changes on all of the model or to listen for single attribute changes. The appropriate place to add handlers to models is the initialize function. Once you add handlers in the initialize function, every instance of the model will have the same handlers. Listing 5-8 shows how to add event handlers to a model.

Listing 5-8. Wiring Event Handlers to the change Event

```
var Car = Backbone.Model.extend({
        defaults: {
                speed: 0,
                type: "no type"
        },
        initialize: function() {
                this.on("change", function() {
                        console.log("Model was changed");
                });
                this.on("change:type", function() {
                        console.log("Model type attribute was changed");
                });
        }
});

var bmw = new Car();
bmw.set("type", "bmw"); // prints "Model type attribute was changed" and "Model was changed"
bmw.set("speed", 80);   // prints "Model was changed"
```

In this example, we added two event handlers on the change event and on the type attribute change event. You can see that the syntax to add a handler to a specific attribute follows this convention: change:attributename. Another thing to notice is the order of the events. The specific event is called before the general event. This means that the event on the type property will be triggered first and the general change event later.

Models are the heart of any application because they are the data structures that hold the application data. Without data there wouldn't be an application. In this section we explored how to create models using the Backbone.js Model API. Now that we have covered all the basics on models, it is time to move on to views.

Views

Views in Backbone.js are objects that represent the logic behind a specific view. Views don't include the view markup and they use template engines to help separate the markup from the view logic. For the markup, Backbone.js uses the Underscore.js template engine. The separation between the markup and the logic helps to separate logic from presentation and is considered a good practice. This is why Backbone.js's views were created in the first place.

Once you want to create a view, you use the Backbone.View.extend function. This is very similar to what you did to create models; later on you will see that it is also similar to creating collections and routers. The extend function receives an options object that enables you to configure the view and to add logic to it. Listing 5-9 shows a simple use of the extend function.

Listing 5-9. Creating a Simple View

```
var CarView = Backbone.View.extend({});

var carView = new CarView();
```

The previous view isn't interesting because it doesn't do anything: it is just an empty view.

Defining a View

When you want to add logic to your view you will pass the extend function an options object. The following options can be passed to the view:

- model: The model that the view is bound to.

- collection: The collection that the view is bound to.

- el: The DOM element that the view is bound to. The element can be attached to the DOM or to a virtual DOM element.

- id: The ID of the view. If you don't pass your own ID, Backbone will autogenerate one.

- className: The class name to use on the view DOM element.

- tagName: The tag name of the view DOM element.

- attributes: The attributes of the view DOM elements.

- events: An options object that configures all the DOM events that the view handles. For this options object you will set all the view DOM events to handlers.

Listing 5-10 shows how to set some of the previous options.

Listing 5-10. Creating a Customized View

```
var CarView = Backbone.View.extend({
        model: Car,
        tagName: "div",
        events: {
                "click #changeSpeed": "changeSpeed"
        },
        changeSpeed: function() {
                this.model.set("speed", this.model.get("speed") + 10);
        }
});

var bmw = new Car({ type: "bmw" });
var carView = new CarView(bmw);
```

In this example you probably noticed a few interesting things. First, the events object convention ("eventname selector") is the name of the event and a DOM selector for the element that the event would be added to. Also, you can see that the event we attach gets the name of the event handler function, changeSpeed in the example, which should also be a part of the view. This is the convention for adding event listeners to DOM events; underneath, Backbone.js uses jQuery to add the event handlers that exist on the view object.

Still, the previous example won't result in anything interesting because it doesn't include markup or a way to render the markup. This is where the render function and the Underscore.js template engine come into the picture.

Rendering the View

The render function's default behavior is doing nothing. You must override the function in order to tell Backbone.js how to render the view. With the render function you use the template and the view model in order to render the HTML. Also, a very important convention in the render function is to return the current context, meaning using the this keyword in order to enable chained calls.

Listing 5-11. Adding the render Function

```
var CarView = Backbone.View.extend({
        model: Car,
        tagName: "div",
        template: _.template($('#car-template').html()),
        events: {
                "click #changeSpeed": "changeSpeed"
        },
        render: function() {
                var html = this.template(this.model.toJSON());
                // here you attach the html
                return this;
        },
        changeSpeed: function() {
                this.model.set("speed", this.model.get("speed") + 10);
        }
});

var bmw = new Car({ type: "bmw" });
var carView = new CarView(bmw);
```

In this example you can see that we added a `template` property to the view that uses the Underscore.js `template` function to compile a template. The template here is a script tag with the `car-template` ID. Another thing to notice is that the `render` function uses the model `toJSON` function to get a JSON object and later on runs the compiled template on the JSON object to generate HTML.

■ **Note** From this example and in the future, you can use the following template, which should be a part of the HTML:
`<script id="car-template" type="text/template"><div><%= type %></div></script>` You can also add this template to the HTML pane in jsFiddle if you use it.

Once you use the template engine and the model and you have generated the HTML, you should add it to the markup. This is where the `el` property of the view comes into play. The `el` view property refers to the DOM element that the view would be rendered to. There are two ways to associate the `el` with a DOM element: create a new in-memory element or reference an existing DOM element.

Creating a new in-memory element is done by setting the `id`, `tagName`, and `className` view properties while extending the `Backbone.View` object. By default, all the in-memory elements are created as `div` elements but you can change that behavior by setting the `tagName` property. Listing 5-12 adds the implementation of the view from Listing 5-11 as the last part of the puzzle:

Listing 5-12. An Entire render Function `http://jsfiddle.net/gilf/W8G99/`

```
var CarView = Backbone.View.extend({
        model: Car,
        tagName: "div",
        template: _.template($("#car-template").html()),
        events: {
                "click #changeSpeed": "changeSpeed"
        },
        render: function() {
                this.$el.html(this.template(this.model.toJSON()));
                return this;
        },
        changeSpeed: function() {
                this.model.set("speed", this.model.get("speed") + 10);
        }
});

var bmw = new Car({ type: "bmw" });
var carView = new CarView(bmw);

console.log(carView.el); // prints [object HTMLDivElement]
```

You might ask yourself what `$el` is. While the `el` property is the `HTMLElement`, the `$el` is a cached jQuery object that wraps the `el` element. The `$el` is very handy because it caches that element and you can use the jQuery API on the cached element. In the previous example I used the `html` function to add the entire generated HTML into the `el` element.

The second el option is to refer to an existing element. In order to do that, add an el property with a selector to the options object that you pass to the Backbone.View.extend function. Listing 5-13 assumes that you have an element with the car ID in your DOM:

Listing 5-13. Setting the el Element http://jsfiddle.net/gilf/BJv52/

```
var CarView = Backbone.View.extend({
        model: Car,
        el: "#car",
        template: _.template($("#car-template").html()),
        events: {
                "click #changeSpeed": "changeSpeed"
        },
        render: function() {
                this.$el.html(this.template(this.model.toJSON()));
                return this;
        },
        changeSpeed: function() {
                this.model.set("speed", this.model.get("speed") + 10);
        }
});

var bmw = new Car({ type: "bmw" });
var carView = new CarView(bmw);

console.log(carView.el); // prints the type of HTML object included in the el
```

You can use any selector when setting the el element as long as it will result in an existing element.

Last but not least, the view object can have an initialize function like models. You can use the initialize function to initialize any aspect of the view. One of the common things that you can do with the initialize function is to listen to model change events. In order to do that you are advised to use the listenTo function. You will learn about the listenTo function later when we cover events. Listing 5-14 shows how to add the initialize function to the previous example.

Listing 5-14. Adding the initialize Function

```
var CarView = Backbone.View.extend({
        model: Car,
        el: "#car",
        template: _.template($("#car-template").html()),
        initialize: function() {
                console.log("car view intialized");
        },
        events: {
                "click #changeSpeed": "changeSpeed"
        },
        render: function() {
                this.$el.html(this.template(this.model.toJSON()));
                return this;
        },
```

```
        changeSpeed: function() {
                this.model.set("speed", this.model.get("speed") + 10);
        }
});
```

In the example, whenever a new `CarView` instance is created, "car view initialized" is printed in the developer tools console. Of course, you can provide more meaningful initialization in the function.

Views are used to separate the logic of the presentation and the presentation itself. Backbone.js does a really good job in helping us do this separation by using the `Backbone.View` object. Now that you understand how to use views, the next step is to learn about the collection object, which will allow us to manipulate a collection of models and help us create more meaningful data structures in our applications.

Collections

The collection object represents a set of models. Because there are no domain models that include only single entities, collection objects can be very handy. Backbone collections help to wrap a set of models and expose a lot of very helpful API functions. They also help to manage changes that occur in the collections and to synchronize those changes.

As with models and views, when you want to create a collection you use the `Backbone.Collection.extend` function. In contrast to the previous objects, you must specify in the options object which model type the collection will hold. You can do that using the model option.

Listing 5-15. Creating a Collection Object `http://jsfiddle.net/gilf/t6mLh/`

```
var Car = Backbone.Model.extend({
        defaults: {
                speed: 0,
                type: "no type"
        }
});

var CarList = Backbone.Collection.extend({
        model: Car
});

var carList = new CarList();
```

You can see here that we have a `Car` model and its car collection. When you create a collection instance, the collection is empty. You can create a collection with data by passing an array of model instances to the constructor of the collection like in Listing 5-16.

Listing 5-16. Creating a Collection Object with Data `http://jsfiddle.net/gilf/sHFqc/`

```
var Car = Backbone.Model.extend({
        defaults: {
                speed: 0,
                type: "no type"
        }
});
```

```
var CarList = Backbone.Collection.extend({
        model: Car
});

var bmw = new Car({ type: "bmw" });
var carList = new CarList([bmw]);
```

Collection APIs

The collection object exposes several useful APIs that you can use to query and manipulate the object. The main API functions that you will probably use are as follows:

- `add`: Adds a new model to the collection. You can pass the function a model object or an array of models that you want to add. Because a collection is a set, you can't add a model that already exists to the collection. On the other hand, you can pass an options object with the `merge` property set to `true` and that will instruct the collection that you want to merge a model into an existing model. Adding models triggers the change event of the collection object.

- `remove`: Removes a model from the collection. You pass the model instances that you want to remove from the collection. Removing models from the collection triggers the `remove` event.

- `get`: Returns the model that corresponds to the given ID, `cid`, or model.

- `at`: Returns the model that exists in the given index.

- `models` property: Gives you raw access to the array of models that is wrapped by the collection object. While you should use `get` or `at` for accessing models, sometimes if it is necessary you can use this property for direct access.

- `length property`: Indicates the number of models currently stored by the collection.

■ **Note**　There are three more main API functions, `fetch`, `create`, and `sync`, which will be explained in detail in Chapter 9 when we create the whole SPA and integrate the client and the server.

Listing 5-17 shows how to use some of the previous API functions.

Listing 5-17. Using Collection API Functions http://jsfiddle.net/gilf/FrwZb/

```
var Car = Backbone.Model.extend({
        defaults: {
                speed: 0,
                type: "no type"
        }
});

var CarList = Backbone.Collection.extend({
        model: Car
});
```

```
var bmw = new Car({ type: "bmw", id: 1 });
var honda = new Car({ type: "honda", id: 2 });

var carList = new CarList([honda]);
console.log(carList.length); // prints 1

carList.add(bmw);
console.log(carList.length); // prints 2

var car1 = carList.get(1);
console.log(car1.get("type")); // prints bmw
console.log(car1 === bmw);     // prints true
```

In the previous code, we created a collection of cars and added only the honda object. Later on, we printed the length of the collection, which is 1. Once we added the bmw object the length of the collection became 2. Using the get function with 1 will return the bmw object that includes an ID with value 1.

Underscore.js Collection Functions

One of the reasons that Backbone.js depends on Underscore.js is the collection object. The collection exposes 28 different Underscore.js utility functions like each, indexOf, and filter. All of these functions add to the rich API of the collection and enable you to do almost any collection operation on the object.

Listing 5-18. Using Collection Underscore.js API Functions http://jsfiddle.net/gilf/bdztw/

```
var Car = Backbone.Model.extend({
        defaults: {
                speed: 0,
                type: "no type"
        }
});

var CarList = Backbone.Collection.extend({
        model: Car
});

var bmw = new Car({ type: "bmw", speed: 100, id: 1 });
var honda = new Car({ type: "honda", speed: 80, id: 2 });

var carList = new CarList([bmw, honda]);

carList.each(function(car) {
  console.log(car.get("type"));
}); // prints bmw and honda

var filteredCars = carList.filter(function(car) {
        return car.get("speed") > 90;
});
```

```
for (var i = 0; i < filteredCars.length; i++) {
    console.log(filteredCars[i].get("type"));
} // prints bmw

console.log(carList.indexOf(bmw));    // prints 0
console.log(carList.indexOf(honda)); // prints 1
```

In the previous code, you saw the use of some Underscore.js functions. Underscore.js collection functions can be very handy for manipulating and shaping the data inside the collection. Knowing how to use those functions can be very helpful when you program against a Backbone.js collection. Once you are familiar with the Backbone.js collection APIs, it is time to move on to the collection events.

Collection Events

The collection object has three major events that enable us to handle changes to the collection:

- add: Triggered whenever a model object is added to the collection.

- remove: Triggered whenever a model is removed from the collection.

- change: Triggered whenever any change on a model happens. You can add event handlers to specific change events by using the change:modelProperty convention.

When you want to add one of these event handlers, you can use the on function. Listing 5-19 shows how to wire the previous events.

Listing 5-19. Using Collection Events http://jsfiddle.net/gilf/pfm5y/

```
var Car = Backbone.Model.extend({
        defaults: {
                speed: 0,
                type: "no type"
        }
});

var CarList = Backbone.Collection.extend({
        model: Car
});

var bmw = new Car({ type: "bmw", speed: 100, id: 1 });
var honda = new Car({ type: "honda", speed: 80, id: 2 });

var carList = new CarList();

carList.on("add", function(car) {
        console.log("adding " + car.get("type"));
});
carList.on("remove", function(car) {
        console.log("removing " + car.get("type"));
});
carList.on("change", function(car) {
        console.log(car.get("type") + " changed");
});
```

```
carList.add([bmw, honda]); // prints adding bmw and adding honda
carList.remove(honda);     // prints removing honda
bmw.set("speed", 80);      // prints bmw changed
```

In this section you learned how to use Backbone.js collections. Collections are a vital part of a domain model and that is why they were implemented in Backbone.js. Backbone.js collections include various API functions that can help you create your collection's desired functionality. Now that you understand how to create model collections, it is time to jump into events.

Events

Backbone.js includes an event model that is exposed through the Events object. While you don't need to use the Events object directly, you use it in all the other Backbone.js main objects. Any one of the main Backbone.js objects is extended with the Events object by definition. You already saw that in models, views, and collections. The Events object is also mixed to the Backbone object itself and that means you can use it as an event aggregator. You can also extend any object by using the _.extend function to create your own object with an event aggregator.

Listing 5-20. Creating Your Own Event Aggregator http://jsfiddle.net/gilf/6Tu8n/

```
var evtAggregator = _.extend({}, Backbone.Events);
```

The Events API

The Events object exposes several options to handle events:

- **on:** Binds an event handler to a named event. It receives three arguments: the name of the event, a callback function, and a context object that is used to invoke the callback.

- **off:** Removes the binding of the given event handler from the event. It receives the same three arguments as the on function.

- **trigger:** Triggers a named event. The function receives two arguments: the name or names of the events to trigger and arguments that would be passed to the callback. If you want to pass more than one event to trigger the object, you should use a space-delimited list of event names.

- **once:** Binds an event handler to a named event like in the on function. The difference between on and once is that once is called only one time and after it is called the handler is removed.

Listing 5-21 shows an example of using the Events API.

Listing 5-21. Using the Events API http://jsfiddle.net/gilf/2kMh7/

```
var evtAggregator = _.extend({}, Backbone.Events);

function handler() {
        console.log("handler triggered");
}

evtAggregator.on("myCustomEvent", handler);

evtAggregator.trigger("myCustomEvent"); // prints handler triggered

evtAggregator.off("myCustomEvent", handler);
```

listenTo and stopListening

There are two special API functions in the Events object:

- listenTo: Enables one object to listen to another object's events. It receives three arguments: the object to observe, the name of the event, and the callback function.

- stopListening: Removes a handler that was added by the listenTo function. It includes the same arguments as listenTo. You can also call stopListening without passing parameters and it will remove all the callbacks from an object.

The on and off functions are set on the current object to listen to its events and later on to handle them. On the other hand, listenTo and stopListening allow an object to observe other object events. It is very handy whenever you want to decouple one object from another instead of calling a function directly on the object.

Listing 5-22. Using the listenTo and stopListening Functions http://jsfiddle.net/gilf/yEzXv/

```
var a = _.extend({}, Backbone.Events);
var b = _.extend({}, Backbone.Events);

a.listenTo(b, "myCustomEvent", function () {
        console.log("my custom event triggered");
});

b.trigger("myCustomEvent"); // prints my custom event triggered

a.stopListening();
```

View Events

Views include two kinds of events: DOM events and events triggered by the Events API. Having two different kinds of event options can confuse developers, and this is why it is important to understand the difference between the two options.

DOM events are events that are triggered by a user interaction. In Backbone.js you saw that you should use the view events property when you extend the view in order to handle DOM element events. When the handler of these events is called, the execution context is the view instance. You can go back to Listing 5-10 to see how to add DOM events in a view.

Events that are triggered by the Events API are triggered on objects rather than on DOM elements. Also, the execution context, which is the object that the event will be triggered on, is passed as an argument to the Events API functions. If the execution context is not passed, the execution context is the listener itself. In most cases, you will bind events by using the Events API in the initialize function of the object. Listing 5-23 shows how to do that.

Listing 5-23. Using Events in a View http://jsfiddle.net/gilf/ceR4f/

```
var CarView = Backbone.View.extend({
        el: "#car",
        template: _.template($("#car-template").html()),
        initialize: function() {
                this.on("myCustomEvent", this.callback);
        },
        events: {
                "click #changeSpeed": "changeSpeed"
         },
```

```
        render: function() {
                this.$el.html(this.template(this.model.toJSON()));
                return this;
        },
        changeSpeed: function() {
                this.model.set("speed", this.model.get("speed") + 10);
        },
        callback:function() {
                console.log("my custom event triggered");
        }
});

var carView = new CarView();
carView.trigger("myCustomEvent"); // prints my custom event triggered
```

■ **Note** For other details about the Events APIs, you can go to the Backbone.js web site:
`http://backbonejs.org/#Events`.

As you have seen, Backbone.js includes an event model, which can help you trigger events on objects. The event model becomes very helpful when you want to track changes on models, collections, and views. The Backbone.js event model basics are now covered, and we can drill down into the last part of Backbone.js objects: the Router object.

Routing

As mentioned in Chapter 4, front-end routing is the most important part of building an SPA. The existence of a routing mechanism in a web application is the main difference between a modern web application and an SPA. Backbone.js includes a Router object, which implements a routing mechanism that you can use.

The Router object provides all the glue to enable routing in the front end. It uses the HTML5 History API underneath and includes a fallback and transparent translation in legacy browsers. The Router object handles routing using the # sign, which is added to the URL. Every navigation event in the application that uses the # sign in the URL will result in translation by the router and is pushed into the `window.history` object using the `window.history.pushState` function. This is what enables us to move backward and forward in the application and to create deep links.

In an application there must be at least one route that is used as the home route. For each route, you need to define a callback function that will be triggered when the user navigates to the route.

To create a router, extend the `Backbone.Router` object.

Listing 5-24. Creating a Simple Router `http://jsfiddle.net/gilf/GRLTk/`

```
var AppRouter = Backbone.Router.extend({});
```

In the router, you define actions that will be triggered when route navigation occurs. In order to do this, you pass a `routes` object to `Backbone.Router.extend` (see Listing 5-25).

Listing 5-25. Configuring Router Routes

```
var AppRouter = Backbone.Router.extend({
        routes: {
                "": "home",
                "about": "about"
        },
        home: function() {
                console.log("home route triggered");
        },
        about: function() {
                console.log("about route triggered");
        }
});
```

In the example we define two different routes: home and about. The home route is defined to run when no routing was supplied. This will occur when you navigate to the application without putting anything in the URL, like in this URL: http://mywebsite/ or this one: http://mywebsite/#. The about route will occur when you navigate to the following URL: http://mywebsite/#about. When you navigate to one of these options, the relevant callback will be triggered.

Configuring Routes

The previous routes were very simple. But what if you want to pass parameters or you want to match any URL with a common denominator? There are two conventions that come in very handy for this: *splat and :param.

In order to pass parameters to a route, you use the :param route convention. You can pass any number of parameters as long as they are mapped to the route action. For example, the route "car/:id" will match an http://mywebsite/#car/1 URL. The action associated with that route should receive an id argument. Listing 5-26 shows this.

Listing 5-26. Configuring a Route with Parameters http://jsfiddle.net/gilf/uLF2n/

```
var AppRouter = Backbone.Router.extend({
        routes: {
                "": "home",
                "about": "about",
                "car/:id": "car"
        },
        home: function() {
                console.log("home route triggered");
        },
        about: function() {
                console.log("about route triggered");
        },
        car: function(id) {
                console.log("car route triggered with id: " + id);
        }
});
```

Navigating to http://mywebsite/#car/1 will print to the console "car route triggered with id: 1."

The *splat route convention enables you to define a route that can get anything written after the * sign as an action parameter. For example, the route "car/*imagePath" will match the http://mywebsite/#car/images/bmw.jpg URL. The action in the previous example should include an imagePath parameter. Listing 5-27 shows how to configure a route using *splat.

Listing 5-27. Configuring a Route with *splat `http://jsfiddle.net/gilf/ruXQ5/`

```
var AppRouter = Backbone.Router.extend({
        routes: {
                "": "home",
                "about": "about",
                "car/*imagePath": "car"

        },
        home: function() {
                console.log("home route triggered");
        },
        about: function() {
                console.log("about route triggered");
         },
        car: function(imagePath) {
                console.log("car route triggered with imagePath: " + imagePath);
        }
});
```

Navigating to `http://mywebsite/#car/images/bmw.jpg` will print to the console "car route triggered with imagePath: images/bmw.jpg."

Router APIs

The `Router` object includes two API functions:

- `route`: Creates a custom route. It receives three parameters: the route string, the name of the action to trigger, and an optional callback function. If the callback is omitted the router will trigger the function with the passed name. Otherwise, the router will trigger the `route:name` event.

- `navigate`: Updates the URL and adds it to the browser history. The function receives a URL and an options object. There are two options that you can configure: `trigger` and `replace`. If the `trigger` option is set to `true`, the router will trigger the route action function. If the `replace` option is set to `true`, the URL wouldn't be added to the browser's history.

Listing 5-28 shows how to use these API functions.

Listing 5-28. Using the Router API `http://jsfiddle.net/gilf/XxSS2/`

```
var AppRouter = Backbone.Router.extend({
        routes: {
                "": "home",
                "about": "about"
        },
        home: function() {
                console.log("home route triggered");
        },
        about: function() {
                console.log("about route triggered");
        },
```

```
        car: function(id) {
                console.log("car route triggered with id: " + id);
        }
});

var router = new AppRouter();
Backbone.history.start(); // prints home route triggered

router.route("car/:id", "car"); // creates a custom route with a parameter
router.navigate("car/1", {trigger: true}); // prints car route triggered with id: 1
```

■ **Note**   For other details about the Router APIs, you can go to the Backbone.js web site: `http://backbonejs.org/#Router`.

Backbone History

One thing that you probably noticed in the previous example is the call to the `Backbone.history.start` function. This function starts history management by monitoring the `hashChange` event and triggering the relevant actions. You should use this function when all the application routes have been configured. `Backbone.history.start` can receive an options object to determine how to use the history. The options object includes four optional configurations: `pushState`, `hashChange`, `root`, and `silent`.

- pushState: If the `pushState` option is set to `true`, it indicates that you want to use the HTML5 History API `pushState` function.

- hashChange: If the `hashChange` option is set to `false`, browsers that don't support the HTML5 History API will get full-page refreshes when changing the state.

- root: The `root` option is used to set a navigation root other than `""` (the default navigation).

- silent: Set the `silent` option to `true` if the server renders the entire first web page. Setting `silent` to `true` won't trigger the first `""` or root navigation.

Listing 5-29 shows how to use some of the options.

Listing 5-29. Using the Backbone.History `http://jsfiddle.net/gilf/3s2CQ/`

```
var AppRouter = Backbone.Router.extend({
        routes: {
                "": "home",
                "about": "about"
        },
        home: function() {
                console.log("home route triggered");
        },
        about: function() {
                console.log("about route triggered");
        }
});

var router = new AppRouter();
Backbone.history.start({silent: true, pushState: true});

router.navigate("about", {trigger: true}); // about route triggered
```

Routing and Views

Now that we know how views and routing work in Backbone.js, it is time to combine the two. Most of the time when you use routing you will navigate from one page to another in the application. When a route event occurs, this is the place where you render the next page to show the user. Listing 5-30 shows what a more realistic router will look like.

Listing 5-30. A More Realistic Router Example

```
var AppRouter = Backbone.Router.extend({
        routes: {
                "": "home",
                "about": "about"
        },
        home: function() {
                var view = new HomeView();
                $('#main').html(view.render().el);
        },
        about: function() {
                var view = new AboutView();
                $('#main').html(view.render().el);
        },
});

var router = new AppRouter();
Backbone.history.start();
```

In this example the single page will have an element with a main ID, which will be used as the main SPA fragment. In the route actions, we create new views and we render them into the main fragment.

The example might look very simple at first glance, but it includes two problems. The first problem is the Backbone.js event-driven behavior. We add event listeners in a view but where do we remove them? The second problem is in the router itself. In our opinion, routers are not responsible for acting as application controllers but in the previous example the router also includes the actions to perform after the route occurs.

Handling Zombie Views

The first problem was view events. When you add event handlers and you don't remove them you can find yourself with zombie views. Zombie views are views that hang in memory because there is an event handler reference that didn't allow the JavaScript garbage collector to clean the view from memory. The first sign that you have a zombie view is when you trigger an event and it is triggered twice or three times and so on.

If we write a router like in Listing 5-30, every route leads to the creation of a new view, but the previous view is not cleaned. So how would you clean a view?

The way to clean views from memory is using their remove function. The view's remove function will remove the entire view and also clean up view event handlers. You can also use the unbind function on the view to make sure that all the events were cleaned. The problem is where to use the function. One answer to that is in the router. But this means that you need a reference to the current view in the router. This is where an application controller comes into play.

Creating an Application Controller

As we wrote, routers should not be responsible for performing actions. Performing route actions is a role that should be a part of an application controller. That controller should also include the current view in order to help us remove views from memory when we perform navigation. Listing 5-31 is a suggestion for how to add an application controller.

Listing 5-31. An Application Controller http://jsfiddle.net/gilf/qzkLG/

```
/* In the HTML you should have the following elements and templates:
<div id="main"></div>
<script id="home-template" type="text/template">
    <h1>home</h1>
</script>
<script id="about-template" type="text/template">
    <h1>about</h1>
</script>
*/


var HomeView = Backbone.View.extend({
    tagName: "div",
        template: _.template($('#home-template').html()),
        render: function() {
        this.$el.html(this.template({}));
                return this;
        }
});
var AboutView = Backbone.View.extend({
    tagName: "div",
        template: _.template($('#about-template').html()),
        render: function() {
        this.$el.html(this.template({}));
                return this;
        }
});

var AppController = {
        currentView: null,
        home: function() {
            var self = this;
            var view = new HomeView();
            self.renderView.call(self, view);
        },

        about: function (id) {
            var self = this;
            var view = new AboutView();
            self.renderView.call(self, view);
        },
```

```
        renderView: function(view) {
            this.currentView && this.currentView.remove();
            $('#main').html(view.render().el);
            this.currentView = view;
        }
    }


var AppRouter = Backbone.Router.extend({
        routes: {
                "": "home",
                "about": "about"
        },
        initialize: function() {
            var routeName;
            for (var route in this.routes) {
                routeName = this.routes[route];
                this.route(route, routeName, $.proxy(AppController[routeName], AppController));
            }
        }
});

var router = new AppRouter();
Backbone.history.start();
```

The main two things to notice in the example are the AppController object and the changes in the router. The AppController will hold the current view and includes a renderView function. The renderView function is responsible for removing the existing view and replacing it with the new view to show. The router object includes an initialize function that dispatches all the routes to the AppController object functions.

The result of running this code in jsFiddle should look like Figure 5-1.

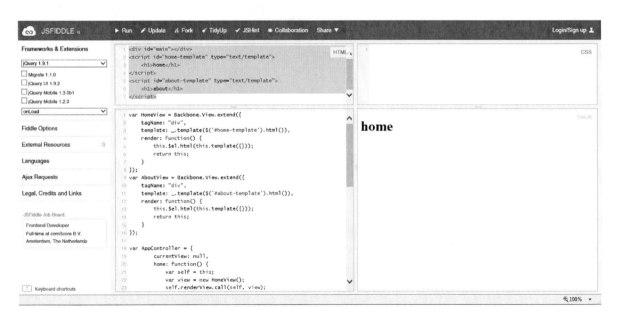

Figure 5-1. *The result of running AppController in jsFiddle*

■ **Note**   There are excellent Backbone.js plug-ins like Marionette, which adds abilities and features like the AppController to Backbone.js. While this book won't cover Backbone.js plug-ins, we encourage you to take a look at the Marionette web site: `http://marionettejs.com/`.

The last part of this chapter will cover how to use Backbone.js with the RequireJS library to create a more meaningful and structured application.

Backbone.js and RequireJS

In Chapter 3, you learned about RequireJS and how it can help you create a modular JavaScript application. Backbone.js imposes object structure in the application but it doesn't include ways to load modules or define modules. Combining both Backbone.js and RequireJS can help you develop a much more robust solution.

The first thing that you will want to do is to divide the parts of your application into modules. Our suggestion is to create each view, model, collection, and router in its own file and then later use RequireJS to load them.

The division into modules raises the problem of how to manage the files in the filesystem. There are two main options: create a folder for each kind of Backbone.js object or create logical module separation.

Creating a folder for each Backbone.js object is simple. In the application you will have `models`, `views`, `collections`, and `routers` folders. This option is suitable for small applications because when the application grows up it is very hard to maintain the files. Figure 5-2 shows how application folders can look.

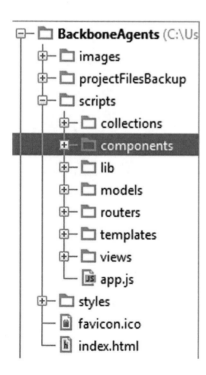

Figure 5-2. *Creating a folder for each kind of Backbone.js object*

Dividing the files into logical modules is more suitable for medium to large applications. In this option each logical application module gets its own folder and inside of the folder you have folders for models, views, and collections. For example, if the application has a search module, all the parts written for that module should be inside the search folder. Figure 5-3 shows this second option.

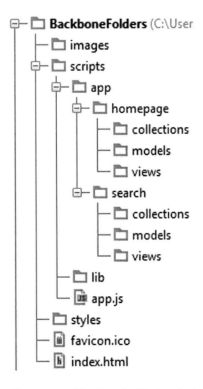

Figure 5-3. *Dividing the files into logical modules*

■ **Note**   The previous options are the ways that we order our application filesystem. Any way that you choose is fine as long as the other developers in the project and you can manage the application files.

Once you set the division into folders it is time to add RequireJS. Backbone.js and also Underscore.js were not created with module definition, and the first thing to do is to use the requirejs.config to create a shim for them (Listing 5-32).

Listing 5-32. Creating a Shim for Backbone.js and Underscore.js

```
requirejs.config({
    //By default load any module IDs from scripts/lib
    baseUrl: 'scripts/lib',

    shim: {
        'backbone': {
            deps: ['underscore', 'jquery'],
```

```
        exports: 'Backbone'
    },
    'underscore': {
        exports: '_'
    }
    }
});
```

In this example the `baseUrl` is set to the `libraries` folder. Once we have the shims in place, you will add the relevant paths to load the modules you are writing. Listing 5-33 uses the Figure 5-2 folders order.

Listing 5-33. Adding Paths to the Configuration

```
requirejs.config({
    //By default load any module IDs from scripts/lib
    baseUrl: 'scripts/lib',
    paths: {
        models: '../models',
        collections: '../collections',
        views: '../views',
        routers: '../routers',
        components: '../components'
    },
    shim: {
        'backbone': {
            deps: ['underscore', 'jquery'],
            exports: 'Backbone'
        },
        'underscore': {
            exports: '_'
        }
    }
});
```

Now that everything is configured and set, we can start using the `define` function to create modules and load them later, according to dependencies.

Let's take the example from Listing 5-31 and use it with RequireJS. Every object should be placed in its own file and defined by using RequireJS. The next listing, 5-34, shows you the definitions of all the parts using RequireJS.

Listing 5-34. The Modules Using RequireJS

```
define(['jquery', 'underscore', 'backbone'], function($, _, Backbone) {
        var HomeView = Backbone.View.extend({
        tagName: "div",
                template: _.template($('#home-template').html()),
                render: function() {
                this.$el.html(this.template({}));
                        return this;
                }
        });
        return HomeView;
});
```

```
define(['jquery', 'underscore', 'backbone'], function($, _, Backbone) {
        var AboutView = Backbone.View.extend({
        tagName: "div",
                template: _.template($('#about-template').html()),
                render: function() {
                this.$el.html(this.template({}));
                        return this;
                }
        });
        return AboutView;
});
define(['jquery', 'underscore', 'backbone'], function ($, _, Backbone) {
        var AppController = {
        currentView: null,
        home: function() {
            var self = this;
            require(['views/homeView'], function (HomeView) {
                var view = new HomeView();
                self.renderView.call(self, view);
            }
        },

        about: function (id) {
            var self = this;
            require(['views/aboutView'], function (AboutView) {
                var view = new AboutView();
                self.renderView.call(self, view);
            }
        },

        renderView: function(view) {
                this.currentView && this.currentView.remove();
                $('#main').html(view.render().el);
                this.currentView = view;
                }
        }
        return AppController;
});
define(['jquery', 'underscore', 'backbone', 'components/appController'], function ($, _, Backbone,
AppController) {
        var AppRouter = Backbone.Router.extend({
                routes: {
                        "": "home",
                        "about": "about"
                },
                initialize: function() {
                        var routeName;
```

```
                        for (var route in this.routes) {
                            routeName = this.routes[route];
                            this.route(route, routeName, $.proxy(AppController[routeName],
AppController));
                        }
                },
                start: function () {
                        Backbone.history.start();
                }
        });
        return new AppRouter();
});
```

In Listing 5-34, the mapping to files is as follows:

- HomeView is located in a homeView.js file under the views folder.

- AboutView is located in an aboutView.js file under the views folder.

- AppController is located in an appController.js file under the components folder.

- AppRouter is located in a router.js file under the routers folder.

▓ **Note** Pay attention to the use of the require function in the AppController. We use the require function to load views only when they are needed. Another thing to notice is that we added a start function on the router that triggers the Backbone.History.start function.

Once the application is set and all the modules exist in their own files, you should start the application with the Backbone.History.start function. This can be done after the web page is loaded. The following code in Listing 5-35 can be a part of the application bootstrap file.

Listing 5-35. The Application Bootstrap

```
requirejs.config({
    //By default load any module IDs from scripts/lib
    baseUrl: 'scripts/lib',
    paths: {
        models: '../models',
        collections: '../collections',
        views: '../views',
        routers: '../routers',
        components: '../components'
    },
    shim: {
        'backbone': {
            deps: ['underscore', 'jquery'],
            exports: 'Backbone'
        },
        'underscore': {
```

```
                exports: '_'
            }
        }
    }
});

require(['routers/router'], function (router) {
    $(document).ready(function (){
        router.start();
    });
});
```

In this section we covered how to integrate Backbone.js and RequireJS in order to create a modular implementation of the basics that you learned. In most of the applications that you build, you will combine libraries and frameworks to implement your solution.

Summary

In this chapter you were introduced to the Backbone.js library and to its components: models, views, collections, events, and routers. Backbone.js is a very simple but powerful library that helps to impose structure in the SPA. Understanding Backbone.js basics can help you to understand other big MV* frameworks like AngularJS or Ember.js. It will also help you to understand SPA functions and major components.

Now that you have the knowledge of how to develop a basic SPA it is time to move on and write a real-world SPA. In the next chapter you will be introduced to our sample application, TheAgency, which is going to show you a real SPA and how it is built. You will use all the tools learned from all the previous chapters.

CHAPTER 6

■ ■ ■

Creating a Single Page Application Step by Step

In this chapter, we are going to create a single page application (SPA) step by step. The SPA that we are creating is called TheAgency, and it is going to manage agents in an intelligence agency. Throughout the chapter, you will use all the tools you have learned up until now, such as Backbone.js, RequireJS, and Underscore.js. One exception, however, is that the SPA won't be built with a back end, because we haven't covered back-end development yet.

■ **Note** In Part III of this book, we will cover back-end development in SPAs.

Just to get you into application creation mode, Figures 6-1, 6-2, and 6-3 show what you are going to build.

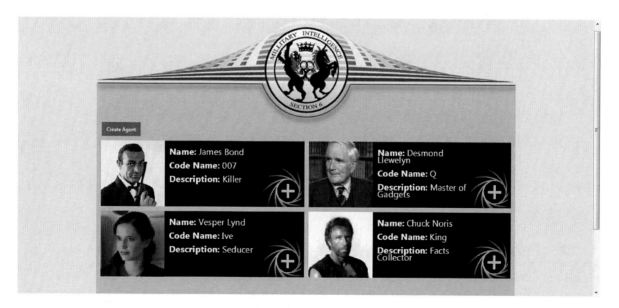

Figure 6-1. *TheAgency home page*

Figure 6-2. *TheAgency Agent Details page*

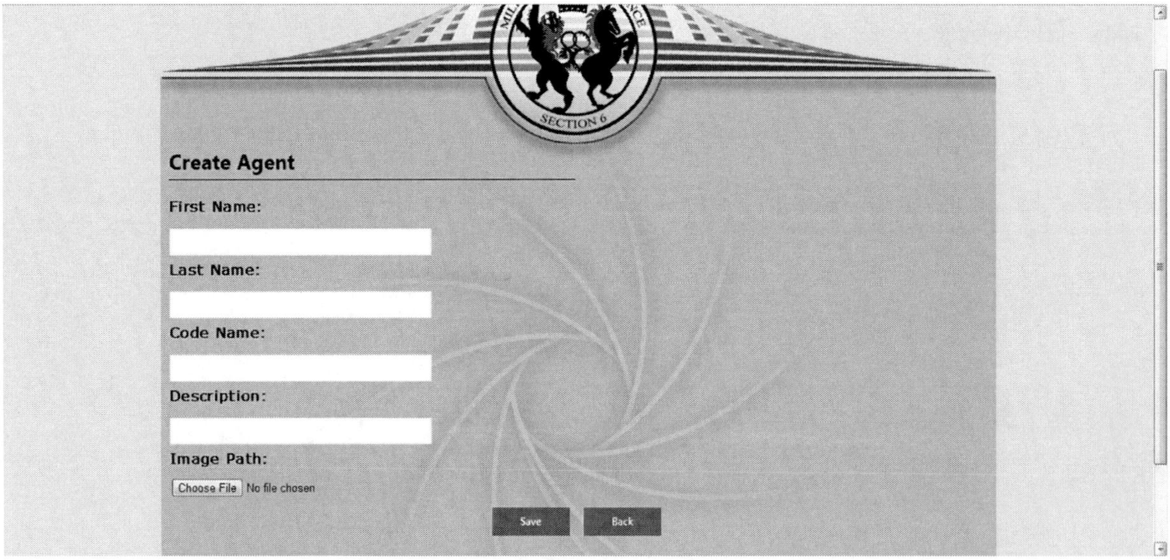

Figure 6-3. *TheAgency Create Agent page*

On the TheAgency home page, you will be able to view all TheAgency agents' minimized details and figures. You can also go to an agent's details page by clicking the adjacent plus sign. The last thing that you can do on the home page is click the Create Agent button and navigate to the Create Agent page.

On the Agent Details page, you will be able to edit the agent details. You will also be able to allocate assignments to an agent. Each assignment might be in one of two states: fulfilled or unfulfilled. You can toggle the assignment state. The last thing that you can do on the Agent Details page is delete an agent.

On the Create Agent page, you will be able to add a new agent to the app. Now that you have seen what you are going to develop, it's time to get to work and write TheAgency front end.

Choosing an IDE

Up until now, you didn't have to use an integrated development environment (IDE) in order to create and run the code examples that you encountered in the previous chapters. All you had to do was use a console inside the browser developer tools, such as Chrome DevTools, Firebug, and IE Developer Tools, or use a web site such as jsFiddle.

Because we are starting to build a more realistic application, it is time to start writing our solution more professionally and use an IDE. There are many good web development IDEs that you can use to create SPAs. Any web development IDE will give you a development environment and will include a lot of tools to write, re-factor, test, and run your application. It is crucial to choose an IDE that fits your needs, and there are many good web development IDEs out, such as the following:

- *WebStorm*: A web IDE from JetBrains that is considered to be one of the best web IDEs. We have used it on several projects, and it has proved to be a very valuable development environment.

- *Visual Studio*: An IDE from Microsoft that is dedicated to the Microsoft development platform. Visual Studio includes tools to create web applications with the .NET environment, but it can also be used to write stand-alone web applications.

- *Eclipse*: An IDE that was created by IBM but is now an open-source IDE. It is mostly used on the Java development platform, and it includes numerous plug-ins that add support to other languages. As with the other IDEs, Eclipse includes the ability to create web applications.

■ **Note**   There are other good IDEs, such as Netbeans, Aptana, and Sublime Text (with plug-ins), that can also be used as web development IDEs.

We are going to use ASP.NET Web API later on as TheAgency's back end, and this is why we picked Visual Studio as the IDE for the book. On the other hand, all the things that we are going to implement in this chapter also can be implemented in other IDEs, and we encourage you to use the IDE that you prefer.

■ **Note**   Important disclosure: TheAgency front-end project was developed in WebStorm IDE. Later on, we moved the project into Visual Studio to align it to the ASP.NET Web API back end.

All the chapter's code can be created in any IDE, but the sources that come with this book are in a Visual Studio solution.

With single page applications, it is now easy to split the project into front-end code and server-side code. We use that approach very often while developing an SPA.

Preparing the Solution Folders

Once you select your IDE, the first thing that you are going to do is decide how to divide your solution folders. In Chapter 5, we showed you two ways and also mentioned that you can choose your own way, as long as all the developers in your project align with it. For TheAgency, we picked the folder for each Backbone.js object kind and used it to order our solution folders.

Creating the Solution Folder Structure

Open your IDE and create a new empty web application. Name the newly created web application **TheAgency**. In the new web application, create the solution folders, as shown in Figure 6-4.

Figure 6-4. *Solution Explorer in Visual Studio*

Inside the solution, you will have three folders: images, scripts, and styles. In the images folder, you will put all the application images. In the scripts folder, you will put all the application JavaScript files. In the styles folder, you will put all your CSS files. The scripts folder is also divided into Backbone.js object kinds folders, such as collections, models, routers, and views. We also added a folder called lib, to hold all the libraries that we are going to use, and a components folder, to hold all the modules that aren't related to Backbone.js.

Adding the JavaScript Libraries

Once you've created the project structure, it is time to download all the libraries that we are going to use and add them into the lib folder, which exists under the scripts folder. Some developers prefer to use the vendor name instead of lib, as we did. You can look at HTML5 Boilerplate, which is a boilerplate template for an HTML5 web site structure, for an example of that. You should download jQuery, Underscore.js, Backbone.js, and RequireJS.

■ **Note**   You probably downloaded the libraries in the previous chapters, but if you didn't, following are the URLs for the libraries' web sites: http://jquery.com (jQuery web site), http://underscorejs.org (Underscore.js web site; pay attention to download underscore version, which is >= 1.5.0), http://backbonejs.org (Backbone.js web site), and http://requirejs.org (RequireJS web site).

Another option, which exists only in Visual Studio, is to use NuGet package manager to install all the library packages. Because we are not covering NuGet in this book, use this option only if you know how to use NuGet. There is a third option for non–Visual Studio projects, which is to use the Yeoman and Bower package manager. Again, use it only if you are familiar with the tool.

In our project, we use a Backbone.js plug-in called Backbone.ModalDialog. We will use this plug-in to create modal dialogs that interact with the user. You can download the plug-in from the following URL: https://github.com/GarethElms/BackboneJSModalView.

■ **Note**   The Backbone.ModalDialog plug-in was created by Gareth Elms, who holds its copyright. There are other ways to create modal dialogs, but we wanted to use a plug-in.

Once you have all the libraries, put them in the lib folder. Figure 6-5 shows how the solution should look after you've added the libraries.

Figure 6-5. *Solution Explorer in Visual Studio, after adding the libraries*

Adding the HTML Page, Application Main Script, Styles, and Images

The last thing that we are going to add is the index.html page, which will act as the application single page, the app.js main script, the project's CSS files, and project images.

Add a new HTML file in the application root and call it index.html. To the file add the HTML code as shown in Listing 6-1.

Listing 6-1. index.html Basic Structure

```
<!DOCTYPE html>
<html lang="en">
<head>
    <meta charset="UTF-8">
    <title>TheAgency</title>
    <link href="favicon.ico" rel="shortcut icon" type="image/x-icon" />
    <link href="styles/site.css" rel="stylesheet" type="text/css" />
    <link href="styles/modern.css" rel="stylesheet" type="text/css" />
    <script data-main="scripts/app.js" src="scripts/lib/require.js"></script>
```

```
        <meta name="viewport" content="width=device-width" />
    </head>
    <body>
        <header>
            <img id="pagetitleImage" alt="MI6 Agents" src="images/MI6PageHeader.png" />
        </header>
        <div id="body">
            <section id="main" class="content-wrapper main-content clear-fix">
            </section>
        </div>
    </body>
</html>
```

As you can see, we have a basic web page with a header and a div with body id. Inside the div with body id, we have a section with the main id, which is going to be used as the main section that is replaced while navigating from one page to another. That section is going to act as the SPA shell.

Another thing to notice is the use of RequireJS to bootstrap the application using the app.js file, which is the setting of the data-main attribute.

Now that we have the need for app.js, let's create it. In the scripts folder, add a new JavaScript file and call it app.js. For the time being, add only the RequireJS configuration inside of it, as shown in Listing 6-2.

Listing 6-2. app.js First Implementation

```
requirejs.config({
    //By default load any module IDs from scripts/lib
    baseUrl: 'scripts/lib',
    paths: {
        models: '../models',
        collections: '../collections',
        views: '../views',
        routers: '../routers',
        components: '../components',
        modalDialog: 'backbone.ModalDialog'
    },
    shim: {
        'backbone': {
            deps: ['underscore', 'jquery'],
            exports: 'Backbone'
        },
        'underscore': {
            exports: '_'
        }
    }
});
```

The most interesting thing in the app.js is the use of shims to load both Underscore.js and Backbone.js. You can also see that we configure the modalDialog as another RequireJS module.

After we've added the basic HTML and script, you should add the styles and images that we are going to use. Because this book concentrates mainly on JavaScript, we decided to add the CSS and images as assets that you can download. You can download all the CSS files and images from the following URL: http://bit.ly/1m6nL3h. Now that we have added all the basic things we require for our SPA, the project folders should look like Figure 6-6.

Figure 6-6. Solution Explorer in Visual Studio, after adding the index.html, app.js, CSS files, and images

It is time to see how the application looks when we set the environment. You can run `index.html` and see the following result (Figure 6-7), which is the main application page without anything on it:

Figure 6-7. *The main page, after setting the environment*

Now we are ready to write our SPA.

Crafting the Models

We will begin by defining our models. Every model should be implemented in its own file and located under the models folder, which exists in the scripts folder. TheAgency has two kinds of models: an agent and the agent's tasks. Every agent has a name, code name, an image, and a description. Every agent can also have zero to an infinite number of tasks. A task has a description and an indicator, whether it is complete or not.

The agent model will be implemented in the agent.js model file, and the task model will be implemented in the task.js model file.

Agent Model Implementation

Let's start with the agent implementation (Listing 6-3).

Listing 6-3. agent.js Implementation

```
define(['backbone', 'collections/tasks'], function (Backbone, Tasks) {
    var agent = Backbone.Model.extend({
        defaults: {
            agentID: 0,
            codeName: '',
            firstName: '',
            lastName: '',
            imagePath: '',
            description: '',
```

```
            tasks: new Tasks()
        },
        idAttribute: 'agentID',
        validate: function(attrs, options) {
            if (attrs.firstName.length == 0 || attrs.lastName.length == 0) {
                return "Name must include first name and last name!";
            }
        }
    });

    return agent;
});
```

As you can see, the agent definition is straightforward. The agent model includes default values to its properties, and it also includes a task collection. We will implement the task collection later.

An agent model also has its idAttribute set to the agentID, which is going to be the identifier property of the agent. An agent model includes a validate function, which will check that no one can create an agent without a first name and a last name. Also, pay attention that the model is defined using the RequireJS define function.

Task Model Implementation

The code in Listing 6-4 shows how to implement a task.

Listing 6-4. task.js Implementation

```
define(['backbone'], function (Backbone) {
    var task = Backbone.Model.extend({
        defaults: {
            taskID: 0,
            description: '',
            isComplete: false
        },
        idAttribute: 'taskID',
        validate: function(attrs, options) {
            if (attrs.description.length == 0) {
                return "You must add a description!";
            }
        },
        toggleComplete: function() {
            this.set("isComplete", !this.get('isComplete'));
        }
    });

    return task;
});
```

Once a task is created, it is not complete, and this is why we set its default isComplete property to false. The task model identifier will be taskID, and therefore, we set the idAttribute to it. A task must have a description, and we use the validate function to check that no task can be created without a description. Also, a task has a toggleComplete function, which toggles its isComplete property.

Both of the models are very simple. After you implement the models, your solution should have two new files in the models folder. Now that we have our models, it is time to move on to the model collections.

Adding Collections

Every model in the application will have a corresponding collection. Each collection will be created in its own file. The first collection will be the agent collection, which will be created in the `agents.js` file. The second collection that we will have is the task collection, which will be created in the `tasks.js` file. Both of the collection files will be created inside the `collections` folder.

The Agent Collection

The code in Listing 6-5 is the definition of the agent collection.

Listing 6-5. agents.js Implementation

```
define(['backbone', 'models/agent'], function (Backbone, Agent) {
    var Agents = Backbone.Collection.extend({
        model: Agent,
        create: function(options) {
            this.push(new Agent(options));
        }
    });

    return Agents;
});
```

As you can see, the agent collection is configured to hold agent models. We set the model property to `Agent` in order to tell Backbone.js that the collection is an agent collection. You can also see that we have created a utility function called `create`, which is used to add a new agent model to the collection. The last interesting thing in the implementation is the dependency that we have on the agent model. We use RequireJS to load that dependency and set the loaded model definitions to the `Agent` variable using the RequireJS `define` function.

The Task Collection

The code in Listing 6-6 is the definition of the task collection.

Listing 6-6. tasks.js Implementation

```
define(['backbone', 'models/task'], function (Backbone, Task) {
    var Tasks = Backbone.Collection.extend({
        model: Task
    });

    return Tasks;
});
```

As opposed to the agent collection, the task collection is much simpler. We only set the collection's model to be of Task type and nothing more. As in the agent collection, the task collection is dependent on the Task model, and we use RequireJS to load the Task definitions.

Now that we have our collections set, the next step is to generate some mock data that we will use in the application.

Creating a Data Service and Generating Mock Data

In this chapter, we won't have a back end. That means that all the application's initial data will be created using a mock data generator. Also, we will save the data with the HTML5 Web Storage API, in order to persist it for later use. In order to do that, we introduce a data-service object.

The data-service purpose will be to generate the initial application data, to enable us to get that data and save it back to localStorage. Later on, when we have a back end, it will be easier to re-factor the data-service implementation for real front-end and back-end communication.

The data service will be added into the components folder in a dataService.js file. Listing 6-7 is the definition of the data-service module.

Listing 6-7. dataService.js Implementation

```
define(['collections/agents', 'collections/tasks'], function (Agents, Tasks) {
    // Sets the maximum agent id to use later in the application
    function setMaxAgentID(agents) {
        app.agentID = _.max(agents,function (agent) {
            return agent.agentID;
        }).agentID;
    }

    // Sets the maximum task id to use later in the application
    function setMaxTaskID(tasks) {
        app.taskID = _.max(tasks,function (task) {
            return task.taskID;
        }).taskID;
    }

    function getAgentsFromCache() {
        var agentsString = localStorage.getItem("agents");
        if (!agentsString) {
            generateInitialData();
            agentsString = localStorage.getItem("agents");
        }
        return JSON.parse(agentsString);
    }

    function generateInitialData() {
        var agents = [
            { id: 1, agentID: 1, codeName: '007', firstName: 'James', lastName: 'Bond', imagePath:
            'images/JamesBondImage.png', description: 'Killer', tasks: [{ id: 1, taskID: 1, description:
            "Kill Goldfinger", isComplete: true }, { id: 2, taskID: 2, description: "Kill Renard",
            isComplete: true }]},
            { id: 2, agentID: 2, codeName: 'Q', firstName: 'Desmond', lastName: 'Llewelyn', imagePath:
            'images/LDesmond.png', description: 'Master of Gadgets', tasks: [{ id: 3, taskID: 3,
            description: "Create a new James Bond car", isComplete: false }, { id: 4, taskID: 4,
            description: "Create a missle launcher pen", isComplete: false }]},
            { id: 3, agentID: 3, codeName: 'Ive', firstName: 'Vesper', lastName: 'Lynd', imagePath:
            'images/VesperLynd.png', description: 'Seducer', tasks: [{ id: 5, taskID: 5, description:
            "Seduce James Bond", isComplete: true }]},
```

```
        { id: 4, agentID: 4, codeName: 'King', firstName: 'Chuck', lastName: 'Noris', imagePath:
          'images/ChuckNoris.png', description: 'Facts Collector', tasks: [{ id: 6, taskID: 6,
          description: "Rule the world", isComplete: true }]}
    ];
    localStorage.setItem("agents", JSON.stringify(agents));
}

var DataService = {
    getData: function () {
        var agents = getAgentsFromCache(),
            tasks = [];

        _.each(agents, function (agent) {
            _.each(agent.tasks, function (task) {
                tasks.push(task);
            });
            agent.tasks = new Tasks(agent.tasks);
        });

        // will be used as our client side models storage
        app.agents = new Agents(agents);
        setMaxAgentID(agents);
        setMaxTaskID(tasks);
    },
    saveData: function (agents) {
        localStorage.setItem("agents", JSON.stringify(agents.toJSON()));
    }
};

return DataService;
});
```

■ **Note** You probably noticed an app object, which we use to set different properties, such as agents, agentID, and taskID. The app object is a namespace that will be created in the app.js file, which you will see very soon.

Let's explore what is going on in the data-service module. The module encapsulates the following functions:

- setMaxAgentID: The function receives an agents array, extracts the maximum agent id in that array, and sets it to an app.agentID property. The maximum agent id will enable us to generate client ids for agents.

- setMaxTaskID: The function receives a task array, extracts the maximum task id in that array, and sets it to an app.taskID property. The maximum task ID will enable us to generate client IDs for tasks.

- getAgentsFromCache: The function checks if localStorage holds a key/value pair that corresponds to the agents key. If it doesn't, the function will generate the application initial data using the generateInitialData function. The function returns the stored agents in JSON representation.

- generateInitialData: The function generates initial data for four agents.

Except for the encapsulated utility function, we also create a DataService object, which includes two main functions: getData and saveData. When we have a back end, these two functions will be replaced with real API functions. For now, they are sufficient.

The getData function runs only once in the application, when the application starts, and its role is to get the data from localStorage (using the getAgentsFromCache function) and to set app.agents, app.agentID, and app.taskID properties.

The saveData function is going to run every time we save something in our application. It receives an agent collection, turns it into JSON representation using the toJSON function, and serializes it into a string, using the JSON. stringify function. Once we have the agent collection string representation, it is saved into the localStorage.

Now that we have the data service, we can create a bootstrapping behavior in the app.js file (see Listing 6-8).

Listing 6-8. app.js After Adding the Data Service

```
requirejs.config({
    //By default load any module IDs from scripts/lib
    baseUrl: 'scripts/lib',
    paths: {
        models: '../models',
        collections: '../collections',
        views: '../views',
        routers: '../routers',
        components: '../components',
        modalDialog: 'backbone.ModalDialog'
    },
    shim: {
        'backbone': {
            deps: ['underscore', 'jquery'],
            exports: 'Backbone'
        },
        'underscore': {
            exports: '_'
        }
    }
});

var app = app || {};

require(['components/dataService'], function(dataService) {
    $(document).ready(function() {
        dataService.getData();
    });
});
```

In the app.js file, we create a namespace called app, which is used as a cache for general things such as the agent collection. After that, we load the data-service module, using the RequireJS require function, and in its callback, we use the jQuery ready function to wait for the DOM content to load, and only then do we run the data service's getData function.

Now that we have data in the application, we are ready to move to the next phase, which is to create the application router.

Adding Front-End Routing

At the end of Chapter 5, we offered you an example for creating a router and for an application controller that we called AppController. We will use that knowledge to implement the application router. Later on, we will describe the AppController and how you should build it.

The Router

In the application, we will have only three routes: home, details, and create agent. The home route will navigate to the home page, where all the agents are shown. The details route will navigate to a specific agent's details. The create agent route will navigate to the Create Agent page.

The router module should be created in its own file, called router.js, and exists in the routers folder. Listing 6-9 provides the code for the implementation of the router.

Listing 6-9. router.js Implementation

```
define(['jquery', 'underscore', 'backbone', 'components/appController'], function ($, _, Backbone,
AppController) {
    var router = Backbone.Router.extend({
        routes: {
            '': 'home',
            'details/:id': 'details',
            'createAgent': 'createAgent'
        },

        initialize: function() {
            var routeName;
            for (var route in this.routes) {
                routeName = this.routes[route];
                this.route(route, routeName, $.proxy(AppController[routeName], AppController));
            }
        },

        start: function () {
            Backbone.history.start();
        }
    });

    return new router();
});
```

In the router, the routes are very simple, and the only interesting route is the details route, which takes an id parameter. Another thing to notice is that we added the call to Backbone.history.start into the router. We will use the start function, when the DOM is loaded, to start running the router. You can also see that we load an AppController, which exists in the components folder, so let's create that.

The Application Controller

Once we have our router set, it is time to implement the application controller. The AppController module file is created in the components folder under the name appController.js. The application controller is very similar to the application controller that we showed in Chapter 5, only the route's functions change.

Listing 6-10 is the application controller implementation.

Listing 6-10. appController.js Implementation

```
define(['jquery', 'underscore', 'backbone'], function ($, _, Backbone) {
    var AppController = {
        currentView: null,
        home: function() {
            var self = this;
            require(['views/homeView'], function(HomeView) {
                var view = new HomeView();
                self.renderView.call(self, view);
            });
        },

        details: function (id) {
            var self = this;
            require(['views/detailsView'], function (DetailsView) {
                var agent = app.agents.get(id),
                    view = new DetailsView({ model: agent });

                self.renderView.call(self, view);
            });
        },

        createAgent: function () {
            var self = this;
            require(['views/createView'], function (CreateView) {
                var view = new CreateView();

                self.renderView.call(self, view);
            });
        },

        renderView: function(view) {
            this.currentView && this.currentView.remove();
            $('#main').html(view.render().el);
            this.currentView = view;
        }
    }

    return AppController;
});
```

Now we are ready to change the app.js again and add the routing support. Listing 6-11 shows the app.js file after that change.

Listing 6-11. app.js with Routing Support

```
requirejs.config({
    //By default load any module IDs from scripts/lib
    baseUrl: 'scripts/lib',
    paths: {
        models: '../models',
        collections: '../collections',
        views: '../views',
        routers: '../routers',
        components: '../components',
        modalDialog: 'backbone.ModalDialog',
        templates: '../templates'
    },
    shim: {
        'backbone': {
            deps: ['underscore', 'jquery'],
            exports: 'Backbone'
        },
        'underscore': {
            exports: '_'
        }
    }
});

var app = app || {};

require(['routers/router', 'components/dataService'], function (router, dataService) {
    $(document).ready(function (){
        dataService.getData();
        router.start();
    });
});
```

Figure 6-8 shows you how the solution should look at present.

Figure 6-8. *The current solution state*

We have data structures, data, and routing in our application, and now it is the time to create the UI.

Creating Views

In this part, we will create the application views. Each view will have a corresponding template, except for the home view, which renders the agent tiles. Each template will be created as a script tag inside the index.html file. The first view that we are going to create is the AgentTileView.

The AgentTileView

The AgentTileView will render a single agent tile, which is used in the application home page. It will be created in the agentTileView.js file, which exists in the views folder. Listing 6-12 is the template for agentTileView.

Listing 6-12. AgentTileView Template

```
<script type="text/template" id="agent-tile-template">
    <div id="tilecontainer">
        <div class="tile double bg-color-gray">
            <div class="tile-content">
                <div class="image">
                    <img src="<%- imagePath %>" class="place-left" id="agentImage" alt="Agent Image"/>
                </div>
                <a id="<%- agentID %>" href="#/details/<%- agentID %>" class="moreDetails"></a>
                <div class="agentDetails">
                    <span class="agenteDetailesHeaders">Name:</span>  <%- firstName %> <%- lastName %>
                </div>
                <div class="agentDetails">
                    <span class="agenteDetailesHeaders">Code Name:</span>  <%- codeName %>
                </div>
                <div class="agentDetails">
                    <span class="agenteDetailesHeaders">Description:</span>   <%- description %>
                </div>
            </div>
        </div>
    </div>
</script>
```

As you can see, each tile will include the agent details and the agent image. The template itself exists inside a script tag with agent-tile-template ID, which will be used by the AgentTileView. The last interesting thing in the template is the boldfaced code, which creates a link to the details page of each agent. Notice that when you create a link, it should have the # sign and all the relevant parts, as in the case of the agent ID in our example.

The code in Listing 6-13 shows how the AgentTileView will look.

Listing 6-13. AgentTileView

```
define(['jquery', 'underscore', 'backbone'], function ($, _, Backbone) {
    var agentTileView = Backbone.View.extend({
        template: _.template($('#agent-tile-template').html()),
        render: function() {
            this.$el.html(this.template(this.model.toJSON()));
            return this;
        }
    });

    return agentTileView;
});
```

The implementation is very straightforward. All the view requires is that the template be set to the HTML in the agent-tile-template script tag. Also, the view includes a render function that only renders the model it gets with the template.

The HomeView

Once we have the AgentTileView, we can create the application home page. The home page view will be responsible for rendering the list of agents as agent tiles and for putting them inside the main section. The HomeView will exist in the homeView.js file, which is part of the views folder.

Listing 6-14 shows how the HomeView should look.

Listing 6-14. HomeView

```
define(['jquery', 'underscore', 'backbone', 'views/agentTileView', "routers/router"],
    function ($, _, Backbone, agentTileView, Router) {
    var homeView = Backbone.View.extend({
        tagName: 'div',
        initialize: function() {
            this.collection = app.agents;
        },
        render: function() {
            this.$el.empty();
            this.$el.append(this.addCreateAgentButton());
            this.collection.each(function(item) {
                this.addOne(item);
            }, this);
            return this;
        },
        addCreateAgentButton: function() {
            var btn = document.createElement('input');
            btn.type = 'button';
            btn.value = 'Create Agent';
            btn.className = 'default';
            btn.id = 'btnCreateAgent';
            btn.addEventListener('click', function() {
                Router.navigate('#/createAgent', {trigger: true});
            }, false);
            return btn;
        },
        addOne: function(agent) {
            var view = new agentTileView({ model: agent });
            this.$el.append(view.render().el);
        }
    });

    return homeView;
});
```

In the code, there are a few interesting things to note.

- The initialize function sets the view's collection to the app.agents AgentCollection.

- The render function renders the list of agent tiles. First, we empty the HomeView $el. After that, we add to the $el the create button that is used to navigate to the CreateAgentView, and then we iterate over the agent collection and add all the agent tiles, using the addOne function.

- The addCreateAgentButton function creates a button input type that is used to navigate to the CreateAgentView. You can see how to add an event listener that uses the Router object to navigate to a relevant view.

- The addOne function receives an agent argument and creates an AgentTileView for that agent. After we have the view, the function will append its el to the $el of the HomeView.

Now that we have the HomeView, you can run the application and see the home page in action, as in Figure 6-9.

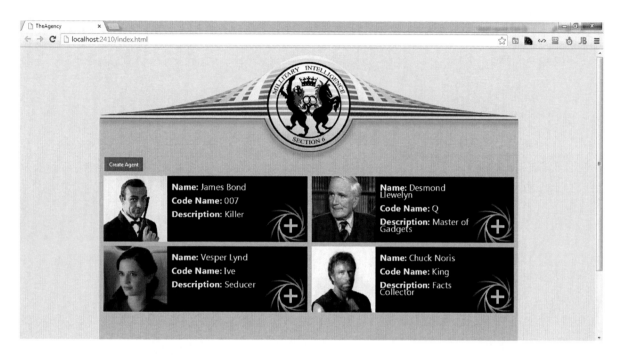

Figure 6-9. *The HomeView after first run*

The TaskView and EditModalView

In order to build the DetailsView, we will first have to create the TaskView and the EditModalView, which are used by the DetailsView. We will start with the TaskView.

The TaskView

The TaskView is responsible for showing a single task and enabling us to change the task state from complete to incomplete and vice versa. The TaskView should be created in a taskView.js file, which should exist in the views folder. In the following code (Listing 6-15), you can see the task template:

Listing 6-15. TaskView Template

```
<script type="text/template" id="task-template">
    <td><%- description %></td>
    <td><% if (isComplete) {%>
        <img src="images/Completed.png" alt="completed" />
        <% } else { %>
```

```
        <img src="images/NotCompleted.png" alt="in progress" />
        <% } %>
    </td>
</script>
```

As you can see, the template has a `task-template` id. Each task will be created as a table row, and the template will generate the table cells for each task. If a task is complete, we use the `Completed.png` image; otherwise, we use the `NotCompleted.png` image.

Listing 6-16 shows how the `TaskView` is implemented.

Listing 6-16. TaskView

```
define(['jquery', 'underscore', 'backbone', 'components/dataService'],
    function ($, _, Backbone, dataService) {
    var taskView = Backbone.View.extend({
        template: _.template($('#task-template').html()),
        tagName: 'tr',
        events: {
            'click td': 'toggleTask'
        },
        render: function() {
            this.$el.html(this.template(this.model.toJSON()));
            return this;
        },
        toggleTask: function (event) {
            this.model.toggleComplete();
            dataService.saveData(app.agents);
            this.render();
        }
    });

    return taskView;
});
```

In the code, note the following:

- The view `tagName` property is set to `tr`, to generate the table row for each task.

- An event listener is added to all the table cells, to toggle a task.

- The `toggleTask` function will use the model's `toggleComplete` function to toggle the task from complete to incomplete. Also, we use the `DataService` object's `saveData` function to save the current data state, once a task is toggled. Last but not least, once a task is toggled, we re-render the view.

The EditeModalView

The `EditModalView` is going to use a Backbone.js plug-in called `Backbone.ModalDialog`, to show a model dialog that is used to edit the agent's details (except for the image). The `EditModalView` should be created in an `editModalView.js` file, which should exist in the `views` folder.

The Backbone.ModalDialog plug-in is a new Backbone.js view, which is called Backbone.ModalView, and you can extend it using its extend function. The Backbone.ModalDialog creates a modal dialog that can be created and hidden when needed. It has two main functions, showModal and hideModal, which are used to show and hide the modal dialog. It also includes a built-in modal UI that you can use or override.

▪ **Note**   You can create your own Backbone.js plug-ins as long as you stay aligned to Backbone.js functionality.

In the EditModalView, we will use the template shown in Listing 6-17.

Listing 6-17. EditModalView Template

```
<script type="text/template" id="edit-template">
    <div class='modal-header'>Edit Agent</div>
    <div id="validationError" class="red"></div>
    <form>
        <label for="txtFirstName">First Name: </label><input id="txtFirstName" type="text"
        value="<%- firstName %>"/><br />
        <label for="txtLastName">Last Name: </label><input id="txtLastName" type="text"
        value="<%- lastName %>"/><br />
        <label for="txtCodeName">Code Name:</label><input id="txtCodeName" type="text"
        value="<%- codeName %>"/><br />
        <label for="txtDescription">Description: </label><input id="txtDescription" type="text"
        value="<%- description %>"/><br/>
        <input id='saveEditButton' type='button' value='Save' />
    </form>
</script>
```

The template has an edit-template id, and it includes a form that will be used to edit the agent details. Note, too, that we have a validationError div, which will be used to notify the user if the model doesn't pass the agent custom validation.

The following code in Listing 6-18 is the EditModalView itself.

Listing 6-18. EditModalView

```
define(['jquery', 'underscore', 'backbone', 'modalDialog', 'components/dataService'],
    function ($, _, Backbone, ModalView, dataService) {
    var editModalView = Backbone.ModalView.extend({
        name: 'editAgentView',
        template: _.template($('#edit-template').html()),
        render: function() {
            this.$el.html(this.template(this.model.toJSON()));
            return this;
        },
        events: {
            'click #saveEditButton': 'updateAgent'
        },
        updateAgent: function (event) {
            event.preventDefault();
```

```
                if(this.model.set(this.getCurrentFormValues(), {validate:true}))
                {
                    dataService.saveData(app.agents);
                    this.hideModal();
                }
                else {
                    $('#validationError').text(this.model.validationError);
                }
            },
        getCurrentFormValues: function() {
            return {
                firstName: $('#txtFirstName').val(),
                lastName: $('#txtLastName').val(),
                codeName: $('#txtCodeName').val(),
                description: $('#txtDescription').val()
            };
        }
    });

    return editModalView;
});
```

In the code, the following are of interest:

- The `EditModalView` is extending the `Backbone.ModalView`.

- An event handler is added to the save button, and it is triggering the `updateAgent` function.

- The `updateAgent` function is preventing the form from submitting it's content. In addition, it is trying to set the model with the current form values. Because we send the `set` function the option of validate, which is set to true, validation will occur before setting the model. If the validation succeeds, we save the current state of the data, using the `DataService` object, and hide the modal dialog. If validation fails, we notify the user by setting the text content of the `validationError` div with the model `validationError`.

- The `getCurrentFormValues` returns an object that includes all the values of the text boxes in the form. Make sure that the returned object includes the same agent model properties.

The DetailsView

Now that we have both the `TaskView` and the `EditModalView`, it is time to create the `DetailsView`. The `DetailsView` should be created in a `detailsView.js` file, which should exist in the `views` folder.

In the `DetailsView`, there are two panes: the agent details in the left pane and the agent task list in the right pane. You can edit the agent details using the edit button. You can delete the agent using the delete button. You can also navigate back to the `HomeView` using the back button. In the tasks pane, there is a text box in which you can write a new task. Pressing Enter will add the task to the agent's task list.

In the `DetailsView`, we will use the template in Listing 6-19.

Listing 6-19. DetailsView Template

```
<script type="text/template" id="details-template">
    <div>
        <img class="whirl" src="images/whirl.png" />
        <div class="float-left">
            <h2>Agent Details</h2>
            <div class="seperatorDiv"></div>
            <fieldset>
                <legend>Agent</legend>
                <div class="display-field">
                    <img src="<%- imagePath %>" alt="Agent Image"/>
                </div>
                <div style="float: left">
                    <div class="display-label">
                        First Name: <br />
                        Last Name: <br />
                        Code Name: <br />
                        Description:
                    </div>
                </div>
                <div>
                    <div id="agentDetails" class="display-field">
                        <%- firstName %><br />
                        <%- lastName %><br />
                        <%- codeName %><br />
                        <%- description %>
                    </div>
                </div>
            </fieldset>
        </div>
        <div class="float-left assignment-padding">
            <h2>Assignments</h2>
            <div class="seperatorDiv"></div>
            <table id="taskTable">
                <tr>
                    <td colspan="2"><input id="txtNewTask" type="text" autofocus="autofocus" /></td>
                </tr>
            </table>
        </div>
        <div class="clear align-center">
            <input id="btnEditAgent" type="button" value="Edit" class="default"/>
            <input id="btnDeleteAgent" type="button" value="Delete" class="default"/>
            <input id="btnBack" type="button" value="Back" class="default"/>
        </div>
    </div>
</script>
```

In the HTML, note the following:

- We use a `fieldset` to hold all the details of the agent. In the `fieldset`, we use Underscore.js to extract the model data and use it.

- The task text box uses the `autofocus` attribute, which was added in the HTML5 specifications. The `autofocus` indicates to the browser that when the page is loaded, it should focus on the text box.

- At the bottom of the view, you can see the three buttons that will be exposed by the view.

The following code (Listing 6-20) is the `DetailsView` itself:

Listing 6-20. DetailsView

```
define(['jquery', 'underscore', 'backbone', 'views/editModalView', 'views/taskView', 'models/task',
'routers/router', 'components/dataService'],
    function ($, _, Backbone, EditModal, TaskView, Task, Router, dataService) {
    var detailsView = Backbone.View.extend({
        template: _.template($('#details-template').html()),
        tagName: 'div',
        events: {
            'click #btnEditAgent': 'editAgent',
            'click #btnDeleteAgent': 'deleteAgent',
            'click #btnBack': 'back',
            'keypress #txtNewTask': 'addNewTask'
        },
        $cache: {
            taskTable: null,
            EnterKey: 13
        },
        initialize: function() {
            this.listenTo(this.model, 'change', this.modelChanged);
        },
        render: function() {
            this.$el.html(this.template(this.model.toJSON()));
            this.$cache.taskTable = this.$el.find('#taskTable');
            this.model.get('tasks').each(function(task) {
                this.addTask(task);
            }, this);
            return this;
        },
        addTask: function(task) {
            var view = new TaskView({ model: task });
            this.$cache.taskTable.append(view.render().el);
        },
        editAgent: function(event) {
            var view = new EditModal({ model: this.model });
            view.render().showModal();
        },
        deleteAgent: function() {
            if (confirm('Are you sure you want to delete the agent?')) {
                app.agents.remove(this.model);
                dataService.saveData(app.agents);
```

```
                Router.navigate('#/', {trigger: true});
            }
        },
        back: function() {
            Router.navigate('#/', {trigger: true});
        },
        addNewTask: function(event) {
            var txt = $('#txtNewTask');
            if (event.which !== this.$cache.EnterKey || !txt.val().trim()) {
                return;
            }

            app.taskID++;
            this.model.get('tasks').add(new Task({ id: app.taskID, taskID: app.taskID, description:
            txt.val() }));
            dataService.saveData(app.agents);
            txt.val('');
            this.render();
        },
        modelChanged: function() {
            this.render();
        }
    });

    return detailsView;
});
```

Of note in the DetailsView are the following:

- The view includes four DOM events—editAgent, deleteAgent, back, and addNewTask. They are added in the events option.

- The view includes a cache property. The property is used to cache DOM elements or properties that are going to be used during the view life cycle. You should cache DOM elements if you are going to use them a lot. This is why we cache the task table. Note that if you want to cache DOM elements, you should do so in the render function, as before that, they might not be available, because they weren't created yet.

- In the initialize function, we add an event listener to the model change event, using the listenTo function.

- In the render function, several things occur. First, we use the template and the model to render the $el. After the $el exists, we find the task table and cache it. Then we iterate the model's tasks and render each of them, using the addTask function.

- The addTask function just adds the given task to the task table by rendering a TaskView for the given task and appending it to the task table.

- The editAgent function creates the EditModal view and displays it using its showModal function.

- The deleteAgent function first checks whether the user really wants to delete the agent, using the JavaScript confirm function. To delete the agent, we use the agent collection remove function. After the agent is removed, we use the DataService to save the current data state and navigate back to the HomeView, using the #/ route.

- The back function only navigates to the HomeView using the #/ route.

- The addNewTask function is responsible for creating a new task and inserting it into the model's task collection.

- The modelChanged function, which is called when the model is being changed, just re-renders the view according to the new model.

You can run the application and navigate to the details view by clicking the plus sign (+) at the right corner of each agent tile. Figure 6-10 shows how the DetailsView should look when you navigate to James Bond's details.

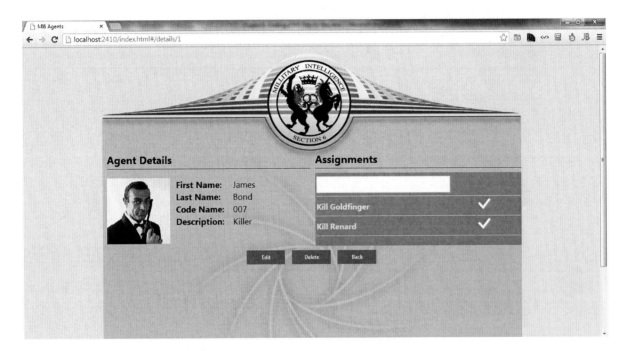

Figure 6-10. *James Bond Agent Details page*

Figure 6-11 shows how EditModal will look when you click the edit button.

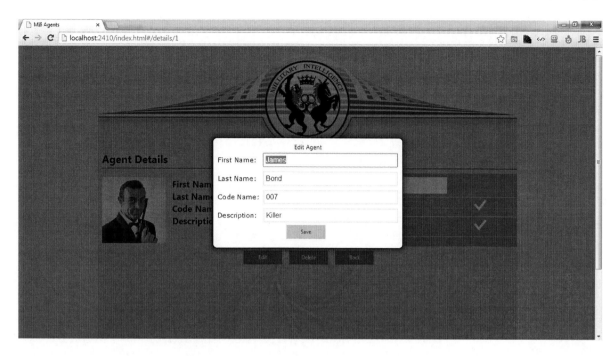

Figure 6-11. *Editing agent James Bond*

Figure 6-12 illustrates what the delete confirmation will look like.

Figure 6-12. *Confirming whether to delete James Bond*

The CreateView

The last view that we are going to create is the CreateView. The CreateView is responsible for creating a new agent. It includes text boxes in which to add the agent details and a file input type with which to add the agent picture. In order to save the image, we will use HTML5 File API.

CreateView should be created in a createView.js file in the views folder. The following template (Listing 6-21) is used by CreateView.

Listing 6-21. CreateView Template

```html
<script type="text/template" id="create-template">
    <div>
        <img class="whirl" src="images/whirl.png" />
        <div class="float-left">
            <h2>Create Agent</h2>
            <div class="seperatorDiv"></div>
            <fieldset>
                <legend>Agent Details</legend>
                <div>
                    <div id="validationError" class="red"></div>
                    <div>
                        <form>
                            <label for="txtFirstName">First Name: </label><input id="txtFirstName"
                            type="text" value="<%- firstName %>" /><br />
                            <label for="txtLastName">Last Name: </label><input id="txtLastName"
                            type="text" value="<%- lastName %>" /><br />
                            <label for="txtCodeName">Code Name:</label><input id="txtCodeName"
                            type="text" value="<%- codeName %>" /><br />
                            <label for="txtDescription">Description: </label><input
                            id="txtDescription" type="text" value="<%- description %>" /><br/>
                            <label for="txtImage">Image Path: </label><input id="txtImage"
                            type="file" value="<%- imagePath %>"/>
                        </form>
                    </div>
                </div>
            </fieldset>
        </div>
        <div class="clear align-center">
            <input id="saveEditButton" type="button" value="Save" class="default"/>
            <input id="btnBack" type="button" value="Back" class="default"/>
        </div>
    </div>
</script>
```

The template itself is very simple and doesn't include anything special. The code in Listing 6-22 is CreateView itself.

Listing 6-22. CreateView

```
define(['jquery', 'underscore', 'backbone', 'models/agent', 'routers/router', 'components/
dataService'],
    function ($, _, Backbone, Agent, Router, dataService) {
    var createView = Backbone.View.extend({
        template: _.template($('#create-template').html()),
        tagName: 'div',
        initialize: function () {
          this.model = new Agent();
        },
        render: function() {
            this.$el.html(this.template(this.model.toJSON()));
            return this;
        },
        events: {
            'click #saveEditButton': 'createAgent',
            'click #btnBack': 'back'
        },
        createAgent: function (event) {
            event.preventDefault();
            var self = this,
                id;

            if(this.model.set(this.getCurrentFormValues(), {validate:true}))
            {
                id = ++app.agentID;
                this.model.set({ agentID: id, id: id});
                $.proxy(this.handleImageFile(function () {
                    app.agents.add(self.model);
                    dataService.saveData(app.agents);
                    Router.navigate('#/', {trigger: true});
                }), this);
            }
            else {
                $('#validationError').text(this.model.validationError);
            }
        },
        handleImageFile: function (callback) {
            var file = document.getElementById('txtImage').files[0],
                reader  = new FileReader(),
                self = this;

            if (file) {
                reader.onloadend = function () {
                    self.model.set({ imagePath: reader.result });
                    callback();
                }
                reader.readAsDataURL(file);
            }
            else {
                callback();
```

```
            }
        },
        back: function() {
            Router.navigate('#/', {trigger: true});
        },
        getCurrentFormValues: function() {
            return {
                firstName: $('#txtFirstName').val(),
                lastName: $('#txtLastName').val(),
                codeName: $('#txtCodeName').val(),
                description: $('#txtDescription').val()
            };
        }
    });

    return createView;
});
```

Note especially the following in the `CreateView` code:

- The `initialize` function sets the model to be a new agent, with no data.

- The view has two DOM events for creating an agent and for going back to `HomeView`.

- The main view function is the `createAgent` function. In the function, we first prevent the default behavior of posting the data by using the `event.preventDefault` function. Later on, we try to set the form values into the model and trigger the model validation. If validation fails, we notify the user by setting the text content of the `validationError` div with the model `validationError`. If the validation succeeds, we set the model's ID to be the ID according to the next ID in the `app.agentID` property. After setting the ID, we set the image file. The `handleImageFile` function receives a callback, because its implementation is asynchronous. After `handleImageFile` completes its asynchronous run, it will call the callback, which is adding the new agent to the agent collection, save the data, using `DataService`, and navigate back to `HomeView`.

- The `handleImageFile` function first tries to extract the file from the file input type. If there was a file in the file input type, we use the `FileReader` object, which exists in the HTML5 File API. The `FileReader` enables developers to read files in a few ways—as Data URL, as text, as binary string, and as an array buffer. We use the Data URL format, which will enable us to save the file's content as a URL that an image tag can use. In order to transform the file we received into a data URL, we use the `FileReader` `readAsDataURL` function. That function will read the file content asynchronously. Only when the `loadend` event is called on the `FileReader` will we be able to get the data URL. This is why we add an `onloadend` event handler, which sets the model's `imagePath` property to the `reader.result` that will be the data URL. Then we call the callback that the `handleImageFile` received.

■ **Note** Data URL is a scheme that is used to put data online on a web page. Data URL's main use is to encode small images that can be embedded into web pages. Data URLs can help you avoid HTTP requests for those small images, because the images will be embedded inside the web page. On the other hand, you shouldn't use Data URL for big images, because it will only make your web page HTML bigger.

`localStorage` capacity is limited by browsers. Saving images as Data URL inside `localStorage` can cause its capacity to become full very quickly. If that occurs, you will receive a quota exceeded error. Despite this, we chose the Data URL option, because, later, the images will be saved to the back end.

- The `back` function navigates back to `HomeView`.

- `getCurrentFormValues` returns an object that includes all the values of the text boxes in the form. Ensure that the returned object includes the same agent model properties.

You can run the application and navigate to the `CreateView` by clicking the Create Agent button. Figure 6-13 shows how `CreateView` should look.

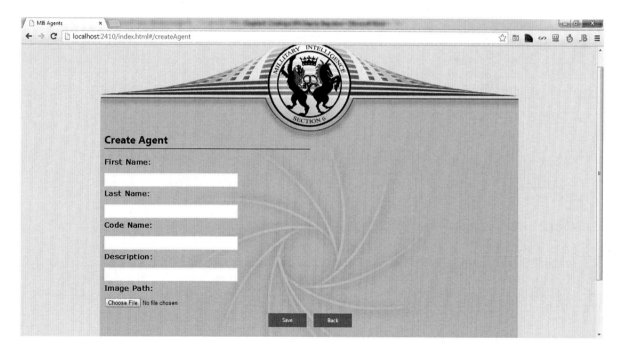

Figure 6-13. *CreateView*

The end solution should resemble Figure 6-14.

Figure 6-14. *The end solution*

The application front end is now operational, and you can navigate between the application pages, add new agents, delete agents, and edit agents. You can also add tasks to agent and toggle their status from complete to incomplete. You can also open Google Chrome DevTools and then the Resources tab to take a look at localStorage. Figure 6-15 shows the localStorage stored data.

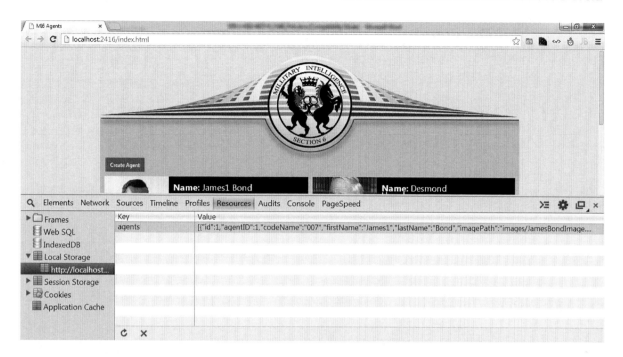

Figure 6-15. *Using Chrome DevTools to look at the stored data*

Congratulations! You have just created an SPA for the first time.

Summary

In this chapter, we built an SPA using Backbone.js, RequireJS, jQuery, and Underscore.js. The SPA includes the ability to view and manipulate agents and tasks in an intelligence agency. Although the application is small, it includes most of the concepts that you will require in order to master SPA front-end creation.

While the application we built can work on its own and without a back end, due to its mock data, in most applications, you will have an SPA back end. Also, we still haven't covered communication options for SPAs. We will cover those in Part III of the book.

PART III

Building the Back End

■ ■ ■

CHAPTER 7

Creating a Back-End Service with ASP.NET Web API

Hypertext transfer protocol (HTTP) is an application-level protocol, originally designed to transfer hypertext-based resources over networks. Today, HTTP is widely adopted and has become one of the most popular protocols for building web applications and services over the Internet.

■ **Note** The current version of HTTP is 1.1. The new version of HTTP, version 2.0, has been in development by the IETF (Internet Engineering Task Force) for the past several years. The new version focuses on the efficiency of HTTP and aims to provide performance enhancements to the protocol, for example, by adding header compression. At present, there is no exact date as to when HTTP 2.0 will be released and when browsers will fully support it.

To develop HTTP-based services using the .NET Framework, we will use ASP.NET Web API, which is the first fully featured framework within the .NET Framework for developing HTTP-based services.

In this chapter, you will learn what HTTP-based services are and how to create them with ASP.NET Web API. We will also continue to develop our agency solution and add ASP.NET Web API code to it to create the SPA back end.

■ **Note** ASP.NET Web API was preceded by the WCF (Windows Communication Foundation) framework, which is part of the .NET Framework. Although WCF is capable of creating HTTP-based services, ASP.NET Web API provides a wider control over HTTP, a more testable pipeline, an enhanced tracing support, and better support for content negotiation and media types—a concept you will learn in this chapter. To better understand the history of ASP.NET Web API and WCF, consider reading the article "WCF or ASP.NET Web APIs? My two cents on the subject" on CodeProject at `www.codeproject.com/Articles/341414/WCF-or-ASP-NET-Web-APIs-My-two-cents-on-the-subjec`.

Introduction to HTTP-Based Services

A service is a software component that exposes a set of managed resources to the purpose of querying and manipulation. For example, a service that manages gadgets will enable the end user to retrieve a list of gadgets, either full or subset, add new gadgets, and change prices of gadgets.

HTTP-based services are services that use HTTP not only as a transport medium but as an application-level protocol. For example, HTTP-based services may use the HTTP caching headers to inform end users that the response can be cached for a specific duration.

When we design and create HTTP-based services, there are four parts of HTTP we must take into consideration—unified resource identifiers (URIs), verbs, status codes, and content negotiation.

URIs

Every resource our service manages has to have a unique identifier. You are probably familiar with the idea of uniquely identifying a resource by using a sequential number or a GUID (globally unified identifier). For example, if you manage both gadgets and agents, you would probably have an agent with ID *1*, and a gadget with ID *1*. The difference between the two IDs is the context you use them in: gadgets or agents.

A URI is a uniform way to uniquely identify all the resources our services manage. For example, the agent with ID 1 may have any of the following URIs:

- `/agents/1`

- `urn:agent:1`

- `http://api.theagency.org/agents/1`

With HTTP-based services, URIs not only specify the identity of a resource, they also locate it over the network. URIs for HTTP-based services have the general form `"http://" host [":" port] / [resource path]`.

The address listed last in the preceding examples is constructed of the following fragments:

1. The `http://` prefix. For secured locators, you can use `https://`.

2. The host `api.theagency.org`. The hostname should be accessible from the client computer.

3. The default port for HTTP, which is port 80. If the resource is accessible from a different port, you would need to specify it in the URI. For example, if the resource is accessible over port 81, the address should be `http://api.theagency.org:81/agents/1`.

4. The resource path `/agents/1`. This is the part your service has to analyze to know you are looking for an agent with ID 1.

■ **Note** A URI that defines the location of a resource is also known as a URL (unified resource locator). A URI that only defines the identity of a resource, without its location, is also known as a URN (unified resource name). When constructing HTTP-based services, it is common to use URLs, not URNs.

For collections, you create URIs that contain only the root path, without the specific resource identifier, such as `http://api.theagency.org/agents/`. Calling such URIs will normally return a list of resources.

Because you are likely familiar with URLs, you're probably asking yourself what the place of the query string in URIs is. There is controversy concerning whether to use query strings as part of the URI, such as `http://api.theagency.org/agents?id=1`, or whether they should only be used to filter a collection of resources; for example, using the URI `http://api.theagency.org/agents?name=d` to represent a filter that returns all agents whose name begins with the letter *d*. Because there is no right or wrong with URI design (unless you are a fanatic of the subject), we will leave this decision to your discretion.

Your service can also express URIs as relative addresses, also known as URI references, such as `/agents/1`. With relative addresses, it is up to the client to resolve the URI reference to an absolute URI.

■ **Note** You should select the type of resource identifier wisely. Identifier types such as GUID and sequential numbers are considered unique. When selecting a property of the resource as the identifier, make sure it is unique in your context. For example, the URI reference `/agents/david` or `/agents/EdwardH` may not guarantee uniqueness if you manage hundreds of agents. In some cases, you might even select two properties as the resource's identifier. For example, `/cities/salem` might not be unique if you manage USA census data, as there are more than a dozen places called Salem in the United States. Instead, you might want to use a URI such as `/censusdata/nebraska/salem` or `/censusdata/salem/NE`.

Among the first things we have to design when creating new HTTP-based services are the URI templates of our resources. It might sound reasonably simple, but there are caveats, even with such an easy task. For example, how will you define the URI for an agent's car? Would it be a URI that only represents the car, such as `/cars/COOL-CAR` (the resource identifier is the car's license plate), or a URI that also expresses the ownership, such as `/agents/1/cars/COOL-CAR`? It really depends on how you treat cars in the service. Are they individual entities or subordinates of the agent entity?

■ **Note** For additional examples and information on URI design, check the "Resource Naming" article at `www.restapitutorial.com/lessons/restfulresourcenaming.html`.

HTTP Verbs

When calling a service, we use URI to locate the specific resource we need. HTTP verbs, also referred to as HTTP methods, are action-like semantics of HTTP. Each of the verbs available in HTTP signifies a different action you perform on a resource, such as retrieve, upsert (insert/update), or delete. For example, the GET verb is used for retrieving resources, whereas the DELETE verb is used for deleting resources. For each verb, HTTP defines two properties.

- *Safety*: A verb is considered safe if calling it does not change the resource's state or data. For example, it is expected that calling a service using the GET verb will only return the resource's data, without changing the data in the system.

- *Idempotency*: A verb is considered idempotent if the side effect of sending a single request to the service is the same as sending multiple requests. For example, sending a request with the DELETE verb will result in the resource being deleted. Even after we send the request multiple times, the resource will still be in the deleted state (or removed entirely from the system). Idempotency doesn't necessarily mean all requests will result with the same response. When sending a DELETE request, it is reasonable that the second response and those that follow will return an erroneous result, because the resource no longer exists.

Table 7-1 lists the common HTTP verbs, their usage, and whether they are safe and idempotent.

Table 7-1. *HTTP Verbs and Their Usage*

Verb	Description	Safe	Idempotent
GET	Used for retrieving a representation of a resource (its data)	Yes	Yes
HEAD	Used for retrieving information about a resource without getting its data. The response will contain the same HTTP headers as in a GET request, but without the message's body.	Yes	Yes
PUT	Used for either adding or updating a resource (depends if the resource already exists)	No	Yes
DELETE	Used for deleting a resource	No	Yes
POST	Used for adding a resource or requesting an action on an existing resource. See additional details below.	No	No
OPTIONS	Used for querying which HTTP verbs and headers are supported for a given resource	Yes	Yes
PATCH	Used for updating part of an existing resource. See additional details below.	No	Yes

HTTP POST

The POST verb is the least structured HTTP verb. You can use POST to accomplish different tasks, such as the following:

- Add a resource or a subordinate to a collection, when you don't know the new resource's URI, for example, POSTing to `http://api.theagency.org/agents` to add a new agent resource or to `http://api.theagency.org/agents/1/tasks` to add a task resource to an existing agent. The response should contain the URI of the newly created resource, so clients can retrieve the resource later.

■ **Note** The PUT verb is also used when creating new resources; however, when you send a PUT request, the URI you use is the one that identifies the new resource. For example, sending a PUT request to `http://api.theagency.org/agents/2` will create a new agent with ID 2.

- Perform an action that changes the state of a resource. For example, POSTing to `http://api.theagency.org/agents/1/retire` will change the agent's status to `retired`. A POST request can also have parameters, either in the query string or in the message's body. For example, POSTing to `http://api.theagency.org/agents/1/increaseSalary?amount=1000` will increase the agent's salary by $1,000 US.

HTTP PATCH

The PATCH verb is not part of the original HTTP 1.1 but was added later to accommodate the need to perform partial updates. With PUT, you can only update a resource by sending a complete replacement of it, even if you only want to update one or two properties. Sending a request with the PATCH verb allows you to send partial representation of the resource that contains only the properties you want to update.

■ **Note** Handling PATCH in a .NET-based service is not a simple task. By default, deserializing a partial resource representation to an object will result in *null* values for reference-type properties or default scalar values for value types. This behavior of the serializer makes it unclear whether you have to set the resource's property to its default value or ignore the property and leave it with its current value. To properly handle partial updates, you will need a different approach that is not based on the standard serialization process. An example of such an approach, using dynamic objects, is demonstrated in the following link: `https://gist.github.com/benfoster/4488755`.

Status Codes

Status codes are three-digit numbers returned as part of the response message. The status code describes the result of processing the request. Status codes are divided into five classes, or categories, as described in Table 7-2.

Table 7-2. *HTTP Status Code Categories*

Category	Usage	Examples
1xx (Information)	Represents an informational response about the state of the connection	101 (Switching protocols)
2xx (Successful)	Indicates that the request was successfully received and accepted by the server	200 (OK) 201 (Created) 204 (No Content)
3xx (Redirection)	Indicates that additional action should be taken by the client to complete the request	301 (Moved permanently) 304 (Not modified)
4xx (Client Error)	Indicates that there is a problem with the request, either with the address, the headers, or the message's body	400 (Bad request) 401 (Unauthorized) 404 (Not found)
5xx (Server Error)	A category of codes referring to server-side errors that occurred during the processing of the request	500 (Internal server error) 503 (Service unavailable)

When you design the service, it is important to return proper status codes. For example:

- If you received a PUT request and created a new resource, the response should be 201 (Created).

- If you received a PUT request for an existing resource, respond with a 200 (OK) with the updated resource or return an empty response with status code 204 (No content).

- If you changed the template of your URIs and you receive a URI with the old template, consider returning a 301 (Moved permanently) response with the new address of the resource.

- If you are requested to delete a resource (using the DELETE verb), respond with either a 200 (OK) response and include the deleted resource in the message's body, a 202 (Accepted) response, if the deletion process was logged but has yet to occur, or a 204 (No content) response, if you deleted the resource and there is no content to return.

■ **Note** For a detailed list of which status code to return for each verb, refer to the "Method Definitions" page in the HTTP RFC at www.w3.org/Protocols/rfc2616/rfc2616-sec9.html. You can also find a complete list of HTTP status codes in the RFC at www.w3.org/Protocols/rfc2616/rfc2616-sec10.html.

Content Negotiation

HTTP is designed to transfer various types of resources in messages, such as hypertext (HTML), scripts, images, JSON, and XML. To support the different types of message formats, HTTP uses Multipurpose Internet Mail Extensions (MIME) types, also known as media types. The MIME type describing the message's body part is located in the message's *Content-Type* HTTP header and is constructed of three parts: type, subtype, and an optional type-specific parameter.

For example, the type text indicates a human-readable text and can be followed by a subtype such as html, which indicates HTML content. The MIME type will be written as text/html, as shown in Listing 7-1.

Listing 7-1. An HTTP Response Containing an HTML File

```
HTTP/1.1 200 OK
Content-Type: text/html
Server: Microsoft-IIS/8.0
Content-Length: 50

<html>
        <body>
                Hello World!
        </body>
</html>
```

Type-specific parameters can be added after the subtype and are prefixed by a semicolon. For example, the text type can have a charset parameter, such as text/html; charset=UTF-8.

The Content-Type header can be present in both request and response and can have a different value in each of them. For example, if you send a PUT or a POST request with a message body, you will have to set the Content-Type HTTP header to the media type of the body.

With HTTP-based services, media types have another use—to express the format of the response you wish to receive. To inform the service of which format you want the response to have, include the Accept HTTP header in the request and set its value to the requested media type. The process of requesting a specific format is also known as *content negotiation.*

Listing 7-2 shows how to send a JSON request to a service and to request that the response will use the XML format.

Listing 7-2. Adding the Accept HTTP Header to a Request

```
POST http://localhost:2410/api/agents/1/tasks HTTP/1.1
Accept: application/xml
Content-Type: application/json
Content-Length: 79
Connection: Keep-Alive
Host: localhost:2410

{"taskID":0,"description":"Locate nuclear bomb","agentID":1,"isComplete":false}
```

■ **Note**   The preceding example is quite abnormal, as you would usually use the same media type in the request and the response. An exception to this might occur in the event you want a different representation of the data. For example, you might send a JSON message and get back either the image that represents the data or a CSV (comma-separated values) file containing a list of entities.

If your client can handle responses of different media types, you can specify those media types in the Accept header, separated with a comma. For example, if your client supports both JSON and XML responses, you can set the Accept header to application/xml, application/json.

The Accept header is part of the Accept-* HTTP headers that define the content negotiation between the client and the service. In addition to the Accept header, you can also use the following:

- Accept-Charset: This specifies the character set that is acceptable in the response, such as UTF-8, ANSI, ASCII, and ISO character sets.

- Accept-Encoding: This specifies the content-coding of the response. This header informs the service which compression formats the client supports. For example, Accept-Encoding: gzip, deflate means that the client knows how to decompress responses that use either the gzip or deflate compression formats. If the service supports any of these formats, it may compress the content to decrease the size of the response.

- Accept-Language: This specifies the preferred languages for the response content. The value can contain one or more comma-separated ISO language codes. If the client supports multiple languages but prefers a specific language, you can specify it by using quality values. For example, setting the Accept-Language header to fr, en; q=0.8, de-DE; q=0.6 means that the client prefers French but also accepts English and, optionally, German.

■ **Note**   For more details on how to construct each of the Accept-* headers, refer to the header field definitions section in the HTTP RFC at www.w3.org/Protocols/rfc2616/rfc2616-sec14.html.

When designing HTTP-based services, consider which types of Accept-* headers you want to support. For example, if you choose to support the Accept-Language headers, make sure you have localized resources for error messages and other strings. If you choose to support the Accept header, make sure you have the proper serializers for types such as JSON and XML, and that you know how to generate other media types, such as images, CSV content, or RSS.

RESTful Services

The term *Representational State Transfer* (REST) describes an architectural style that takes advantage of HTTP's resource-based nature. Until now, we have explained the basic concepts of HTTP-based services—URIs, verbs, status codes, and content negotiation. REST complements HTTP-based services by adding two important capabilities: resource discoverability and state management.

Resource Discoverability

A simple example for resource discoverability can be found in the Atom format. An Atom feed is a resource that has its own URIs, which contain a list of items. Feed items are resources themselves, with their own URIs. Their URIs are published as links in the feed representation. Publishing URIs of items in the feed entries makes the items discoverable for clients. Listing 7-3 shows a response containing an Atom feed for a list of agents.

Listing 7-3. Returning a List of Agents As an Atom Feed

```
HTTP/1.1 200 OK
Cache-Control: no-cache
Content-Type: application/atom+xml
Content-Length: 1331

<?xml version="1.0" encoding="utf-8"?>
<feed xmlns="http://www.w3.org/2005/Atom">
    <title type="text">Agents Feed</title>
    <id>uuid:2043537d-42aa-4976-a981-7fe18047b541;id=1</id>
    <updated>2014-03-03T21:10:37Z</updated>
    <entry xml:base="http://localhost:2410/api/agents/1">
        <id>uuid:2043537d-42aa-4976-a981-7fe18047b541;id=2</id>
        <title type="text">James Bond</title>
        <updated>2014-02-13T23:10:37+02:00</updated>
        <content type="text">Killer</content>
    </entry>
    <entry xml:base="http://localhost:2410/api/agents/2">
        <id>uuid:2043537d-42aa-4976-a981-7fe18047b541;id=3</id>
        <title type="text">Desmond Llewelyn</title>
        <updated>2013-11-29T23:10:37+02:00</updated>
        <content type="text">Master of Gadgets</content>
    </entry>
    <entry xml:base="http://localhost:2410/api/agents/3">
        <id>uuid:2043537d-42aa-4976-a981-7fe18047b541;id=4</id>
        <title type="text">Vesper Lynd</title>
        <updated>2013-11-29T23:10:37+02:00</updated>
        <content type="text">Seducer</content>
    </entry>
    <entry xml:base="http://localhost:2410/api/agents/4">
        <id>uuid:2043537d-42aa-4976-a981-7fe18047b541;id=5</id>
        <title type="text">Chuck Noris</title>
        <updated>2013-11-29T23:10:37+02:00</updated>
        <content type="text">Facts Collector</content>
    </entry>
</feed>
```

A client can show the list of entries to the end user and have them select which item they want to watch. The URI of the item will be extracted from the entry and used to retrieve that item's data.

State Management

To manage the state of resources, RESTful services use links to describe what can be done with the resource. The links, often referred to as hypermedia controls, are embedded into the representation of the resource. For example, the representation of an agent can include links you can use when you want to delete the agent, add a task to the agent, or upload a new photo of the agent. Listing 7-4 shows a response containing an agent with hypermedia controls (links).

Listing 7-4. Returning an Agent with Hypermedia Controls

```
HTTP/1.1 200 OK
Cache-Control: no-cache
Content-Type: application/json; charset=utf-8
Content-Length: 594

{
  "agentID": 1,
  "codeName": "007",
  "firstName": "James",
  "lastName": "Bond",
  "imagePath": "images/JamesBondImage.png",
  "description": "Killer",
  "Links": [
    {
      "Rel": "Delete",
      "Link": "http://localhost:2410/api/agents/1"
    },
    {
      "Rel": "UploadPhoto",
      "Link": "http://localhost:2410/api/agents/1/photo"
    }
  ]
}
```

A resource may also change its hypermedia controls over time, as its state changes. For example, if you delete an agent, you might still be able to retrieve its representation—if it was not removed from the database—but the link to delete the agent would not appear in the representation. It's most likely that a deleted entity will not have any links at all, because the entity is no longer updatable—unless it is a link to revive the agent.

Instead of creating your own representation for hypermedia controls, you can use the Hypertext Application Language (HAL) media type, which extends XML and JSON, to support embedding of hypermedia controls in resources.

■ **Note** To learn more about HAL and how to use it with ASP.NET Web API, read the article "Building Hypermedia Web APIs with ASP.NET Web API" on MSDN Magazine at `http://msdn.microsoft.com/en-us/magazine/jj883957.aspx`.

If you apply the practices of REST to your HTTP-based services, your services can be referred to as *RESTful* services.

ASP.NET Web API Basics: Routing, API Controllers, and Actions

With ASP.NET Web API, you can create HTTP-based services that utilize HTTP verbs and URIs. ASP.NET Web API provides the support for fully interoperable services that can be consumed by many platforms, due to wide support of HTTP in various environments.

Based on HTTP characteristics, the ASP.NET Web API uses HTTP headers to help clients determine the format of data they expect to get back from the service. ASP.NET Web API supports generating responses in the JSON and XML formats, without requiring any special handling in your service code.

Before you start learning how to create HTTP-based services with ASP.NET Web API, you should get to know some of the terminology of ASP.NET Web API.

- *Routing*: The mechanism that maps requests to code, based on the request URI and the HTTP verb.

- *API Controller*: The class where you implement your service. You will usually create an API controller, or *controller* for short, for each of your resource types. For example, for the agency model, which handles agents and tasks, we will have two API controllers: one for handling agent-related actions and another to handle an agent's tasks.

■ **Note**   ASP.NET MVC also uses the term *controller*. Therefore, use the term *API controllers* to refer to services created with ASP.NET Web API, so there won't be any confusion.

- *Actions*: These are the public methods in your API controller. Actions, also known as *action methods*, are invoked by the API controller, based on the request, the HTTP verb, and the routing data.

Creating an ASP.NET Web API Project

If this is the first time you are using ASP.NET Web API, you probably want to try it out. Follow the steps below to create an ASP.NET Web API project in Visual Studio 2013.

■ **Note**   For the following exercise, you will have to use Visual Studio 2013. If you have Visual Studio 2012, you will find it difficult to execute the steps as requested, because Visual Studio 2012 has different dialogs to create the ASP.NET Web API project. In addition, Visual Studio 2012 uses an older version of the ASP.NET Web API NuGet package, which generates different code than the one generated with Visual Studio 2013. For information how to use Visual Studio 2012 to create ASP.NET Web API projects, visit the page accessed by the following link: www.asp.net/web-api/videos/getting-started/your-first-web-api.

CREATING AN ASP.NET WEB API PROJECT IN VISUAL STUDIO 2013

In this section, you will use Visual Studio 2013 to create a new ASP.NET Web API project.

1. Open Visual Studio 2013 and select File ➤ New ➤ Project.

2. In the **New Project** dialog, select Installed ➤ Templates ➤ Visual C# ➤ Web ➤ ASP.NET Web Application.

3. Enter the location and name for the new project and click OK.

4. In the **New ASP.NET Project** dialog, select the *Web API* template and click OK, as shown in Figure 7-1. Wait for the project to be created.

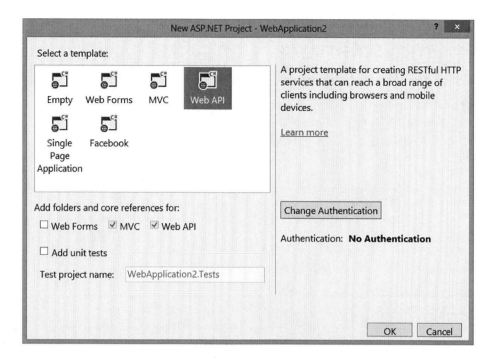

Figure 7-1. *Selecting the Web API project template*

If you look at the Solution Explorer window, you will see the standard structure of an MVC project—the Controllers, Views, and Models folders. This is because the project you created is actually an MVC project, with additional classes and configuration for ASP.NET Web API. (In Figure 7-1, you can see that both the Web API and MVC boxes are checked.)

Now let's run this new project and see what is going on in the browser.

1. Press Ctrl+F5 to run the web application. A browser will open after a short while.

2. In the top menu, click the **API** link. You will see a help page showing a list of URIs you can use and their supported HTTP verbs.

3. Click any of the links in the help page to see detailed documentation for the selected action.

The help page is constructed by using ASP.NET MVC, but the information it displays is extracted from your API controllers and action methods by using the ASP.NET Web API Help Pages mechanism.

■ **Note**   This book does not cover the topic of ASP.NET Web API Help Pages. If you want to learn how to create help pages for your API controllers, refer to the article at the following link:

www.asp.net/web-api/overview/creating-web-apis/creating-api-help-pages.

Let's call one of the action methods.

4. In the browser's address bar, change the address to
    http://localhost:{port}/api/values (the {port} should be the port you currently
    see in the address bar for the running web application) and press Enter.

5. If you are using Internet Explorer, you should see an open/save dialog at this point. Click Open
    and, if required, select Notepad as the viewer application. Other browsers, such as Chrome
    and Firefox, support displaying the response message body in the browser window, as shown
    in Figure 7-2.

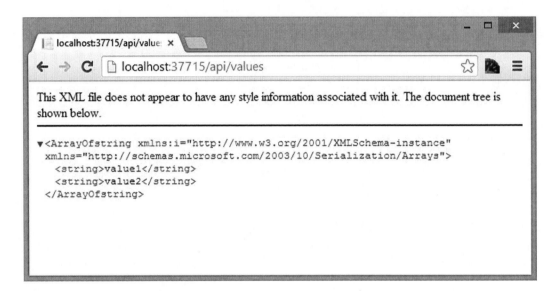

Figure 7-2. *Response of a GET request*

As you can see, sending a GET request to the /api/values URI resulted in an XML response. We will see later on
how you can control the format of the response and decide whether it would be an XML or a JSON format.

Preparing the TheAgency Solution for ASP.NET Web API

The previous exercise created a new ASP.NET Web API project, but we already have a web application, which we
created in Chapter 6. To create a back end in our solution, we have to add three things, as follows, before we add our
ASP.NET Web API services:

1. The ASP.NET Web API assemblies

2. The model classes for Agent and Task

3. A database class that represents our database

■ **Note** In this book, we do not refer to a specific technique for managing resource data, such as Entity Framework or NHibernate. It is up to you, the reader, to decide which framework you wish to use. ASP.NET Web API is capable of using any data framework that can produce serializable entities.

Open the solution you developed in Chapter 6, and let's start creating the back end of our SPA.

Adding ASP.NET Web API Assemblies

There is only one thing you need to do to add the ASP.NET Web API assemblies to your web application project: install the ASP.NET Web API NuGet package in your project. To install the NuGet package, perform the following steps:

1. In the Solution Explorer window, right-click the web project, then click **Manage NuGet Packages**.

2. In the **Manage NuGet Packages** dialog, select **Online**, and search for the **ASP.NET Web API** NuGet package.

3. Locate the **Microsoft ASP.NET Web API** NuGet package and install it.

■ **Note** The name of the package may include a version number. When we wrote this book, the full name of the NuGet package was *ASP.NET Web API 2.1*.

Adding Model Classes

Before we create our API controllers for the Agent and Task, we must have those entity types on the back end. In the Solution Explorer window, add a folder named *Models* to the project. Add two files to the folder: Agent.cs and Task.cs. Open the Task.cs file and add the following properties from Listing 7-5 to the class:

Listing 7-5. Creating the Task Entity

```
public int TaskID { get; set; }

public string Description { get; set; }

public bool IsComplete { get; set; }
```

Next, open the Agent.cs file, and add the following properties (Listing 7-6) to the class.

Listing 7-6. Creating the Agent Entity

```
public int AgentID { get; set; }

public string CodeName { get; set; }

public string FirstName { get; set; }
```

```
public string LastName { get; set; }

public string ImagePath { get; set; }

public string Description { get; set; }

public IList<Task> Tasks { get; set; }
```

Add a Database Management Class

As explained, we will not use a database in this project. Instead, we will use an in-memory list of agents and tasks. In the Models folder, add a new class named Database, and add the following code (Listing 7-7) to it.

Listing 7-7. Creating the In-Memory Database Class

```
public static List<Task> Tasks = new List<Task> {
    new Task{TaskID=1, Description="Kill Goldfinger", IsComplete=true},
    new Task{TaskID=2, Description="Kill Renard", IsComplete=true},
    new Task{TaskID=3, Description="Create a new James Bond car", IsComplete=false},
    new Task{TaskID=4, Description="Create a missle launcher pen", IsComplete=false},
    new Task{TaskID=5, Description="Seduce James Bond", IsComplete=true},
    new Task{TaskID=6, Description="Rule the world", IsComplete=true}
};

public static List<Agent> Agents = new List<Agent> {
    new Agent{AgentID=1, CodeName="007", FirstName="James", LastName="Bond",
ImagePath="images/JamesBondImage.png", Description="Killer"},
    new Agent{AgentID=2, CodeName="Q", FirstName="Desmond", LastName="Llewelyn",
ImagePath="images/LDesmond.png", Description="Master of Gadgets"},
    new Agent{AgentID=3, CodeName="Ive", FirstName="Vesper", LastName="Lynd",
ImagePath="images/VesperLynd.png", Description="Seducer"},
    new Agent{AgentID=4, CodeName="King", FirstName="Chuck", LastName="Noris",
ImagePath="images/ChuckNoris.png", Description="Facts Collector"},
};

static Database()
{
    Agents[0].Tasks = new List<Task> { Tasks[0], Tasks[1] };
    Agents[1].Tasks = new List<Task> { Tasks[2], Tasks[3] };
    Agents[2].Tasks = new List<Task> { Tasks[4] };
    Agents[3].Tasks = new List<Task> { Tasks[5] };
}

public static Task AddTask(Task newTask)
{
    int newId = Tasks.Max(t => t.TaskID) + 1;
    newTask.TaskID = newId;
    Tasks.Add(newTask);
    return newTask;
}
```

```
public static Agent AddAgent(Agent newAgent)
{
    int newId = Agents.Max(a => a.AgentID) + 1;
    newAgent.AgentID = newId;
    Agents.Add(newAgent);
    return newAgent;
}
```

Now our project is ready for some ASP.NET Web API code.

Routes and Controllers

One of the first challenges when developing HTTP-based services with ASP.NET Web API is mapping HTTP requests to the server code. The mapping between the two ends should be based on the request's URI and the HTTP method. The process of mapping the URI and HTTP method is called routing and is comprised of two parts.

1. Identifying the API controller class that should be used

2. Identifying the class method that should be invoked

ASP.NET Web API routes are defined by using the MapHttpRoute extension method. Follow these steps to add routing instructions to our project:

1. Add a new *Global Application Class* (global.asax) to the project. Open the class, and add a using directive for the System.Web.Http namespace.

2. Add the code in Listing 7-8 to the Application_Start method.

Listing 7-8. Configuring a Route for ASP.NET Web API

```
var config = GlobalConfiguration.Configuration;

config.Routes.MapHttpRoute(
    name: "DefaultApi",
    routeTemplate: "api/{controller}/{id}",
    defaults: new { id = RouteParameter.Optional }
);

GlobalConfiguration.Configuration.Formatters.JsonFormatter.SerializerSettings.ContractResolver =
    new CamelCasePropertyNamesContractResolver();
GlobalConfiguration.Configuration.EnsureInitialized();
```

The MapHttpRoute method has the following parameters:

- Name: Each route has a name. You can use that name to access the route information from inside your code. For example, you can use the route to generate new URLs and include those URLs in your responses. We will see an example for that when we create the action method for HTTP POST in the Agents API controller.

- routeTemplate: The template is a string representing the relative URI of the route. The routing mechanism checks each URI it receives and locates the route with a template that matches the URI structure. Route strings can have placeholders in them, in the form of {placeholder_name}. The routing mechanism maps the value of the placeholder in the URI to a route variable. In your action methods, you can access the placeholder values of the current request. You can also set the values of placeholders when you use routes to create new URLs.

■ **Note**   If a URI matches two routes, the first route added to the `Routes` collection will be selected.

- `Defaults`: You can use this parameter to specify default values for placeholders. You can also use this parameter to specify which placeholders are not mandatory, as shown in the preceding example.

■ **Note**   The route shown in the above example is the default route created by Visual Studio when you create a new ASP.NET Web API project. You can find this code in the project's `App_Start` folder, in the `WebApiConfig.cs` file.

After calling the `MapHttpRoute` method, we set the JSON serializer's `ContractResolver` property to a contract resolver that uses camel-case property names. By default, the JSON serializer will serialize property names of objects by using their original names, which in C# are Pascal case. Because in JavaScript we use camel casing, we choose to change the convention for property names in the serializer.

The last line of code calls the `EnsureInitialized` method. This call is required to signal ASP.NET Web API that we configured its pipeline.

■ **Note**   If you look at the generated code in the new ASP.NET Web API project we created previously, you will notice there is no direct call to the `EnsureInitialized` method. This method is internally invoked from the `GlobalConfiguration.Configure` static method, which is called in the `global.asax` file.

After ASP.NET Web API receives a request that matches the template in the route, it looks for an API controller class that matches the value of the `{controller}` placeholder. The lookup process searches for a class that does the following:

1. Derives from the `System.Web.Http.ApiController` class

2. Bears a class name that matches the placeholder's value (case insensitive) and has the suffix `Controller`

For example, the relative URI `api/agents/1` will be evaluated against the template defined in the earlier example `api/{controller}/{id}`. ASP.NET Web API will look for a controller that is named `AgentsController`.

In our web application project, create a folder named `Controllers`. Add a new class to the folder and name it `AgentsController`. Open the `AgentsController.cs` file and replace its content with the code in Listing 7-9.

Listing 7-9. Creating the AgentsController Class

```
using System;
using System.Collections.Generic;
using System.Linq;
using System.Web;
using System.Web.Http;
using TheAgency.Models;
```

```
namespace TheAgency.Controllers
{
    public class AgentsController : ApiController
    {
        public IEnumerable<Agent> GetAll()
        {
            return Database.Agents;
        }

        public Agent Get(int id)
        {
            Agent agent = Database.Agents.SingleOrDefault(a => a.AgentID == id);
            return agent;
        }

        public void Delete(int id)
        {
            Agent agent = Database.Agents.SingleOrDefault(a => a.AgentID == id);
            Database.Agents.Remove(agent);
        }
    }
}
```

The AgentsController class currently contains three methods: -GetAll, Get, and Delete. The next section will explain how ASP.NET Web API decides which method to invoke when it receives a request to the Agents API controller.

Routing Requests to Controller Actions

After ASP.NET Web API chooses a controller, it can start to handle the next step: choosing the method that will handle the request. The selection of the action method is performed by the ApiController base class.

The mapping between the request and the action method is handled in the base class by calling an implementation of the IHttpActionSelector interface. The default implementation of the interface is provided by ASP.NET Web API in the form of the ApiControllerActionSelector class.

■ **Note**   You can create your own implementation of the IHttpActionSelector interface to replace the default action selector. If you want to learn more about how to customize the ASP.NET Web API pipeline, consider reading the book *Pro ASP.NET Web API*, by Tugberk Ugurlu, Alexander Zeitler, and Ali Kheyrollahi (Apress, 2013).

The ApiControllerActionSelector class uses the following information to map between requests and action methods:

- *HTTP method*: The action selector will look for action methods in your API controller that match the HTTP method of the request. A method will consider a match if

  - Its name is identical, or prefixed with the name of the HTTP method. For example, methods named GetAll or Get will both be considered a match for HTTP GET requests.

- The method is decorated with the [AcceptVerbs] attribute, and the attribute is set to support the required HTTP method. For example, the [AcceptVerbs("GET", "DELETE")] attribute specifies that the decorated method supports both the GET and the DELETE HTTP methods.

- The method is decorated with an attribute that implements the IActionHttpMethodProvider interface, and the attribute matches the requested HTTP method. There is an attribute for each of the known HTTP methods, such as [HttpGet], [HttpPost], and [HttpPatch].

■ **Note** If a method's name does not start with any HTTP method name, and the method is not decorated with the [AcceptVerbs] or the [Http*] attributes, the method is assumed to support the HTTP POST method.

- *Request URI*: The action selector will look up the {action} placeholder in your routing template to find the name of the action method you want to invoke. A method in the API controller will be considered a match if any of the following applies:

  - The method name matches the value of the placeholder.

  - The method name is prefixed with the HTTP method name, followed by the value of the placeholder.

  - The method is decorated with the [ActionName] attribute, and the attribute is set to the value of the placeholder.

■ **Note** The comparison of the method name and placeholder value is case insensitive.

For a given request, the ApiControllerActionSelector will go over the controller's methods and perform the following filtering to locate the required action method:

1. Locate all the methods in the API controller that match the HTTP method of the request.

2. If there is a value for the {action} placeholder, filter out all the methods that do not match the placeholder value.

■ **Note** The ApiControllerActionSelector class only checks public methods in your API controller class. If you have a public method in your class that you don't want to be a part of the selection process, decorate it with the [NonAction] attribute.

After filtering the list of methods, it is possible that the list will have more than one matching method. For example, for the Agents API controller, a GET request can use either the GetAll or the Get method. In this case, the ApiControllerActionSelector class will check the parameters passed in the request and locate the method that can accept the most parameters. If after this process there are more than one matching methods, the action selector will throw an InvalidOperationException exception, stating there were multiple actions that were found for the request.

> ■ **Note** Parameter name matching is case insensitive and ignores the order of the parameters in the method
> declaration. Parameter matching is based on the URI and the message's body and depends on which HTTP method
> your request uses. For example, for GET requests, any complex parameter will be deserialized from the request's
> query string. For POST and PUT requests, the same complex parameter will be deserialized from the message's
> body. For more information on parameter binding in ASP.NET Web API, refer to the article at
> www.asp.net/web-api/overview/formats-and-model-binding/parameter-binding-in-aspnet-web-api.

In our web application project, open the AgentsController class and replace the Delete method declaration
with the code as shown in Listing 7-10.

Listing 7-10. Updating the Delete Method Declaration

```
[HttpDelete]
public void RemoveAgent(int id)
```

Next, add the code in Listing 7-11, which adds a new agent.

Listing 7-11. The CreateAgent Method

```
public Agent CreateAgent(Agent newAgent)
{
    // Extract the image from the image string
    string regEx = "data:(.+);base64,(.+)";
    Match match = Regex.Match(newAgent.ImagePath, regEx);
    if (match.Success)
    {
        // Get the content-type of the file and the content
        string imageType = match.Groups[1].Value;
        string base64image = match.Groups[2].Value;

        if (imageType != null && base64image != null)
        {
            // Verify the content-type is an image
            string imageRegEx = "image/(.+)";
            match = Regex.Match(imageType, imageRegEx);
            if (match.Success)
            {
                // Get the file extension from the content-type
                string fileExtension = match.Groups[1].Value;
                // Get the byte-array of the file from the base64 string
                byte[] image = Convert.FromBase64String(base64image);

                string path = HttpContext.Current.Server.MapPath("~/images");
                string fileName = newAgent.FirstName + newAgent.LastName;

                // Generate a unique name for the file (add an index to it if it already exists)
                string targetFile = fileName + "." + fileExtension;
                int index = 0;
                while (File.Exists(Path.Combine(path, targetFile)))
```

155

```
                {
                    index++;
                    targetFile = fileName + index + "." + fileExtension;
                }

                // Write the image to the target file, and update the agent with the new image path
                File.WriteAllBytes(Path.Combine(path, targetFile), image);
                newAgent.ImagePath = "images/" + targetFile;

                newAgent = Database.AddAgent(newAgent);

                return newAgent;
            }
        }
    }
    throw new InvalidOperationException();
}
```

Most of the preceding code is meant to handle the image that is sent to the service in the ImagePath property. The image is sent as a data-uri string, which contains the media type of the image, and a base64 string representation of the image.

■ **Note**   After you add this code, you will need to add the System.Text.RegularExpressions and System.IO namespaces to the *using* section at the beginning of the file.

The AgentsController class now has four action methods. Table 7-3 shows the request that matches each of the action methods and the parameters it uses.

Table 7-3. Mapping of the Request's URL and HTTP Method to the Controller's Action Methods and Their Parameters

HTTP Method	Request URL	Action Method	Matched Parameters
GET	/api/agents	GetAll	--
GET	/api/agents/1	Get	id = 1
DELETE	/api/agents/1	RemoveAgent	id = 1
POST	/api/agents	CreateAgent	newAgent = request's body

As you might have noticed, our ASP.NET Web API route does not use the {action} placeholder in the route template. Although supported, we recommend that you refrain from using the {action} placeholder as it prevents you from creating "clean" URIs.

For example, instead of having an agent represented as a single URI, /api/agents/1, and then using HTTP verbs to retrieve and manipulate it, you will have to use different URIs to express what you wish to do, such as /api/agents/ get/1 and /api/agents/delete/1.

Responses and Content Negotiation

Reexamine the method declaration in the `AgentsController` class. You will notice that the methods return model objects, such as `Agent` or `IEnumerable<Agent>`, and not an XML or a JSON document.

The part of serializing the returned object is handled by the ASP.NET Web API pipeline. The content negotiation process of ASP.NET Web API and the resulting output depends on the `Accept-*` HTTP headers set in the request and the media type formatters configured in your project.

ASP.NET Web API has built-in support for both the XML and JSON formats. If your client requests any of those types in the `Accept` HTTP header, ASP.NET Web API will use the matching formatter to serialize the returned objects. If the client does not give a specific preference to one of the supported media types, ASP.NET Web API will return its default format, which is JSON.

■ **Note**   If you executed the exercise steps in the beginning of this section, you may have noticed that responses in Chrome and Firefox contained XML bodies, while responses in Internet Explorer are JSON-based. This is because Chrome and Firefox set the `Accept` HTTP header by default to `application/xml`, whereas Internet Explorer does not.

The default formatter in ASP.NET Web API is the JSON formatter, because it is the first formatter in the `GlobalConfiguration.Configuration.Formatters` collection. Changing the default formatter to XML is simply a matter of shifting their order in the collection, as demonstrated in Listing 7-12.

Listing 7-12. Changing the Default Formatter to XML

```
MediaTypeFormatter jsonFormatter = config.Formatters.JsonFormatter;
config.Formatters.Remove(jsonFormatter);
config.Formatters.Add(jsonFormatter);
```

By moving the JSON formatter from the top of the collection to its end, the XML formatter becomes the default formatter.

■ **Note**   Because we write SPA in JavaScript, it is likely that you will only use the JSON formatter. Instead of moving the JSON formatter to make it the default, you might consider simply removing the XML formatter from the collection. To do this, use the following code: `config.Formatters.Remove(config.Formatters.XmlFormatter)`.

The built-in formatters offer some level of configuration. For example, adding the code `config.Formatters.JsonFormatter.Indent = true;` to the ASP.NET Web API configuration method will make the JSON formatter generate indented text, as shown in Listing 7-13.

Listing 7-13. JSON Response Without and with Indentation

Before:

```
HTTP/1.1 200 OK
Cache-Control: no-cache
Content-Type: application/json; charset=utf-8
Content-Length: 263
```

```
{"agentID":1,"codeName":"007","firstName":"James","lastName":"Bond","imagePath":"images/
JamesBondImage.png","description":"Killer","tasks":[{"taskID":1,"description":"Kill Goldfinger",
"isComplete":true},{"taskID":2,"description":"Kill Renard","isComplete":true}]}
```

After:

```
HTTP/1.1 200 OK
Cache-Control: no-cache
Content-Type: application/json; charset=utf-8
Content-Length: 382

{
  "agentID": 1,
  "codeName": "007",
  "firstName": "James",
  "lastName": "Bond",
  "imagePath": "images/JamesBondImage.png",
  "description": "Killer",
  "tasks": [
    {
      "taskID": 1,
      "description": "Kill Goldfinger",
      "isComplete": true
    },
    {
      "taskID": 2,
      "description": "Kill Renard",
      "isComplete": true
    }
  ]
}
```

■ **Note** You may want to add the indentation configuration to our agency web application project—in the `global.asax` file, inside the `Application_Start` method. This will allow you to view the responses more clearly when shown in sniffing tools. Having indentation in the output will not affect the client-side code. However, indentation is not recommended for production environments, as it increases the size of responses.

If you need to support additional media types, you can create a new class that derives from the `MediaTypeFormatter` base class, specify which media types it supports, and implement it to create the required output. To register the new class with the ASP.NET Web API pipeline, add the new class to the configuration's `Formatters` collection. This process will be explained in detail in Chapter 8.

Attribute-Based Routing

In addition to the routing templates that you define in the configuration method, you can add routing templates directly to API controllers and actions by using attributes. Attribute-based routing is useful for cases such as the following:

- Using a different convention to map to controllers

- Adding version support to your controllers and actions

- Supporting multiple action methods for the same HTTP method that vary according to the request's URI

■ **Note**   Attribute-based routing is built into ASP.NET Web API as of version 2.0. If your web application project uses an older version of ASP.NET Web API, consider upgrading it to the latest version, or install the AttributeRouting (ASP.NET Web API) NuGet package.

For example, an agent's tasks are managed in the TasksController class. Instead of using the default api/{controller}/{id} URI, we would like to access tasks by using the URI api/agents/{agentId}/tasks/{id}, where {agentId} is mandatory, and {id} is optional.

To accomplish this, we will decorate the TasksController class with the [RoutePrefix] attribute and each of the action methods with the [Route] attribute. In our project, under the Controllers folder, open the TasksController class and replace its content with the code shown in Listing 7-14.

Listing 7-14. Creating the TasksController with Attribute-Based Routing

```
using System;
using System.Collections.Generic;
using System.Linq;
using System.Web;
using System.Web.Http;
using TheAgency.Models;

namespace TheAgency.Controllers
{
    [RoutePrefix("api/agents/{agentId}/tasks")]
    public class TasksController : ApiController
    {
        [HttpPost]
        [Route]
        public Task AddTask(int agentId, Task newTask)
        {
            Agent agent = Database.Agents.SingleOrDefault(a => a.AgentID == agentId);

            // Create the task and attach it to the agent entity
            newTask = Database.AddTask(newTask);
            agent.Tasks.Add(newTask);
```

```
            return newTask;
        }

        [HttpPut]
        [Route("{taskId}")]
        public void UpdateTask(int agentId, int taskId, Task updatedTask)
        {
            Agent agent = Database.Agents.SingleOrDefault(a => a.AgentID == agentId);
            Task task = agent.Tasks.Where(t => t.TaskID == taskId).SingleOrDefault();

            // Update the task from the database
            task.Description = updatedTask.Description;
            task.IsComplete = updatedTask.IsComplete;
        }
    }
}
```

The [RoutePrefix] attribute decorating the class defines the base URI that applies to all the action methods. The route template also defines the {agentId} placeholder, which means all the methods must have a parameter named agentId.

Each of the action methods in the class has a different route configuration.

- *AddTask*: This method is marked for POST requests and does not set any suffix to the URI. You can invoke this method by sending a POST request to URIs, such as /api/agents/1/tasks, and providing the new task in the request's body.

- *UpdateTask*: This method defines the URI suffix {taskId}, which also acts as a placeholder. You can invoke this method by sending a PUT request to URIs, such as /api/agents/1/tasks/2, and providing the updated task in the request's body.

■ **Note** Attribute-based routing also supports constraints for placeholders. This is a more advanced topic, and it is not covered in this book. To learn more about this feature, refer to the attribute-based routing documentation at www.asp.net/web-api/overview/web-api-routing-and-actions/attribute-routing-in-web-api-2.

To support attribute-based routing, you have to inform ASP.NET Web API that you are using attribute-based routing. In our project, open the Global.asax file and replace the Application_Start method code with the following code (Listing 7-15).

Listing 7-15. Configure ASP.NET Web API for Attribute-Based Routing

```
var config = GlobalConfiguration.Configuration;

config.MapHttpAttributeRoutes();

config.Routes.MapHttpRoute(
    name: "DefaultApi",
    routeTemplate: "api/{controller}/{id}",
    defaults: new { id = RouteParameter.Optional }
);
```

```
config.Formatters.JsonFormatter.Indent = true;
GlobalConfiguration.Configuration.Formatters.JsonFormatter.SerializerSettings.ContractResolver =
    new CamelCasePropertyNamesContractResolver();
GlobalConfiguration.Configuration.EnsureInitialized();
```

The call to the MapHttpAttributeRoutes method is placed before the call to the MapHttpRoute method, to ensure that attribute-based routing is favored over convention-based routing, as it is more specific. This is similar to declaring a try/catch block and having the derived exception types first, before the base Exception type handling.

■ **Note** If you use Visual Studio 2013 to create ASP.NET Web API projects, the call to the MapHttpAttributeRoutes method is automatically added to your configuration code.

You can also mix attribute-based routing with convention-based routing. If you have an API controller that uses convention-based routing, and you need to add an action method to it, which will be invoked for a specific URI, you can use the [Route] attribute without having the controller decorated with the [RoutePrefix] attribute, as shown in Listing 7-16.

Listing 7-16. Adding RSS Support to the AgentsController Class

```
public class AgentsController : ApiController
{
    [Route("api/agents/feed")]
    public IEnumerable<FeedItem> GetAgentsFeed() {}

    public IEnumerable<Agent> GetAll () {}

    public Agent Get (int id) {}
}
```

■ **Note** You do not have to add the following code (Listing 7-16) to your web project, as it will not be used by the SPA front end.

In the preceding example, using the URI /api/agents will invoke the GetAll method. Using the URI /api/agents/feed will invoke the GetAgentsFeed method.

■ **Note** Instead of creating a special method for handling RSS feed requests and assigning a specific URI to the action method, you can add content-negotiation support to the existing GetAll action method, so it will support XML, JSON, and the RSS media types. In the case of the preceding example, we decided to create a separate method, because we will need information regarding each agent, which is not included in the Agent class. For example, we will need the last update date of the agent entity, which we separately retrieve from the database.

The HttpResponseMessage Class

Action methods can return both simple and complex types that are serializable to a format based on the Accept header. Although ASP.NET Web API handles the content negotiation and serialization for you, it is up to you to handle other aspects of the HTTP response message, such as changing the returned status code or adding HTTP headers to the response.

The System.Net.Http.HttpResponseMessage class enables you to set every aspect of the HTTP response message returned by your action method. In order to control the HTTP response, you must change the return type of the action to HttpResponseMessage. Inside the action, you use the Request.CreateResponse or Request.CreateResponse<T> methods to create a new HttpResponseMessage object.

Let's apply this concept to our AgentsController by changing our POST method. We will set the Location HTTP header in the response to the URI of the new agent. Clients can then use this URI to update or delete the resource. Apply the following changes in the AgentsController class:

1. Add a using directive for the System.Net.Http and System.Net namespaces.

2. Locate the CreateAgent method and change its return type from Agent to HttpResponseMessage.

3. Replace the return statement at the end of the CreateAgent method with the code in Listing 7-17.

Listing 7-17. Setting the Location HTTP Header in the Response

```
HttpResponseMessage response = Request.CreateResponse(HttpStatusCode.Created, newAgent);
string uri = Url.Link("DefaultApi",
    new {
        controller = this.ControllerContext.ControllerDescriptor.ControllerName,
        id = newAgent.AgentID
    });
response.Headers.Location = new Uri(uri);

return response;
```

In the preceding code, the response message is created, and its status code is set to Created (201). Next, the URI of the new agent is placed in the Location HTTP header, and the response message is returned.

■ **Note**   The CreateResponse method does not serialize the newAgent object. The serialization is performed by the appropriate media type formatter after the action method completes its execution.

Next, implement the HTTP PUT method by adding the following code (Listing 7-18) to the AgentsController class.

Listing 7-18. Implementing the Action Method for PUT Requests

```
public HttpResponseMessage Put(int id, Agent updatedAgent)
{
    Agent agent = Database.Agents.SingleOrDefault(a => a.AgentID == id);

    // Update the task from the database
    agent.CodeName = updatedAgent.CodeName;
```

```
agent.Description = updatedAgent.Description;
agent.FirstName = updatedAgent.FirstName;
agent.LastName = updatedAgent.LastName;

return Request.CreateResponse(HttpStatusCode.NoContent);
}
```

In the preceding code, the response is created with status code 204 (No Content). We do not have to return the updated agent resource to the client, as it is identical to the agent object the client sent to the service.

Handling Exceptions

In HTTP, errors are communicated to the client by two mechanisms.

- *HTTP status codes*: Status codes provide an application-readable representation of the result of a request. For errors, there are two status code categories: client errors and server errors. Client errors, such as wrong input or unauthorized requests, will return status codes in the 4xx range. Server errors, such as getting an unexpected exception in the server code, or the web application being inaccessible, will result in 5xx status codes.

- *Entity body*: For most error status codes, the HTTP response can contain an entity body. The entity body provides clients with details about the error that occurred. When you manually return an error message from code, you will have to construct the entity body yourself. For unhandled exceptions, ASP.NET Web API creates an error response with information from the unhandled exception. The level of information included in the response for unhandled exceptions changes, depending on whether you are running locally or remotely. Remote users will only receive the error message, while local users will get the full exception information, including stack trace and inner exceptions. You can control whether or not to include details by changing the ASP.NET Web API configuration object's IncludeErrorDetailPolicy property.

■ **Note** If you create your own error response, refrain from including information from the exception object, such as the stack trace and the inner exception, as that data can be sensitive, and it should not reach your client.

Because both aspects of HTTP errors can be set by using the HttpResponseMessage class, you can return errors by changing your method's return type to HttpResponseMessage, and return custom error messages as needed.

However, when you deal with complex execution flows, returning different types of results—entity data and errors—can create a complex method flow. Instead of returning a response message, favor throwing an exception. ASP.NET Web API provides a special exception type for this—System.Web.Http.HttpResponseException. This exception type provides control over the response message by accepting an HttpResponseMessage parameter in its constructor.

To throw an HttpResponseException, follow these steps:

1. Create a new HttpResponseMessage object.

2. Set the status code, headers, and content that you want the error response to have.

3. Throw a new HttpResponseException accepting the HttpResponseMessage as a constructor parameter.

Let us apply this to our `AgentsController` class. Locate the `RemoveAgent` method and replace its implementation with the following code (Listing 7-19).

Listing 7-19. Throwing an HttpResponseException If an Agent Is Not Found

```
Agent agent = Database.Agents.SingleOrDefault(a => a.AgentID == id);

// Verify the agent exists before continuing
if (agent == null)
{
    throw new HttpResponseException(
        new HttpResponseMessage(HttpStatusCode.NotFound)
            {
                Content = new StringContent("Agent not found")
            });
}

Database.Agents.Remove(agent);
```

You can also use the `CreateErrorResponse` extension method to create an `HttpResponseMessage`. Calling the `Request.CreateErrorResponse` method will create a response message with a structured error object, similar to that returned by ASP.NET Web API for unhandled exceptions.

In the `AgentsController` class, locate the `CreateAgent` method and replace the `throw` statement at the end of the method with the code in Listing 7-20.

Listing 7-20. Throwing an HttpResponseException If the Agent Is Malformed

```
throw new HttpResponseException(Request.CreateErrorResponse(
            HttpStatusCode.BadRequest, "Could not deserialize agent"));
```

■ **Note**   To use the `CreateAgent` extension method, make sure you add a `using` directive for the `System.Net.Http` namespace.

If the client sends a POST request with an agent object that is missing a photo, the service will return a 400 (`Bad Request`) response, as shown in Listing 7-21.

Listing 7-21. The Error Response Returned for a New Agent Without a Photo

```
HTTP/1.1 400 Bad Request
Cache-Control: no-cache
Content-Type: application/json; charset=utf-8
Content-Length: 48

{
  "Message": " Could not deserialize agent "
}
```

The entity body in the above response is in fact a representation of the `HttpError` class. The `CreateErrorResponse` has an overload that accepts an `HttpError` object instead of a string. By creating the `HttpError` object yourself, you can add more detail to the error message, including custom properties of your own.

■ **Note** For more information about the HttpError class, visit the ASP.NET Web API exception handling page on
www.asp.net/web-api/overview/web-api-routing-and-actions/exception-handling#httperror.

Handling Unhandled Exceptions

Most service frameworks support creating a custom error handler for any uncaught exception, and ASP.NET Web API
is no different. To create a custom error handler, follow these steps:

1. Create a new class that inherits from the ExceptionFilterAttribute class.

2. In the new class, override the OnException method and provide your logic to construct the
    error response message, as shown in Listing 7-22. To create the response message, use any
    of the techniques described in Listing 7-19 and Listing 7-20.

    Listing 7-22. Creating a Custom Exception Filter

    ```
    public class UnhandledExceptionFilterAttribute : ExceptionFilterAttribute
    {
        public override void OnException(HttpActionExecutedContext context)
        {
            context.Response = context.Request.CreateErrorResponse(
                HttpStatusCode.InternalServerError,
                "There is a problem with the service. Please try again in
    a couple of minutes");
        }
    }
    ```

3. Apply the new exception filter in the required scope, as follows:

    a. *Action level*: Decorate actions with the new custom attribute.

    b. *Controller level*: Decorate controllers with the new custom attribute, as shown in
        Listing 7-23.

    Listing 7-23. Applying the Custom Exception Filter to a Controller

    ```
    [UnhandledExceptionFilter]
    public class MyController : ApiController
    {
        // ...
    }
    ```

    c. *Globally*: Add the exception filter to the Filters collection of the ASP.NET Web API
        configuration object.

■ **Note** You do not have to add the following code (Listing 7-22) to your web project.

■ **Note** The exception filter is part of ASP.NET Web API's Filters mechanism. This mechanism extends the message-handling pipeline for specific actions or controllers. In addition to exception filters, you can create action filters, which execute before and after your action, and authorization filters, which enable you to add custom authorization logic to your controllers and actions.

One of the situations in which we return error messages to clients is when a client sends the wrong input to an action method. Our next topic will explain how to validate the input to decide whether or not it is wrong.

Validating the Input

When you work with data, one of the things you must take care of is input validation. Normally, you would place validation rules in the client side, so that users would be shown validation messages as they enter the information. This provides a better user experience than having to wait for the server to validate the input and return an error message.

However, when building services, especially services that are accessible over the Internet, it is best practice to also validate the input on the service side. Validating on the service side will assure us that even if a user has managed to work around client-side validations, the bad input will not enter the database.

Data Annotations

The .NET Framework has built-in support for input validation, called DataAnnotations attributes. To use these attributes, add, a reference to the System.ComponentModel.DataAnnotations assembly. With data annotations, you can decorate your entity properties with validation attributes and then test a given object to check if it is valid according to the defined attributes.

The System.ComponentModel.DataAnnotations namespace contains a wide list of validations, such as required fields, value ranges for integers, and regular expression formats for strings. You can also create your own custom validation attributes by inheriting from the ValidationAttribute class.

Let's apply some data annotation attributes to our Agent class. First, open the class and add a using directive for the System.ComponentModel.DataAnnotations namespace.

Next, replace the implementation of the CodeName, FirstName, and LastName properties with the code in Listing 7-24.

Listing 7-24. Adding Data Annotations to the Agent Class

```
[Required]
[StringLength(30)]
public string CodeName { get; set; }

[Required]
[RegularExpression("^[a-zA-Z]+$")]
public string FirstName { get; set; }

[RegularExpression("^[a-zA-Z]+$")]
public string LastName { get; set; }
```

The Agent class declares two properties as Required—CodeName and FirstName. The required string properties would fail validation if they had a null or empty value. The CodeName also has the StringLength validation rule, which will fail the test if the string is more than 30 characters long. Finally, the FirstName and LastName properties have the RegularExpression validation attribute, which uses regular expressions to verify string value against a given pattern. The pattern in the above example requires that the names contain only letters.

■ **Note**   To learn more about data annotations and how to create your own custom annotations, refer to the MSDN article at `http://msdn.microsoft.com/en-us/library/dd901590.aspx`.

Validating Input with ASP.NET Web API

After you decorate your entity properties with data annotation attributes, you can use ASP.NET Web API to validate the input. To have ASP.NET Web API validate your input parameters, check the `ApiController`'s `ModelState.IsValid` property in your action method, before executing any business logic. If the value of the property is `true`, the model is valid. If the value is `false`, the model validation has failed, and you should return an error message.

The `ModelState` object itself is a dictionary. When you call the `IsValid` property, the dictionary is populated. The dictionary's keys are the property names, and its values are lists of errors found for each property.

The easiest way to return a list of errors to the client is to use the `Request.CreateResponseError` method, as it has an overload that accepts the `ModelState` object.

To implement this in our web application project, open the `AgentsController` class and add the following code (Listing 7-25) to the beginning of the `CreateAgent` method.

Listing 7-25. Validating a New Agent Before Storing It in the Database

```
if (!ModelState.IsValid)
{
    return Request.CreateErrorResponse(HttpStatusCode.BadRequest, ModelState);
}
```

The `CreateErrorResponse` method creates an error response and outputs a list of invalid properties and the error message reported for each invalid validation.

■ **Note**   For complex code flaws with multiple code paths, favor throwing an `HttpResponseException` over returning an `HttpResponseMessage`.

For example, the POST request shown in Listing 7-26 is missing the agent's first name and has digits in the agent's last name.

Listing 7-26. Sending a POST Request with a Malformed Agent

```
POST http://localhost:2410/api/agents HTTP/1.1
Content-Length: 113
Accept: application/json
Content-Type: application/json

{"agentID":0,"codeName":"008","firstName":"","lastName":"Spartacus123"}
```

Sending the above request to the service will cause the `ModelState.IsValid` to return `false`, and the action method will return an error response, as shown in Listing 7-27.

Listing 7-27. An Error Response Containing Invalid Model State

```
HTTP/1.1 400 Bad Request
Cache-Control: no-cache
Content-Type: application/json; charset=utf-8
Content-Length: 260

{
  "Message": "The request is invalid.",
  "ModelState": {
    "newAgent.FirstName": [
      "The FirstName field is required."
    ],
    "newAgent.LastName": [
      "The field LastName must match the regular expression '^[a-zA-Z]+$'."
    ]
  }
}
```

■ **Note**   The error messages shown in the preceding example are the default error messages of the validation attributes. You can change those messages by setting the `ErrorMessage` parameter of each validation attribute. Globalization is also supported by setting the `ErrorMessageResourceName` and `ErrorMessageResourceType` parameters of the validation attribute.

Validation Filters

As with unhandled exceptions, it would be best if ASP.NET Web API had a special filter that we could use to test the model validation every time an action was invoked. This way, we wouldn't have to add the model validation to each and every action method. Unfortunately, this is not built into ASP.NET Web API, but it is quite simple to build such a filter, as shown in Listing 7-28.

Listing 7-28. Creating a Custom Validation Filter

```
public class ValidationFilter : ActionFilterAttribute
{
    public override void OnActionExecuting(System.Web.Http.Controllers.HttpActionContext actionContext)
    {
        if (!actionContext.ModelState.IsValid)
        {
            actionContext.Response = actionContext.Request.CreateErrorResponse(
                HttpStatusCode.BadRequest, actionContext.ModelState);
        }
        else
        {
            base.OnActionExecuting(actionContext);
        }
    }
}
```

■ **Note** You do not have to add the following code (Listing 7-28) to your web project.

The validation filter, shown in the preceding example, inherits from the `ActionFilterAttribute` class. Action filters, as mentioned previously, are filters that are called before and after invoking an action method. By overriding the `OnActionExecuting` method, we can create custom logic that is executed before the action method. In the case of the validation filter, if the model is not valid, we will create the response message and skip calling the action method.

Much as with the exception filters, we can apply the custom action filter to actions and controllers or apply it globally by adding it the `Filters` collection of the ASP.NET Web API configuration object.

Summary

This chapter is the beginning of your journey into developing HTTP-based services for your SPA back end with ASP. NET Web API. In it, you learned what HTTP-based services are and what makes RESTful services different from HTTP-based services. After understanding the concepts of HTTP-based services, you started to learn how to create HTTP-based services with ASP.NET Web API: how to define routes, create API controllers for our resources, and create action methods that retrieve and manipulate resources.

Next, you learned how to manipulate response message using the `HttpResponseMessage` class and how to handle exceptions by using the `HttpResponseException` class and the `ExceptionFilterAttribute`.

Last, you learned how to validate input parameters by using data annotation attributes and the ASP.NET Web API's `ModelState` object.

The next chapter will also deal with ASP.NET Web API, where you will learn how to create action methods that take advantage of various HTTP concepts, such as content negotiation, streaming, and caching.

CHAPTER 8

Implementing HTTP Concepts with ASP.NET Web API

ASP.NET Web API provides a complete solution for building HTTP services. As such, it offers support for content negotiation, response caching, and streaming content to and from the client.

In this chapter, you will learn how to create a more efficient back-end service for our SPA, by implementing those HTTP concepts.

Content Negotiation

Serialization and deserialization are common tasks when creating and consuming services. Over the years, the .NET Framework offered a variety of serialization mechanisms supporting different formats, such as XML and JSON. However, when creating HTTP-based services, serialization must take HTTP's content negotiation rules into account.

■ **Note**   Content negotiation was discussed in Chapter 7.

ASP.NET Web API has built-in support for content negotiation using media type formatters. Media type formatters are classes derived from the `System.Net.Http.Formatting.MediaTypeFormatter` base class.

Remember the TheAgency solution from Chapter 7, where you created the ASP.NET Web API back end? The action methods that we created return either an entity object, such as `Agent` or `Task`, or return an `HttpResponseMessage` object, which contains an entity object.

The decision to serialize the content as either JSON or XML, the two built-in formats in ASP.NET Web API, is taken by the message-handling pipeline.

■ **Note**   As of ASP.NET Web API 2.1, content negotiation also supports the BSON (binary JSON) media type. Currently, BSON is not supported in browsers and, therefore, is not discussed further in this book. If you want to read more on the advantages of BSON and how to use this format with non-browser clients, refer to the ASP.NET Web API documentation at `www.asp.net/web-api/overview/formats-and-model-binding/bson-support-in-web-api-21`.

Let us create a new media type formatter in the TheAgency solution, which will support serializing the response to a CSV (comma-separated values) format. Each agent will be serialized as a row in a CSV file, containing a first name, last name, and the agent's URI ("self" URI).

After you open the solution, add a new folder named Formatters to the web application. Inside the new folder, add a class called AgentCSVFormatter. Before we begin, add using directives for the namespaces that we will use in the code, as shown in Listing 8-1.

Listing 8-1. Adding using Directives for Namespaces

```
using System.Web.Http.Routing;
using System.Net.Http.Formatting;
using System.Net.Http.Headers;
using System.Net.Http;
using TheAgency.Models;
```

We will begin by deriving our new class from the MediaTypeFormatter base class, as shown in Listing 8-2.

Listing 8-2. Creating the AgentCSVFormatter Class

```
public class AgentCSVFormatter : MediaTypeFormatter
{
    public AgentCSVFormatter()
    {
        this.SupportedMediaTypes.Add(new MediaTypeHeaderValue("text/csv"));
    }
}
```

Each media type formatter has a property, called SupportedMediaTypes, containing all the media types it supports. When you implement a new media type formatter, you first have to populate this property.

■ **Note**   The MediaTypeFormatter base class also supports content negotiation based on the Accept-Charset header. To set the supported charset for your media type formatter, set the SupportedEncodings property of the class. Currently, ASP.NET Web API does not offer built-in support for content negotiation based on the Accept-Language and Accept-Encoding headers. The Accept-Encoding header, which informs the server whether to compress the response or not, is handled automatically by IIS, if you turned on dynamic compression.

Media type formatters, such as XML and JSON, can be used both when deserializing a request and when serializing a response. For the CSV media type formatter, we only want to support serializing to CSV (download), not deserializing CSV content (upload). To specify this behavior, add the code in Listing 8-3 to the class.

Listing 8-3. Overriding the CanReadType Method

```
public override bool CanReadType(Type type)
{
    return false;
}
```

When you design new media type formatters, you must decide whether the formatter will support any type of content or will suit only a set of types. For example, images might be a valid media type when requesting a resource of an employee, but not for a department, in a company.

In our example, it will be quite complex to create a CSV representation for every type of content, as it will require the use of reflection. Therefore, this media type will only support serializing collections of Agent objects. To specify this behavior, add the method shown in Listing 8-4 to the class.

Listing 8-4. Overriding the CanWriteType Method

```
public override bool CanWriteType(Type type)
{
    Type enumerableType = typeof(IEnumerable<Agent>);
    return enumerableType.IsAssignableFrom(type);
}
```

By using the IEnumerable<T> generic type, the media type formatter will support any IEnumerable content, such as List<T>, Array, and HashSet<T>.

Before we add the code to write the CSV content, we have to verify that the content has all the information we need. The first name and last name are part of the agent's properties, but we do not have the agent's URI in the agent object.

To create the URI, we will have to use the UrlHelper class, which requires us to have access to the HTTP request message object.

■ **Note** We already used the UrlHelper class in Chapter 7, when creating a new agent. We used the Link method to set the HTTP Location header in the response to the URI of the newly created agent.

The default behavior of ASP.NET Web API is to use a single instance of your media type formatter in runtime. Because we need our media type formatter to be aware of the current request, we have to change this default behavior. We will do so by adding the code in Listing 8-5 to the class.

Listing 8-5. Overriding the GetPerRequestFormatterInstance Method

```
HttpRequestMessage _request;

public AgentCSVFormatter(HttpRequestMessage request)
{
    _request = request;
}

public override MediaTypeFormatter GetPerRequestFormatterInstance(
    Type type, HttpRequestMessage request, MediaTypeHeaderValue mediaType)
{
    return new AgentCSVFormatter(request);
}
```

■ **Note** If the agent resource had a "self" URI hypermedia control, as required when creating RESTful services, we wouldn't have to generate the URI in the media type formatter. We could manage with a single instance of the formatter, instead of creating a new instance for each request. As an exercise, try using HAL, which was mentioned in Chapter 7, to add hypermedia controls to the agent resource, and then use the "self" URI when constructing the CSV content.

The GetPerRequestFormatterInstance method enables us to return a different instance of our media type formatter for each handled request.

▨ **Note**　After we add the second constructor, which accepts the request object, we can do without the parameter-less constructor. To simplify the demonstration steps, we will use both of the constructors, as you will see shortly.

Finally, we can implement the actual process of reading or writing the data. If we supported deserializing content, we would be required to override the ReadFromStreamAsync method of the base class. However, the CSV media type formatter only supports serializing responses; therefore, we will only override the WriteToStreamAsync method, as shown in Listing 8-6.

Listing 8-6. Overriding the WriteToStreamAsync Method

```
public override async System.Threading.Tasks.Task WriteToStreamAsync(
    Type type, object value, System.IO.Stream writeStream,
    HttpContent content, System.Net.TransportContext transportContext)
{
    var agents = value as IEnumerable<Agent>;

    using (var writer = new System.IO.StreamWriter(writeStream))
    {
        // Write the CSV header
        writer.WriteLine("First name,Last name,Link");
        if (agents != null)
        {
            UrlHelper url = _request.GetUrlHelper();
            // Write the CSV content
            foreach (var agent in agents)
            {
                string agentUrl = url.Link("DefaultApi", new { id = agent.AgentID });
                await writer.WriteLineAsync(
                    string.Format("{0},{1},{2}", agent.FirstName, agent.LastName, agentUrl));
            }
        }
    }
}
```

The first thing to note about the method is that it uses the *async* pattern. If you are writing large quantities of data to the response, you can use asynchronous methods that return a Task object, such as the WriteLineAsync method. Using asynchronous methods can improve the performance of your service and allow it to handle more requests concurrently.

▨ **Note**　It is not always better to use asynchronous calls with async/await. For CPU-intensive processing, or when doing several short-lasting I/O calls, it is sometimes preferable to use synchronous calls, to prevent multiple thread switching. If you do not require the use of asynchronous calls, consider changing the base class from the MediaTypeFormatter class to the BufferedMediaTypeFormatter base class. The later derives from the MediaTypeFormatter class and contains synchronous read and write virtual methods. Asynchronous programming with ASP.NET Web API will be explained in depth in Chapter 11.

The media type formatter is now ready. The last thing we have to do is hook it up to the ASP.NET Web API pipeline. In Chapter 7, we saw that we can control the formatters through the Formatters collection in the global configuration object. We will use the same collection to attach the new formatter to the ASP.NET Web API formatters' pipeline. From the web application, open the global.asax file and add the code shown in Listing 8-7 to the end of the Application_Start method.

Listing 8-7. Adding the New Media Type Formatter to the Configuration

```
config.Formatters.Add(new TheAgency.Formatters.AgentCSVFormatter());
```

To test the new media type formatter, we need to invoke a call to get a list of agents and request that the response will be text/csv. Because our SPA is not yet connected to the ASP.NET Web API back end, we will use Fiddler, an HTTP debugger tool, to manually send a request to get the list of agents as a CSV file, as shown in Figure 8-1.

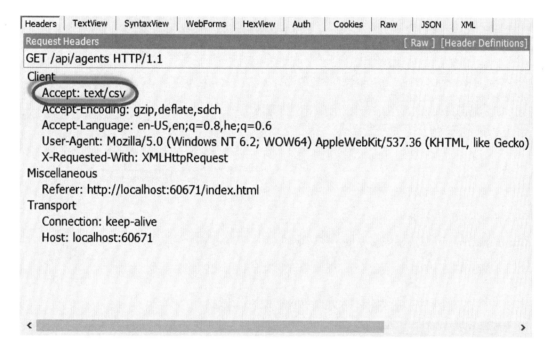

Figure 8-1. *Requesting a list of agents as CSV content*

▧ **Note** The use of Fiddler to debug both front ends and back ends is covered in Chapter 11.

The resulting response is shown in Figure 8-2.

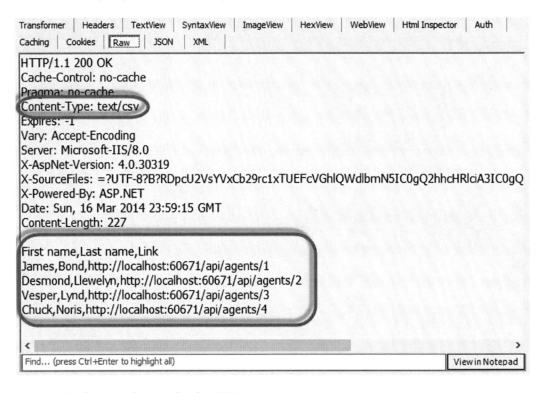

Figure 8-2. *The agents list, serialized as CSV*

You can create media type formatters for various purposes, such as the following:

- Alternative representation of a resource, such as image, video, or a document that represents the resource

- Formats that can be viewed by external applications, such as CSV, RSS, or HTML

- Specialized transfer formats that conserve bandwith or support transport of binary data, such as ProtoBuf, Data-URI, and base64

Caching

The idea of caching server content in the browser is not new. We have been caching static resources, such as HTML pages, script files, and web site images, for years. When it comes to dynamic content, such as resources returned from HTTP services, the concept of local cached copies also applies.

If your service returns a resource that is unlikely to change in the next couple of minutes, days, or even weeks, you can add the required HTTP caching headers to inform the browser that it can cache the response.

After a browser caches a resource, it will not issue a request for that resource, until the cached resource expires. You can control which resources to cache and for how long, by adding caching headers to your responses.

■ **Note** Serving resources from the cache improves the response time of SPA and decreases the load on the server.

Cache-Related Headers

There are several cache-related headers in HTTP, but for ASP.NET Web API services, the two most significant are Cache-Control and Expires.

Cache-Control Header

The Cache-Control header contains instructions that are to be used by the browser. The instructions frequently used with ASP.NET Web API are

- *no-cache*: This setting informs the browser that the response is cacheable but should be revalidated on the subsequent request. Browsers may choose to cache the response, for example, to be used in the case of a network failure. ASP.NET Web API uses this setting by default, for every successful response, unless specified otherwise.

- *no-store*: This setting instructs the browser that it should not store any copy of the response in the cache.

- *max-age*: This setting defines when the browser should revalidate the cached resource. The value for this setting is specified in seconds.

- *Private*: Adding this instruction means that the content should only be cached by the requesting browser. Any shared cache, such as a proxy cache, should not cache this response.

■ **Note**   There are several other instructions for the Cache-Control header, but they are less frequently used with dynamic content, for example, the s-maxage setting, which defines a separate max-age for shared caches. The entire list of Cache-Control settings is available in the HTTP RFC at www.w3.org/Protocols/rfc2616/rfc2616-sec14.html#sec14.9.

Listing 8-8 shows an example of how to set the Cache-Control header in the response so that it will be cached for five minutes and only in the browser.

Listing 8-8. Setting the Cache-Control Header for a Response

```
var cacheControl = new CacheControlHeaderValue {
    Private = true,
    MaxAge = TimeSpan.FromMinutes(5)
};
response.Headers.CacheControl = cacheControl;
```

Setting the CacheControl property will override the default cache settings of ASP.NET Web API. The resulting HTTP response is shown in Listing 8-9.

Listing 8-9. HTTP Response with the Cache-Control Header

```
HTTP/1.1 200 OK
Cache-Control: max-age=300, private
Content-Type: application/json; charset=utf-8
Date: Sat, 22 Mar 2014 12:16:06 GMT
Content-Length: 166
```

```
{
  "agentID": 1,
  "codeName": "007",
  "firstName": "James",
  "lastName": "Bond",
  "imagePath": "images/JamesBondImage.png",
  "description": "Killer",
}
```

Any subsequent call made to the same URI during the five-minute time frame will result in the browser fetching the response automatically from the cache, without contacting the service. After five minutes, the cached content will be considered stale, and any subsequent request to that URI will cause the browser to issue a new request to the service.

Expires Header

The Expires header allows you to specify the exact date and time when the cached response expires. After the response expires, any subsequent request to the resource will cause the browser to submit a request to the service.

■ **Note**   Although you can set expiration by using the Cache-Control header with the max-age setting, it is sometimes more useful to set the expiration to a specific date and time. For example, when dealing with tax-related content, setting the Expires header to the last day of the fiscal year would be easier than setting the max-age to the number of seconds remaining in the current fiscal year.

If the Expires header is included in the response, without the Cache-Control header, the browser must cache the response and set the expiration to the specified value. If both headers are present in the response, the Cache-Control header will take precedence over the Expires header. Listing 8-10 shows how to set the Expires header in the HTTP response message object.

Listing 8-10. Setting the Expires Header in a Response

```
response.Headers.CacheControl = new CacheControlHeaderValue();
response.Content.Headers.Expires =
    new DateTime(DateTime.Today.Year, 12, 31, 23, 59, 59);
```

ASP.NET Web API has a default setting for the Cache-Control header. Because the Cache-Control header takes precedence over the Expires header, we have to clear the Cache-Control header before setting the Expires header. The resulting response is shown in Listing 8-11.

Listing 8-11. HTTP Response with the Expires Header

```
HTTP/1.1 200 OK
Expires: Wed, 31 Dec 2014 21:59:59 GMT
Content-Type: application/json; charset=utf-8
Date: Sat, 22 Mar 2014 12:16:06 GMT
Content-Length: 166
{
  "agentID": 1,
  "codeName": "007",
  "firstName": "James",
```

```
    "lastName": "Bond",
    "imagePath": "images/JamesBondImage.png",
    "description": "Killer",
}
```

■ **Note**   You cannot set the value of the Expires header to more than one year in the future.

If you look closely at the expired time, you will notice it is 21:59:59 GMT, and not 23:59:59, as set in the code. This is because the code example was executed on a server that is using a GMT+2 time zone. Returning an expiration time that is based on the client's time zone is quite complex, because the client's time zone is not passed in the HTTP request headers.

If the response does not contain the Cache-Control or the Expires header, it is up to the browser to decide whether to cache the response. For example, Internet Explorer caches such responses indefinitely and never revalidates them—until the cache is cleared, that is. Chrome, on the other hand, will not cache such responses and will always call the service on subsequent requests.

To force the revalidation behavior in all browsers, ASP.NET Web API returns a default Cache-Control header with no-cache and an Expires header set to -1 (expired).

Cache Headers and Content Negotiation

When using content negotiation, sending a request to the same URI can result in different responses, depending on the Accept-* headers. This means that it is not enough for a browser to cache the response for a request based on the URI alone. In fact, browsers can store several responses for the same request URI, if you inform them which request headers are used for the content negotiation.

■ **Note**   Browsers use the request's headers for the variations, not the response's, because when sending subsequent requests, the browser relies on the request to detect if the response is already cached or not.

To inform browsers how to vary responses, add the Vary HTTP header to the response and set it to the names of the Accept-* headers that you use for content negotiation, as shown in Listing 8-12.

Listing 8-12. Setting the Vary Header for Cached Responses

```
var cacheControl = new CacheControlHeaderValue {
    Private = true,
    MaxAge = TimeSpan.FromMinutes(5)
};
response.Headers.CacheControl = cacheControl;
response.Headers.Vary.Add("Accept");
```

Adding the last line will inform the browser that it should cache responses varied by the request's URI and the value of the Accept header. For example, if we have a service that supports the CSV and JSON formats, and the client application requests each of the formats (using the Accept header), the browser would have two different responses in the wcache: one containing a CSV and the other JSON, both for the same URI. The next time the client sends a request to either format, the browser will retrieve the cached response that matches the URI and the value of the Accept header.

Cache Headers and Actions Methods

As the previous examples show, setting the cache headers requires access to the HttpResponseMessage object. Instead of changing all of your cacheable action methods to return an HttpResponseMessage object, you can create an action filter that will apply the header to the response.

■ **Note**   Action filters were introduced in Chapter 7, where we used them to validate the input, before calling the action method.

If you haven't done so already, open the TheAgency solution. In the Solution Explorer window, add a new folder named Filters to the web application project, and in it, create a new class named CachingFilterAttribute. Open the newly created file and replace its content with the code shown in Listing 8-13.

Listing 8-13. Implementing a Cache Filter Attribute

```
using System;
using System.Net;
using System.Web.Http.Filters;
using System.Net.Http.Headers;

namespace TheAgency.Filters
{
    public class CachingFilterAttribute : ActionFilterAttribute
    {
        public int MaxAge { get; set; }

        public CachingFilterAttribute(int maxAge)
        {
            MaxAge = maxAge;
        }

        public override void OnActionExecuted(HttpActionExecutedContext actionExecutedContext)
        {
            var response = actionExecutedContext.Response;

            if (response.StatusCode == HttpStatusCode.OK)
            {
                response.Headers.CacheControl = new CacheControlHeaderValue
                {
                    Private = true,
                    MaxAge = TimeSpan.FromSeconds(MaxAge)
                };
            }
        }
    }
}
```

The OnActionExecuted method will be invoked after the action method completes its execution. Because only successful responses are supposed to be cached, we will only set the cache header if the status code of the response is 200 (OK).

To apply this caching filter attribute to our action method, open the AgentsController.cs file that is under the Controllers folder and decorate the GetAll method with the new attribute, as shown in Listing 8-14.

Listing 8-14. Applying the [CacheFilter] Attribute to an Action Method

```
[TheAgency.Filters.CachingFilter(30)]
public IEnumerable<Agent> GetAll()
{
    return Database.Agents;
}
```

Setting the MaxAge property in the constructor to 30 will instruct the browser to cache the list of agents for 30 seconds. For the next 30 seconds, any subsequent request the SPA sends to retrieve the list of agents will cause the browser to return the cached response, without contacting the service.

To test this, we've run our SPA of TheAgency with an empty cache and then reloaded the application every couple of seconds. The result, as captured by Fiddler's time line graph, is shown in Figure 8-3.

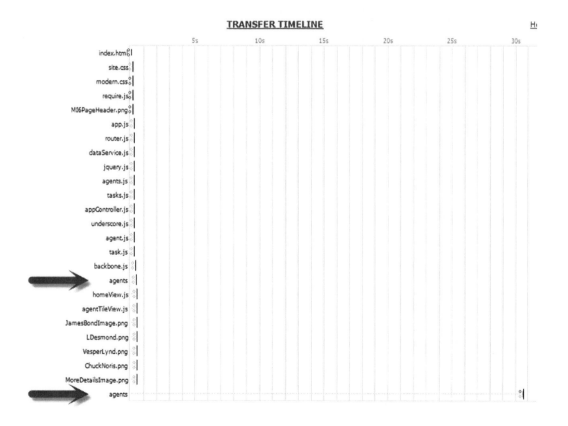

Figure 8-3. *A time line showing the SPA requests over time*

As you can see, the first time the SPA loads, several requests are sent to the server, including the request for the list of agents (indicated by the top arrow). Reloading the SPA afterward results in no requests to the server, because all the content is cached—both the list of agents and the static content. After 30 seconds, reloading the SPA results in a single request—to retrieve the list of agents (indicated by the bottom arrow). All the other static content is still served from the cache.

■ **Note**   Your SPA front end is currently not connected to the service back end. You will learn how to connect the two ends in Chapter 9.

Resource Versioning with ETags

After the cached content on the client-side expires, the browser will send the subsequent request to the server and will replace the cached response with the one it received from the server. For example, we might want to cache a list of countries for ten days, to enable our SPA to load faster. After ten days, the browser will again request the list of countries and will replace its existing cached response with the new list.

But what if after ten days the list of countries doesn't change? We would still receive the entire list of countries, even though the currently cached response is identical to the response we just received from the service.

To solve this issue, HTTP offers us the ETag (entity tag) header, which we can use to represent the version of a resource. The ETag value can be any string that represents a version. It can be a version number, the last update date, or a GUID that we recalculate every time we update the resource.

ETags are handled by browsers and servers in the following way:

1. The browser sends the request to the server. This is the first time, so there are no ETag headers involved.

2. In the service, if the response is cacheable, we add the ETag header to it and set its value to the version of the resource.

3. The browser caches the response along with the ETag value.

4. After the response expires and has to be revalidated, the browser will send the request to the service, along with the value of the ETag. When sending the request, the browser places the version value in a header named If-None-Match.

5. In our service, we pull the version value from the If-None-Match header and compare it to the version of the resource.

    a. *If the versions are different*: Return the new content, along with an updated ETag header. The browser will overwrite the cached response with the new response, including the new ETag value.

    b. *If the version has not changed*: Return an HTTP 304 (Not Modified) response, with no content. The browser will identify the 304 response and use the cached response it had from before.

■ **Note**   If you return a 304 response, add the required caching headers, to make sure the browser updates the expiration date of the cached resource. Otherwise, the cached content will still be considered as expired and will require revalidation on every subsequent request.

The code to create steps 1 and 4 is shown in Listing 8-15. If you want to apply it to our solution, open the AgentsController.cs file and replace the implementation of the Get method with the code in Listing 8-15.

Listing 8-15. Using the ETag Header to Manage Versions of Resources

```
public HttpResponseMessage Get(int id)
{
    Agent agent = Database.Agents.SingleOrDefault(a => a.AgentID == id);

    HttpResponseMessage response;
    EntityTagHeaderValue etag = Request.Headers.IfNoneMatch.FirstOrDefault();
    bool shouldReturnAgent = true;
    if (etag != null)
    {
        string etagValue = etag.Tag.Replace("\"", "");
        string currentVersion = agent.GetHashCode().ToString();
        shouldReturnAgent = (etagValue != currentVersion);
    }

    if (shouldReturnAgent)
    {
        response = Request.CreateResponse(HttpStatusCode.OK, agent);
        response.Headers.ETag = new EntityTagHeaderValue(
            string.Format("\"{0}\"", agent.GetHashCode().ToString()));
    }
    else
    {
        response = Request.CreateResponse(HttpStatusCode.NotModified);
    }

    return response;
}
```

The first request that is sent to the service will not have the If-None-Match header. That is why we set the shouldReturnAgent variable by default to true.

According to the HTTP RFC, ETag values must be wrapped in double quotes. Therefore, when we add the ETag header, we wrap the version with double quotes and remove them when reading the If-None-Match header value.

To get the resource's version, we call the GetHashCode method. If you already have a version or a last-modified property in your entity class, you can use that instead—after converting its value to a string.

To make sure the caching headers are added to both 200 (OK) and 304 (Not Modified) responses, open the CachingFilterAttribute class, and change the condition in the OnActionExecuted method to

```
(response.StatusCode == HttpStatusCode.OK || response.StatusCode == HttpStatusCode.NotModified)
```

Uploads and Downloads

Sometimes, you might find yourself with the need to upload files to a service or to create a service that supports file download.

When handling files or any other binary content in .NET, we normally work with streams, such as FileStream, NetworkStream, or MemoryStream.

Downloading Files from a Service

To return a stream from an action method, create an HttpResponseMessage object and set its content to a StreamContent object, as shown in Listing 8-16.

Listing 8-16. Downloading a File Through an Action Method

```
[Route("api/agents/{id}/SoundTrack")]
public HttpResponseMessage GetAgentSoundTrack(int id)
{
    Agent agent = Database.Agents.SingleOrDefault(a => a.AgentID == id);

    Stream soundTrackStream = GetSoundTrackStream(agent);

    HttpResponseMessage response = Request.CreateResponse(HttpStatusCode.OK);
    response.Content = new StreamContent(soundTrackStream);
    response.Content.Headers.ContentType = new MediaTypeHeaderValue("audio/mpeg3");
    return response;
}
```

The preceding example retrieves the stream by calling the GetSoundTrackStream method and then passes it to the StreamContent object. The StreamContent object is responsible for reading the content from the original stream and, upon completion, closing the original stream and disposing of it.

■ **Note** We intentionally didn't specify how the GetSoundTrackStream method works. It can read a FileStream from the disk, use a NetworkStream to read the content from another service, or construct it in-memory with a MemoryStream. The stream itself can even be a wrapper stream, such as a WavToMp3ConvertStream wrapping a FileStream.

Uploading a File to an Action Method

Receiving a stream from your client is a bit more complex. First, you will have to read the stream from the request message, as streams are not passed as method parameters. Second, when reading the stream from the request, it is recommended that you use asynchronous code, to better utilize the .NET Thread Pool. This process is demonstrated in Listing 8-17.

Listing 8-17. Uploading a File to an Action Method (form submit)

```
public async Task<HttpResponseMessage> Post()
{
    // Check if the request contains multipart/form-data.
    if (!Request.Content.IsMimeMultipartContent())
    {
        throw new HttpResponseException(Request.CreateErrorResponse(
                HttpStatusCode.UnsupportedMediaType, "Request does not contain a photo"));
    }

    string root = HttpContext.Current.Server.MapPath("~/images");
    var provider = new MultipartFormDataStreamProvider(root);
```

```
// Read the file - this will also save the file
await Request.Content.ReadAsMultipartAsync(provider);

// Change the file name from a temp name to the original name
string fileName = provider.FileData[0].Headers.ContentDisposition.FileName.Replace("\"", "");
string tempPath= provider.FileData[0].LocalFileName;
string newPath = Path.Combine(Path.GetDirectoryName(tempPath), fileName);
File.Move(tempPath, newPath);

var response = Request.CreateResponse(HttpStatusCode.Accepted);

return response;
}
```

▨ **Note** If you are also writing the stream to a destination, such as saving it locally to the disk, it is recommended that the write operations are also executed asynchronously. Asynchronous action methods are explained in depth in Chapter 11.

The preceding example matches a scenario in which the client application uses an HTML form to submit a file to the ASP.NET Web API service. When you use form submit to upload files, the browser uploads the content using a special multipart/form-data MIME type. To read the content of such a message, you must do the following:

1. Create a MultipartFormDataStreamProvider object and provide it with the target path on which you want to store the uploaded files (browsers support uploading several files together in a single request).

2. Call the Request.Content.ReadAsMultipartAsync method and pass it the data stream provider object. The method will read each file from the request and pass it to the provider, which will save it to the path you provided.

The code in the preceding example performs another step: changing the file name of the stored file. By default, the data stream provider saves the files using random names. If you prefer to name the file as it is named in the client computer, you have to retrieve the name from the request message and rename the local file.

To access the name of the uploaded file, we used the provider.FileData[index].Headers. ContentDisposition.FileName property. To get the path of the file created in the server, we used the provider.FileData[index].LocalFileName property with a matching index.

▨ **Note** The original file name in the request is wrapped with double quotes, which we removed by using the string.Replace method.

Submitting files using HTML forms is one of the common ways to upload content to a service. Another way of uploading files from browsers is to use the new File API of HTML5. The File API uploads files as binary streams, which makes the process of reading them on the service side a lot easier. Listing 8-18 shows how to read plain binary streams and save them to a file.

Listing 8-18. Uploading a File to an Action Method (HTML5 File API)

```
[HttpPost]
[Route("api/agents/{id}/photo")]
public async Task<HttpResponseMessage> UploadPhoto(int id)
{
    Agent agent = Database.Agents.SingleOrDefault(a => a.AgentID == id);

    Stream imageStream = await Request.Content.ReadAsStreamAsync();

    string path = GetImagePathForAgent(agent);
    using (FileStream fs = new FileStream(path, FileMode.Create))
    {
        await imageStream.CopyToAsync(fs);
        fs.Close();
    }
    imageStream.Close();

    return Request.CreateResponse(HttpStatusCode.Accepted);
}
```

To read the stream from the request, we use the `Request.Content.ReadAsStreamAsync` method. After we retrieve the stream, we simply send it to a destination, which, in the case of the preceding example, is a `FileStream` object.

■ **Note**   For more information on how to use the File API in browsers, refer to the article at
https://developer.mozilla.org/en-US/docs/Using_files_from_web_applications.

Summary

This is the second chapter that deals with ASP.NET Web API. In this chapter, you continued to learn how to create more elaborate services with ASP.NET Web API. You learned how to implement content-negotiation with media type formatters; how to add caching to our services with the `Cache-Control`, `Expires`, and `Vary` HTTP headers; and how to support resource versioning with the `ETag` header. Finally, you learned how to implement file download and upload in our services.

In the next chapters, we will return to the client side, starting by learning how to connect our SPA to the back-end services that we created in Chapters 6 and 7.

CHAPTER 9

▩ ▩ ▩

Communication Between Front and Back End

In the last two chapters, you learned how to create a back-end application programming interface (API) by using ASP.NET Web API. Once you have a fully operational back end, you will probably want to create the front-end-to-back-end integration, in order to achieve a robust solution. In single page application (SPA) development, the integration between the front end and the back end is particularly crucial.

In most of the solutions, you will use Ajax as your main communication option. Most of the MV* frameworks/libraries include modules to handle Ajax requests, which can simplify the integration process. On the other hand, Ajax is not the only solution for communication. There are other ways, such as WebSockets, Server-Sent Events, and WebRTC.

In this chapter, we will start by explaining how to communicate with the back end that you wrote in Chapters 7 and 8. We will also explore the built-in Ajax support that is included in Backbone.js. Then, we will re-factor our application, TheAgency, to use a back end, instead of its current front-end persistence solution. At the end of the chapter, we will discuss other communication options that you can use for front-end and back-end communication.

Our first stop will be Ajax.

Using Ajax to Communicate with the Server

Ajax is the main communication option in SPAs. At its core, Ajax is just a combination of development techniques and the XMLHttpRequest object. You use the XMLHttpRequest object to send an asynchronous HTTP request to a remote server and later on handle the HTTP response and render only the relevant parts in your web page. Because XMLHttpRequest runs in the background, the page is still responsive, and the users can continue to interact with it.

You can create an Ajax request by creating an XMLHttpRequest object, configuring the object, and using its send function. Listing 9-1 shows a simple Ajax request.

Listing 9-1. The XMLHttpRequest Object

```
var xhr = new XMLHttpRequest();
xhr.open("GET", "/api/agents/1");
xhr.readystatechange = function() {
  if(xhr.readyState === XMLHttpRequest.DONE && xhr.status === 200) {
    console.log("The agent data is: " + xhr.responseText);
  }
};
xhr.send();
```

In the preceding code, we first create a new instance of the `XMLHttpRequest` object. Then, we use the `open` function to configure the request to be an HTTP GET request and to set the end point in the server, which is `/api/agents/1`. Once we set the object, we add an event listener to the `readystatechange` event that monitors the state of the `XMLHttpRequest` object. Only when the state of the `XMLHttpRequest` is `DONE` and the status of the response is 200 (which is `OK` status) will we write to the console the response as text.

The preceding code was very short and simple. In real-world scenarios, writing your own Ajax functions can be cumbersome. You will need to configure the HTTP headers in the request, create more sophisticated response parsing, and more. This is why libraries such as jQuery offer Ajax functions support. The code example in Listing 9-2 does the same thing as Listing 9-1, but by using the jQuery `$.get` function.

Listing 9-2. Using the $.get Function

```
$.get("/api/agents/1", function(data) {
        console.log("The agent data is: " + data);
});
```

As you can see, the code is much shorter and very trivial to use. You set the URL and the success callback to the `$.get` function, and jQuery will handle all the details for you.

Today, most web developers don't craft their requests by hand with the `XMLHttpRequest` but use library abstractions. Before we jump into Backbone.js Ajax support, we will first discuss a JavaScript development pattern that is called Promises.

The Promises Pattern

Working with asynchronous code can be very challenging. Because you never know when a callback will be triggered, it can be very hard to implement features that depend on the result of the request. Moreover, asynchronous code in JavaScript can become very bloated. This is where the promises pattern becomes very handy.

A promise/deferred object is an object that defers the execution of its callbacks to the point in time where the operation that is in the promise's context finishes. A promise has three different states: unfulfilled, fulfilled, or failed. When a promise starts, it always begins in the unfulfilled state. Later on, the promise can only move to the fulfilled state or the failed state. As soon as a promise is fulfilled or failed, its value is immutable.

Because a promise defers its callback execution to some point in the future, you can use it to chain asynchronous code blocks as if they were synchronous. Using promises can simplify asynchronous code and help to create a more maintainable code.

■ **Note**   You can read more about the promises specifications in CommonJS wiki: `http://wiki.commonjs.org/wiki/Promises`.

A promise object API mainly includes three functions: `then`, `done`, and `fail`. The `then` function is used to chain callbacks to the promise, and it returns another promise for itself. It receives three callback functions: success, error, and progress. If the promise execution throws an error, the `then` function will run the error callback. If you want to add some functionality while the promise is in progress, you can implement it in the progress callback.

The `done` function resembles the `then` function functionality, but when an error occurs, it will throw the error and will not continue, as opposed to the `then` function. The `fail` function is used to chain callbacks to handle failures.

A lot of JavaScript utility libraries expose a promise implementation. For example, you can create a promise object in jQuery using the `$.Deferred` function. Moreover, all the asynchronous operations that jQuery exposes return a promise object. Let's change the code of Listing 9-2 and write to the console, once the get function finishes. (See Listing 9-3.)

Listing 9-3. Using the $.get Function with a Promise

```
$.get("/api/agents/1", function(data) {
        console.log("The agent data is: " + data);
}).then(function() {
        console.log("hello after the get async operation finished");
});
```

In the preceding example, we chain the then function to the promise that the $.get returns and write text to the console.

Since Ajax is asynchronous, promises can help you write better code. Now that you have a little background about promises, you can go forward and learn about the Backbone.js sync API.

Backbone.js Ajax Support

Backbone.js includes Ajax support by exposing the Backbone.sync function. The Backbone.sync function uses the jQuery ajax function to make Ajax requests to the server, in order to read or save a model or a collection to the server. The Backbone.sync function returns a jqXHR object, which implements jQuery promise API.

The Backbone.sync function can be overridden in order to use other communication or persistence options. For example, Backbone.localStorage is a Backbone.js plug-in that replaces the Backbone.sync Ajax requests with requests to localStorage.

The Backbone.sync function receives three arguments: method, model, and an options object. The method is the type of CRUD (Create/Read/Update/Delete) that you want to perform. It can have four string options.

1. *"create"* will send a POST HTTP request to the server.

2. *"read"* will send a GET HTTP request to the server.

3. *"update"* will send a PUT HTTP request to the server.

4. *"delete"* will send a DELETE HTTP request to the server.

The model is the model that you want to perform the action on. The options object is all the options the jQuery ajax function receives, such as success and error callbacks.

Listing 9-4 shows a code example that uses the Backbone.sync function.

Listing 9-4. Using Backbone.sync

```
Backbone.sync('update', task);
```

This will send a PUT request to the server, with all the task data, as part of the request body.

■ **Note**   You must set the URL property of the task model to the relevant end point in the server. If you forget to set the URL, you will get an error. You can find Backbone.sync documentation on the Backbone.js web site at http://backbonejs.org/#Sync.

Backbone.sync is a low-level function. Backbone.js also includes functions on the model and on the collection objects that enable you to perform Ajax requests. Under the hood, the model and collection Ajax functions will call the Backbone.sync function, and they are used mostly for convenience.

In order to use the Ajax API, you have to set the `url` property of the model or collection to the end point in the server. For example, the end point in the server for agents is `/api/agents`. The `url` property can get a static URL string or a function that can help you to create dynamic URLs.

Models include the following Ajax API functions: `sync`, `fetch`, `save`, and `destroy`. The `sync` function is just a façade to call `Backbone.sync`. The `fetch` function is used to retrieve the server's latest version of the model. The `save` function will save the current state of the model to the server. The `destroy` function will delete the current model from the server. Listing 9-5 shows how to save a task.

Listing 9-5. Saving a Task Using the Model save Function

```
task.save();
```

Collections include the following Ajax API functions: `sync`, `fetch`, and `create`. As in the models, the `sync` function is a façade to call `Backbone.sync`. The `fetch` function will fetch all of the collection from the server. The `fetch` function can be configured with an options object. The `create` function will create a new instance of a model in the collection and will send a POST request to the server also to create the model on the server side. The code in Listing 9-6 shows how to fetch all the agents using the `fetch` function.

Listing 9-6. Fetching Agents Using the Collection fetch Function

```
agents.fetch();
```

Now that we know how to use Backbone.js to communicate with our web API, it is time to re-factor TheAgency to use our back end.

Updating TheAgency

Once we have a functional back end for TheAgency and we understand how to use Backbone.js Ajax support, we can start to re-factor our code to work against the exposed web API. The first object that we are going to change is the `DataService` object.

In TheAgency front-end solution, the `DataService` object has two main API functions: `getData` and `saveData`. Both of these functions worked against `localStorage` to fetch or save the agent collection. Now that you know about the `Backbone.sync` function, you understand that you can use the `Backbone.localStorage` plug-in to fetch or save data to `localStorage`. On the other hand, using `localStorage` means that you won't take advantage of the web API.

■ **Note**   Because we wanted to show how to use HTML5 storage, we implemented a simple solution using our own `DataService` object. If you want to use `localStorage` to manipulate data, you are encouraged to use the `Backbone.localStorage` plug-in, instead of implementing your own solution.

We are going to re-factor the `DataService` object to work against the web API. We will still use the `getData` function in our API, but we will implement a specific API for the operations that we are using in the SPA.

The code in Listing 9-7 is the new version of the `DataService` object.

Listing 9-7. The New Version of the DataService Object

```
define(['collections/agents', 'collections/tasks'],
    function (Agents, Tasks) {
        function adjustTasks(agents) {
            var tasks = [];
```

```
        agents.each(function (agent) {
            _.each(agent.get('tasks'), function (task) {
                task.agentID = agent.get('agentID');
                tasks.push(task);
            });
            agent.set('tasks', new Tasks(tasks));
            tasks.length = 0;
        });
    }
    var DataService = {
        getData: function () {
            var deferred = $.Deferred();
            var agents = new Agents();
            agents.fetch().then(function () {
                adjustTasks(agents);
                app.agents = agents;
                deferred.resolve();
            });
            return deferred.promise();
        },
        addTask: function (task) {
            task.url = '/api/agents/' + task.get('agentID') + '/tasks'
            return task.save();
        },
        updateTask: function (task) {
            task.url = '/api/agents/' + task.get('agentID') + '/tasks/' + task.get('taskID');
            return Backbone.sync('update', task);
        },
        createAgent: function (agent) {
            agent.url = '/api/agents'
            return Backbone.sync('create', agent);
        },
        updateAgent: function (agent) {
            return Backbone.sync('update', agent);
        },
        deleteAgent: function (agent) {
            return agent.destroy();
        }
    };

    return DataService;
});
```

The first change in the object is the lack of setMaxAgentID and setMaxTaskID functions. Since the server is going to manage the identities of models, we don't need to track the ids. We don't need the getAgentsFromCache function either, because the data is originated from the server.

On the other hand, we have a utility function that is called adjustTasks. The responsibility of the function is to translate the task array that we get from the server from JSON format to Task objects.

The new DataService API includes the following functions:

- getData: The function creates a deferred object, which is used to create a promise. After the creation of the deferred object, we use the agent collection's fetch function. Once the data arrives from the server, we use the adjustTasks function and set the app.agents to the agent collection. The last thing to do in the function is to resolve the deferred. The resolve function tells the promise that it is fulfilled. If you want to move a promise to failed state, you use the reject function.

- addTask: The function receives a task and saves it to the server, using the save function. Note that because a task is related to an agent, we set the task URL to include the agentID, as the web API expects.

- updateTask: The function receives a task and uses the Backbone.sync function to update it in the server.

- createAgent: The function creates a new agent in the server using the Backbone.sync function.

- updateAgent: The function updates an agent in the server, using the Backbone.sync function.

- deleteAgent: The function uses the agent's destroy function to delete a given agent.

Once you have the new DataService API, it is time to change the agent and agent collection to include default URL handling. Listings 9-8 and 9-9 show how the agent and the agent collection should look now. Another thing to notice in the agent model is that we don't set the agentID's default value. If you set the agentID to a default value, once you create a new agent, Backbone.js will assume that the agent got its ID from the server and will send a PUT request instead of a POST request when you save the agent.

Listing 9-8. The New Version of Agent Model

```
define(['backbone', 'collections/tasks'], function (Backbone, Tasks) {
    var agent = Backbone.Model.extend({
        url: function () {
            return '/api/agents/' + this.get('agentID');
        },
        defaults: {               codeName: '',
            firstName: '',
            lastName: '',
            imagePath: '',
            description: '',
            tasks: new Tasks()
        },
        idAttribute: 'agentID',
        validate: function(attrs, options) {
            if (attrs.firstName.length == 0 || attrs.lastName.length == 0) {
                return "Name must include first name and last name!";
            }
        }
    });

    return agent;
});
```

Listing 9-9. The New Version of Agent Collection

```
define(['backbone', 'models/agent'], function (Backbone, Agent) {
    var Agents = Backbone.Collection.extend({
        url: '/api/agents',
        model: Agent,
        create: function(options) {
            this.push(new Agent(options));
        }
    });

    return Agents;
});
```

You should also update the task model and remove the default setting of the taskID. Lising 9-10 shows how the task model should look after the change.

Listing 9-10. The New Version of Task Model

```
define(['backbone'], function (Backbone) {
    var task = Backbone.Model.extend({
        defaults: {
            description: '',
            isComplete: false,
            agentID: 0
        },
        idAttribute: 'taskID',
        validate: function(attrs, options) {
            if (attrs.description.length == 0) {
                return "You must add a description!";
            }
        },
        toggleComplete: function() {
            this.set("isComplete", !this.get('isComplete'));
        }
    });

    return task;
});
```

In the app.js, we used to load the data from the localStorage. We will change that behavior to load the data from the server. The following code shows you how the require part of app.js changes. (See Listing 9-11.)

Listing 9-11. The New Version of the app.js require Part

```
require(['routers/router', 'components/dataService'], function (router, dataService) {
    $(document).ready(function () {
        dataService.getData().then(function () {
            router.start();
        });
    });
});
```

As you can see, we use the dataService.getData function to get all the agents. Once the asynchronous call is over, the promise that getData returns is resolved, and we start the router.

Now that all the data structures, the app.js, and the DataService have been re-factored, it is time to handle the changes in the views. We will start with the TaskView's toggleTask function, which includes the only change in the view, as seen in Listing 9-12.

Listing 9-12. The New Version the TaskView toggleTask Function

```
toggleTask: function (event) {
        var self = this;
        this.model.toggleComplete();
        dataService.updateTask(this.model).then(function () {
                self.render();
        });
}
```

In the function, we save the TaskView scope in the self variable. Then we toggle the model value and use the dataService.updateTask function with the current task state. Once the function completes, we render the view.

In the EditModalView, we change the updateAgent function. The code in Listing 9-13 shows how that function will look after the re-factoring.

Listing 9-13. The New Version of the EditModelView updateAgent Function

```
updateAgent: function (event) {
        event.preventDefault();
        var self = this;

        if(this.model.set(this.getCurrentFormValues(), {validate:true}))
        {
                dataService.updateAgent(this.model).then(function () {
                    self.hideModal();
                });
        }
        else {
                $('#validationError').text(this.model.validationError);
        }
}
```

As you can see, once the data is validated, we use the dataService.updateAgent function to update the agent data. Once the server operation completes, the then callback will be called, and the modal will be removed.

The DetailsView includes a few changes in the deleteAgent and addNewTask functions. Listings 9-14 and 9-15 are the new versions of deleteAgent and addNewTask.

Listing 9-14. The New Version of the DetailsView deleteAgent Function

```
deleteAgent: function() {
        if (confirm('Are you sure you want to delete the agent?')) {
                app.agents.remove(this.model);
                dataService.deleteAgent(this.model).then(function() {
                    Router.navigate('#/', { trigger: true });
                });
        }
}
```

Listing 9-15. The New Version of DetailsView addNewTask Function

```
addNewTask: function(event) {
        var txt = $('#txtNewTask'),
            self = this;
        if (event.which !== this.$cache.EnterKey || !txt.val().trim()) {
                return;
        }

        var task = new Task({description: txt.val(), agentID: this.model.get('agentID') });
        this.model.get('tasks').add(task);
        dataService.addTask(task).then(function () {
                txt.val('');
                self.render();
        });
}
```

As you can see, the main changes here are the use of the `DataService` API and the chaining of the then functions to be triggered after the operations succeed.

In `CreateView`, we change the `createAgent` function, as seen in Listing 9-16.

Listing 9-16. The New Version of CreateView createAgent Function

```
createAgent: function (event) {
        event.preventDefault();

        var self = this;

        if(this.model.set(this.getCurrentFormValues(), {validate:true}))
        {
                $.proxy(this.handleImageFile(function () {

                        dataService.createAgent(self.model).then(function (newAgent) {
                                app.agents.add(newAgent);
                                app.agents.get(newAgent.agentID).set('tasks', new Tasks());
                                Router.navigate('#/', { trigger: true });
                        });                    }), this);
        }
        else {
                $('#validationError').text(this.model.validationError);
        }
}
```

In the code, we use the `dataService.createAgent` function to save the newly created agent to the server. The server returns the newly created agent with its server ID and only then do we add the agent to the agent collection. Pay attention to the fact that the server returns an empty array inside the `tasks` property. We fix that in the code and add a new task collection instead.

■ **Note**   You should add the tasks collection, which should be called `Tasks`, as part of the RequireJS `define` function at the beginning of the `createView`.

Now that we finished our re-factoring, you can run the application against your web API and see how it is working.

Working with Other Communication Options

Ajax is probably the main option to use when you want to communicate from an SPA front end to the back end. As we mentioned at the beginning of the chapter, there are other communication options that you should consider when you write a web application. This part of the chapter will introduce some of those options.

Server-Sent Events (SSE)

SSE (Server-Sent Events) is an acronym relating to EventSource JavaScript API. The API enables web servers to push data over HTTP. You can use SSE for a lot of push scenarios, such as, for example, implementing a feed that is updated by server-pushed data.

The data that is pushed to the front end uses a push protocol that must have the `text/event-stream` MIME type. Also, the data must be sent in a format that includes the prefix `data:`, followed by the data itself and a line break at the end of the data. Listing 9-17 shows how a pushed data will look.

Listing 9-17. Data in SSE

```
data: a server message
```

Another way to push data to the front end is by using a named event. A named event message starts with the `event:` prefix, followed by the event name itself and a line break. After the named event line, you must put the data that is sent to the event, using the same `data:` format that we saw previously. The example in Listing 9-18 shows two different events sent to the front end.

Listing 9-18. Using Two Different Named Events

```
event: create
data: create data

event: update
data: update data
```

Up until now, we only discussed how the push protocol should be implemented and did not discuss how clients use the protocol. In order to listen to a named event, the client has to create an `EventSource` object. The `EventSource` object receives a URL to listen to in its constructor. Once the object is instantiated, you can add event handlers for the `message` event. Listing 9-19 is a simple example of creating an `EventSource` object.

Listing 9-19. Creating an EventSource

```
var source = new EventSource(url);
source.addEventListener('message', function (e) {
    console.log(e.data);
}, false);
```

The default event handler is the `message` event, and all data that is pushed without a named event will be pushed to its handler. In the handler, you use the event argument's `data` property to retrieve the sent data for later use. If you want to listen to a named event, you will have to add a handler to the event. Listing 9-20 shows how to listen to the `create` event from Listing 9-18.

Listing 9-20. Creating an EventSource to Listen to the create Event

```
var source = new EventSource(url);
source.addEventListener('create', function (e) {
    console.log(e.data);
}, false);
```

■ **Note**   There are server implementations for SSE, but they are beyond this book's scope.

WebSockets

In the past, when we wanted to create highly responsive web applications, we had to use such solutions as long polling or forever frames. These hacks helped to make our web applications responsive to changes in the server, but they imposed a lot of difficulties and implementation considerations. Today, you can use WebSockets instead to create your interactive application.

WebSockets enable full-duplex communication channels over TCP between clients and servers. WebSockets include a new protocol that overcomes the request-response nature of HTTP and enables close to real-time communication between clients and servers. This behavior can help you create interactive applications such as monitoring applications, live chats, collaborative applications, and very highly responsive forms.

WebSockets are built upon a new protocol. In order to establish a WebSocket connection, the client must send an `HTTP Upgrade` request to a WebSockets server. Once the server agrees to upgrade the request to a WebSockets protocol, it will send the client a `101 Switching Protocols` status code. This is where the TCP sockets both in the client and in the server are opened and the duplex communication will start.

When one of the end points (client or server) decides to close the connection, it will send a closing request, and both of the sockets will be closed. The other end point (the one that didn't trigger the closing request) must reply with its own closing request.

■ **Note**   The implementation of the protocol and how to create a WebSockets server are not in this book's scope. You can read about the WebSockets protocol RFC at `http://tools.ietf.org/html/rfc6455`.

The communication that is transferred between the opened sockets doesn't include overheads such as an HTTP request. Moreover, the data that is sent is raw JSON data, which is serialized and deserialized by the client and the server.

In order to use WebSockets in the front end, you will use the `WebSocket` object. The `WebSocket` object receives a WebSockets server URL in its constructor. The URL should start with `ws://` or `wss://` instead of `http://` and `https://`, because we use a non-HTTP protocol. Once the `WebSocket` object is created, you can add event listeners to open, message, and close events.

The open event is triggered when the socket is opened. The `close` event is triggered when the socket is closed. The `message` event is triggered every time a message arrives from the server. Listing 9-21 is an example of how to create a `WebSocket` object.

Listing 9-21. Creating a WebSocket Object

```
var socket = new WebSocket(url);
socket.onopen = function() {
        console.log('Socket Status: ' + socket.readyState);
}
socket.onmessage = function(e) {
        console.log('Data received: ' + e.data);
}
socket.onclose = function() {
        console.log('Socket Status: ' + socket.readyState);
}
```

As you can see, in the message event, you retrieve the data, using the event argument's data property. Another thing to note is the use of the readyState property of the socket, which can include the following values:

- CONNECTING (0): The connection hasn't been established yet.

- OPEN (1): The connection was established.

- CLOSED (2): The connection has been closed or could not be opened.

In order to send data to the server, you will use the WebSocket's send function. The send function receives as an argument the data that you want to send. Listing 9-22 shows how to send a simple JavaScript object.

Listing 9-22. Sending Data Using the send Function

```
socket.send({ firstName: 'John', lastName: 'Dow'});
```

You don't have to craft your own WebSockets implementation, and there are libraries that can help you to integrate the protocol, such as **Socket.IO** and **ASP.NET SignalR**.

Socket.IO

Socket.IO is a WebSockets façade that uses feature detection to check whether WebSockets are supported in the browser and, if not, uses fallbacks such as long polling, Flash, and more. These fallbacks enable you to concentrate on creating your real-time implementation, without considering how the duplex communication works underneath.

Socket.IO includes two parts: server implementation only for Node.js servers and a client-side library for JavaScript. Both of the APIs, client and server, have the same API, to make the communication as easy as possible.

Once you have chosen to use Socket.IO in the front end, it has a very simple API, which is exposed through the io namespace. You use the connect function, give it your Socket.IO server URL, and then add an event handler to the socket object that the connect function returns. Listing 9-23 is an example showing simple Socket.IO usage in the front end.

Listing 9-23. Using the Socket.IO Client Library

```
var socket = io.connect(url);
socket.on('connect', function () {
        socket.send('message for the server');
        socket.on('message', function (msg) {
                // handle message from the server
        });
});
```

As you can see, when a socket is created using the `io.connect` function, you can add to it event listeners using the on function. In the example, we added the connect event listener, the `message` event listener, and, using the send function, sent a message to the server.

■ **Note**   The server side of Socket.IO is implemented in the Node.js framework, and Node.js is beyond the scope of this book.

ASP.NET SignalR

The SignalR library was influenced by the Socket.IO library. SignalR is a part of ASP.NET, and it is used to add real-time web functionality to web applications that are built with ASP.NET. Like Socket.IO, SignalR includes two parts: a server implementation and a client library. Like Socket.IO, it works with WebSockets, when they are supported in the browser, and has fallbacks such as SSE, forever frames, and long polling.

SignalR handles the connection to the server automatically and chooses the appropriate fallback for you, if needed. You can configure SignalR to create your desired connection type, but that means there will be no guarantee that the library will work in specific browsers.

SignalR includes two different models that you can use for communication: connections and hubs. A connection is a simple end point for sending messages from the client to the server and vice versa. You can use the connection to access low-level functionality of the transport protocol that SignalR is using. A hub is a high-level pipeline that allows both client and server to call methods on each other directly, as if there is no network between them. Sometimes, working with SignalR looks like magic, because you call a function in the front end, and it is dispatched by SignalR to the server side and vice versa.

In order to understand better how SignalR works, we will create a simple chat example.

- Open Visual Studio and create an empty ASP.NET web application with the name `SignalR`.

- Add the SignalR package by running the command `Install-Package Microsoft.AspNet.SignalR` in the NuGet Package Manager Console.

- Make sure to update the jQuery package using the `Update-Package jQuery` command in the NuGet Package Manager Console.

- Add a new class file in the project root and name it `ChatHub`.

- The `ChatHub` inherits from the SignalR Hub class, and it will act as a hub in the application. It will include a Send method that receives name and message parameters and broadcasts them to all the hub clients. In the `ChatHub`, add the code from Listing 9-24.

Listing 9-24. ChatHub Class

```
using System;
using System.Collections.Generic;
using System.Linq;
using System.Web;
using Microsoft.AspNet.SignalR;

namespace SignalR
{
  public class ChatHub : Hub
  {
```

```
    public void Send(string name, string message)
    {
      Clients.All.broadcastMessage(name, message);
    }
  }
}
```

- Add a new class file in the project root and name it Startup. The Startup class acts as the bootstrapper for SignalR, and it is mandatory. It should include a Configuration method that receives IAppBuilder instance and calls its MapSignalR method. In the Startup, add the code from Listing 9-25.

Listing 9-25. Startup Class

```
using Microsoft.Owin;
using Owin;
using SignalR;

namespace SignalR
{
  public class Startup
  {
    public void Configuration(IAppBuilder app)
    {
      app.MapSignalR();
    }
  }
}
```

- Create a new HTML file in the project root and call it index. On the index page, we will create the text box for the chat and a button to send messages in the chat. We will also include jQuery UI Dialog, to receive the username when the page is loading. You can download the plug-in from the jQuery UI web site at http://jqueryui.com/download/. You should pay attention to the <script src="/signalr/hubs"></script>, which is used by SignalR to generate all the communication functionality. In the index HTML, add the code from Listing 9-26.

Listing 9-26. Index.html Implementation

```
<!DOCTYPE html>
<html>
<head>
    <meta charset="UTF-8">
    <title>Simple Chat</title>
    <link href="styles/site.css" rel="stylesheet" />
    <link href="styles/ui-lightness/jquery-ui-1.10.3.custom.min.css" rel="stylesheet" />
</head>
<body>
    <div class="container">
        <input type="text" id="txtMessage" autofocus="autofocus" />
        <input type="button" id="btnSend" value="Send" />
        <dl id="chat">
        </dl>
    </div>
```

```html
        <div id="dialog">
            <form>
                <label for="txtDisplayName">Enter Your Name:</label>
                <input type="text" name="txtDisplayName" id="txtDisplayName"
class="text ui-widget-content ui-corner-all" />
            </form>
        </div>
        <script src="Scripts/jquery-2.0.3.min.js"></script>
        <script src="Scripts/jquery.signalR-2.0.1.min.js"></script>
        <script src="Scripts/jquery-ui-1.10.3.custom.min.js"></script>
        <script src="/signalr/hubs"></script>
        <script src="Scripts/app.js"></script>
    </body>
</html>
```

- Create a new JavaScript file in the Scripts folder and call it app.js.

- In the app.js file, add the code from Listing 9-27.

Listing 9-27. app.js Implementation

```javascript
$(document).ready(function () {
    var txtDisplayName = $('#txtDisplayName'),
        txtMessage = $('#txtMessage'),
        dlChat = $('#chat'),
        chat = $.connection.chatHub;

    chat.client.broadcastMessage = function (name, message) {
        dlChat.append($('<dt/>').text(name)).
            append($('<dd/>').text(message));
    };

    $.connection.hub.start().done(function () {
        $('#btnSend').click(function () {
            chat.server.send(txtDisplayName.val(), txtMessage.val());
            txtMessage.val('').focus();
        });
    });

    $("#dialog").dialog({
        autoOpen: true,
        modal: true,
        buttons: {
            "Ok": function () {
                $(this).dialog("close");
            }
        }
    });
});
```

We have bolded the relevant SignalR parts. In order to start working with SignalR, you will have to use the $.connection and point it to the hub, which in our case, is chatHub. Once we have the hub, we add an event listener to listen to the client.broadcastMessage event. In that event, we update the definition list with a new chat message when it is arriving.

The last part that relates to SignalR in the implementation is the use of the $.connection.hub.start function to start the hub. Once the hub is started, we add an event listener to the send button and use the hub's server property to send a message to the server using the send function.

Now that you have your chat application ready, press F5 and run the project. Open more than one browser instance and copy the URL of the chat to them. Write text in the text box and broadcast it to the other browsers, using the send button, to see how SignalR is working. Figure 9-1 shows how the app might look.

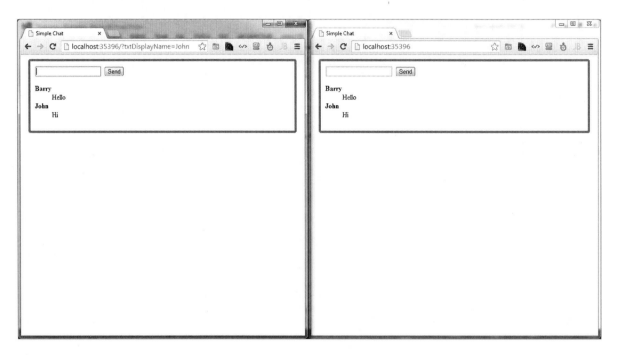

Figure 9-1. *Chat in action*

SignalR can be a very good starting point for creating interactive applications with real-time communication, if you are using ASP.NET. It can help you create SPAs that are updated in real time and highly responsive.

Web Real-Time Communication (WebRTC)

Web Real-Time Communication (WebRTC) is an HTML5 JavaScript API that is used for browser-to-browser real-time video, audio, and data communication.

▓ **Note** WebRTC is still being standardized by W3C while we are writing this book. This is why we won't cover the topic in depth and omit a lot of details, since they might change in the near future. For more details about WebRTC, see www.webrtc.org/.

WebRTC includes three main JavaScript APIs:

- *MediaStream*: API to retrieve stream data from cameras and microphones

- *RTCPeerConnection*: API that enables efficient communication between peers

- *RTCDataChannel*: API to retrieve data that will be broadcast later to other peers

---

■ **Note** Because MediaStream is the only stable API, we won't cover the other two APIs.

The MediaStream API enables developers to read and synchronize streams of media. These streams can originate from cameras (mainly from webcams) and microphones. In order to retrieve the streams, and to be able to broadcast them later using `RTCPeerConnection` to other browsers, you will use the `navigator.getUserMedia` function. Once you've used the function and its success callback is triggered, you will be able to get the live stream of the media you use. Listing 9-28 shows how to use `navigator.getUserMedia` to output a webcam stream to a video element.

Listing 9-28. Using The getUserMedia Function

```
navigator.getUserMedia = navigator.getUserMedia || navigator.webkitGetUserMedia ||
navigator.mozGetUserMedia;

navigator.getUserMedia({audio: false, video: true},
        function(stream) {
                var video = document.getElementById("video");
                video.src = window.URL.createObjectURL(stream);
                video.play();
        },
        function(error) {
                console.log(error);
        });
```

The getUserMedia function receives three arguments: a constraints object, success callback, and error callback. The constraints can have the `audio` and `video` Booleans, which are used to enable video or audio. The success callback gets the stream as a parameter, and in the example, it uses it as the source of the video element. The error callback is used to indicate that an error occurred and to take actions after it occurred.

Once you have a stream or some data that is retrieved by MediaStream or RTCDataChannel, you can use the RTCPeerConnection to communicate with another browser and send it the data. The RTCPeerConnection is the API that coordinates the communication of the browsers using a signaling channel. The signaling channel is provided by a script in the web page or by a remote server.

Because the API doesn't require a plug-in or an application, such as Skype, for example, it can open new web application development possibilities, such as creating video chats or streaming music and files using peer-to-peer connections and in real time.

Choosing Your Communication Option

In this chapter, we discussed a few ways to enable client and server communication. Ajax remains the main communication option to use in web applications, but you shouldn't use Ajax only. When you require more real-time communication, you should use WebSockets. In push scenarios, such as notifications or feed update, you should use SSE, which fit better. If you need peer-to-peer communication, WebRTC might be the option that you should use.

Knowing where each communication option fits can help you create a much better application. For example, in a web game that we built a few months ago, we used both Ajax and WebSockets. WebSockets were used to help players communicate in real time, while Ajax was used for game transactions. The game example shows that you shouldn't be afraid to use more than one communication option in your application.

Summary

When you create your SPA, you will probably have a back end that will be responsible for such things as authentication, authorization, persistency, and more. There are a few methods to enable front-end and back-end communication, which we discussed in the chapter, such as Ajax and WebSockets.

Once you create your SPA, it is your responsibility to choose the relevant communication option to use. If you have a web API back end, the main choice is to use Ajax, but don't restrict yourself to this option.

This chapter concludes the third part of the book. You now have a fully functional SPA that uses Backbone.js in the front end and ASP.NET web API in its back end.

PART IV

Advanced SPA Topics

CHAPTER 10

■ ■ ■

JavaScript Unit Testing

Unit testing is an important and crucial part of the development process. A unit test is a way to evaluate a unit, which is a small piece of code, and determine if it satisfies the relevant requirements. Unit tests help to create robust code that isn't malfunctioning during runtime. They act as a safety net when developers continue to develop a feature and might make changes to existing features. Without unit tests, application developers can't be sure that their changes haven't broken the application logic and requirements.

Having automatic unit tests in any application is considered a best practice. Testing a single page application (SPA) might appear to be a difficult task, but there are efficient ways to accomplish it. In this chapter, you will learn about unit testing in the front end, meet the Jasmine library that helps to create front-end tests, and discover how to use Jasmine to test the application that we built: TheAgency.

Unit Testing in the Front End

Until recently, unit testing in JavaScript was rare. Because developers used JavaScript mostly to handle the UI, they preferred to use manual tests to test their logic. Moreover, there was a lack of unit-testing environments that could support the need for JavaScript unit testing.

Today, when we have SPAs that have a lot of their logic developed in the front end, unit testing in the front end is a must. Writing untestable code might result in an application that is not working as expected, and we can't allow that. The need for unit-testing environments in JavaScript caused a change in developers' mind-sets and resulted in a lot of new JavaScript libraries that filled the gap.

There are many JavaScript unit-testing libraries, and listed below (followed by the relevant URL) are some of the most popular:

- **Jasmine:** `http://pivotal.github.io/jasmine`

- **Mocha:** `http://visionmedia.github.io/mocha`

- **QUnit:** `http://qunitjs.com`

- **Intern:** `http://theintern.io`

All these libraries can help you create your unit tests, but in this chapter, we will focus only on Jasmine library. Before we introduce Jasmine, we will start with a little information about Test Driven Development (TDD) and Behavior Driven Development (BDD).

What Is TDD?

Test Driven Development (TDD) is a development approach that Kent Beck is credited with discovering. TDD determines that a developer should start developing a new feature by writing a failing test. Later on, the developer is responsible for developing the minimal amount of code that will pass the test. Once the test is passed, the developer will re-factor the code for clarity, readability, and non-duplication.

The development process using TDD is as follows:

1.   Create a test.

2.   Run the test and expect the new test to fail.

3.   Write the least code that will make the test pass.

4.   Run the test and verify that all other tests pass now.

5.   Generalize and re-factor for clarity, readability, and non-duplication.

6.   Return to 1.

This cycle is called the "red-green re-factor" cycle, and a developer should run it many times during a single development day. At the end of each cycle, the developer can check in the code, because all of his tests are passing, and he can be sure that he added some functionality to the product.

Now that you know what TDD is, we can explain what BDD is.

What Is BDD?

Behavior Driven Development (BDD) is a development approach developed by Dan North and based on TDD. BDD can use Domain-Driven Design (DDD) and object-oriented analysis and design (OOAD) to create better tests, but these approaches are not mandatory. Combining all the good parts from all the different development approaches (TDD, DDD, and OOAD) provides development teams collaboration tools that can help communicate with business analysts and project owners and later on help to create more robust and high-quality software.

■ **Note**   Domain-Driven Development (DDD) is a development approach that focuses on the core domain and its logic in order to develop a project. It relies on collaboration between developers and domain experts to address domain problems in the project. Object-oriented analysis and design (OOAD) is a development approach that applies object-oriented paradigms and visual modeling to collaborate between business owners and developers.

At its core, BDD specifies that tests should be created for the requirements (behaviors) set by the business owners. By testing the desired behavior, you will create the required software. That means that developers and business analysts should collaborate to specify the desired software behavior. The desired behavior is sometimes called a user story. Once a user story is specified, and the developer understands the need, the developer can check whether the units that he builds meet the expectations.

In BDD, the output of the tests should be readable both to the developer and the business owners. This is why it is important to have meaningful test names and meaningful user story names and descriptions. If the developer or the business owner does not understand the tests or the user stories, they should collaborate again, until they have arrived at a common language.

Because BDD is based on TDD, the process of writing the tests after they have been specified is the same as the process shown earlier.

BDD, like TDD, relies heavily on automation for the testing process. Once you have expectations set, you will want to test them during the development process. You can test the expectation in build processes or whenever testing is needed. This is why automation is very important, and therefore, you will probably use a BDD framework, such as Jasmine, in order to automate testing.

Jasmine Library

Jasmine is one of the popular JavaScript unit-testing libraries. It was created by Pivotal Labs and is described as a BDD framework, which is why we first introduced you to BDD.

Jasmine doesn't depend on any other library or even on the DOM. You can run Jasmine inside a browser, using its spec runner web page, and you can also run it headless, with the help of other frameworks such as Jasmine Headless WebKit.

Before you write your tests, you should start by setting the unit-testing environment.

Setting the Environment

The first thing that you should do to set up the environment is to download Jasmine. The library can be found via the following link: http://pivotal.github.io/jasmine.

We will set up a spec runner web page, which will be responsible for running all the tests that we are going to create. Jasmine comes with a spec runner HTML page, and you must add it to your project. The web page should look like Listing 10-1.

Listing 10-1. Jasmine Spec Runner

```
<html>
<head>
  <title>Jasmine Spec Runner</title>

  <link href="lib/jasmine-1.3.0/jasmine_favicon.png" rel="shortcut icon" type="image/png">
  <link href="lib/jasmine-1.3.0/jasmine.css" rel="stylesheet" type="text/css">
  <script src="lib/jasmine-1.3.0/jasmine.js" type="text/javascript"></script>
  <script src="lib/jasmine-1.3.0/jasmine-html.js" type="text/javascript"></script>

  <!-- include source files here… -->

  <!-- include spec files here… -->

  <script type="text/javascript">
    (function() {
      var jasmineEnv = jasmine.getEnv();
      jasmineEnv.updateInterval = 1000;

      var htmlReporter = new jasmine.HtmlReporter();

      jasmineEnv.addReporter(htmlReporter);

      jasmineEnv.specFilter = function(spec) {
        return htmlReporter.specFilter(spec);
      };
```

```
    var currentWindowOnload = window.onload;

    window.onload = function() {
      if (currentWindowOnload) {
        currentWindowOnload();
      }
      execJasmine();
    };

    function execJasmine() {
      jasmineEnv.execute();
    }
  })();
  </script>
</head>
<body>
</body>
</html>
```

The spec runner first loads the `jasmine.js`, `jasmine-html.js,` and `jasmine.css` dependencies. It also loads a script that generates and configures the environment and after that runs all the tests when the window is loaded. The last part is the place that you put your source files and test files. In the spec runner, these places are marked with HTML comments.

Figure 10-1 shows how a spec runner should look when you run it.

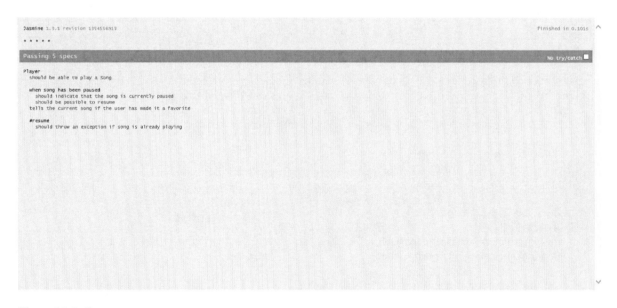

Figure 10-1. *Spec runner*

In Figure 10-1, there are five passing specs, indicating the tests were completed with success. Once you have the environment ready, it is time to write your first tests.

Creating Suites and Specs

When you decide to test a unit in your application, you will create a test suite for it and create test specifications inside the suite.

Specs

A spec is a JavaScript function that tests a part of the unit. Specs are created using the it function. The it function receives two arguments: the name of the spec and the function that the spec is going to run. The name of the spec should be meaningful and should describe the behavior that you are going to test. The name should also be written in plain, simple language and should be readable by anyone, not just by developers.

Listing 10-2 shows a simple spec.

Listing 10-2. A Spec

```
it("A spec that is doing nothing", function() {
});
```

The preceding example is only a spec definition, and it is doing nothing like its spec name indicates.

Suites

A suite is a container of specifications (specs), and it describes what the specifications are verifying.

In order to create a suite, you will use the describe global function. The describe function receives two arguments: the name of the suite and the function with the suite implementation. Listing 10-3 shows a suite definition.

Listing 10-3. Describing a Suite

```
describe("Suite Name", function() {
        // Put here your tests
});
```

The name of the suite should describe what is under test. Suites run in the order that they are described. They can be used as a function scope to all the tests that they include.

Another aspect of suites is that they act as a function scope that contains specs. That means that you can create variables inside suites that will be available to all the specs that share the same function scope. This knowledge is very helpful when you want to share objects or data between specs.

Expectations and Matchers

Specs should include one or more expectations. An expectation is an assertion that can be either true or false. If an expectation returns false, the spec will fail. In order to create an expectation, you use the expect function on the value you want to test and then use an *expectation matcher* function to test that value. An expectation matcher is a Boolean comparison between the actual value and the expected value.

In Listing 10-4, you can see how to use the expect function and some matchers.

Listing 10-4. A Spec with Matchers

```javascript
it("using matchers", function() {
        var a = 12;
        var b = a;
        var c = function () {
        }
        expect(a).toBe(b);
        expect(a).not.toBe(null);
        expect(a).toEqual(12);
        expect(null).toBeNull();
        expect(c).not.toThrow();
});
```

In the preceding code, you can see that the matchers express what they check. For example, the b variable was set to a's value, and therefore, you expect a to be b. You also expect a not to be null, or to be equal to 12. As you can see, the code expresses itself.

You nest specs inside suites, and following (Listing 10-5) is the full example of the previous code:

Listing 10-5. A Suite with a Spec

```javascript
describe("A spec", function () {
        it("that uses matchers", function() {
                var a = 12;
                var b = a;
                var c = function () {
                }
                expect(a).toBe(b);
                expect(a).not.toBe(null);
                expect(a).toEqual(12);
                expect(null).toBeNull();
                expect(c).not.toThrow();
        });
});
```

Creating a Custom Matcher

Jasmine includes a variety of matchers, and you can write your own custom matcher if you need a matcher that isn't provided. If you want to add a custom matcher, you should create a function that receives zero or more arguments. The function should return true if the actual value passes the matcher requirements or false otherwise. The actual value exists in this.actual when the matcher is being run. If you want to add a message, you can use this.message and set it to a function that returns your message. For example, Listing 10-6 is a custom matcher.

Listing 10-6. Adding a Custom Matcher

```
jasmine.Matchers.prototype.toBeGreaterThan = function(expected) {
        var self = this;
        var notText = this.isNot ? " not" : "";

        this.message = function () {
                return "Expected " + self.actual + notText + " to be greater than " + expected;
        }

        return this.actual > expected;
}
```

As you can see, the function is called toBeGreaterThan, and it receives an expected value. It also returns whether the actual value is greater than the expected value. In order to set the right message, we have to understand if the matcher was run with negate context, and this is why we used the this.isNot property. The last step is to add the function to the jasmine.Matchers.prototype, which is an object that includes all the Jasmine matchers.

According to Jasmine documentation, custom matchers should be added in the spec it function or in a beforeEach function (beforeEach is described later). If you want to add them in those functions, you will use the this.addMatchers function (where the this keyword is in a Jasmine execution context) and pass it an options object that each option is a custom matcher, as in Listing 10-7.

Listing 10-7. Adding a Custom Matcher using addMatchers

```
this.addMatchers({
        toBeGreaterThan: function(expected) {
                var self = this;
                var notText = this.isNot ? " not" : "";

                this.message = function () {
                        return "Expected " + self.actual + notText + " to be greater than " + expected;
                }

                return this.actual > expected;
        }
});
```

Setup and Teardown

Sometimes you have to run code before or after a test, in order to initialize or clean up the testing environment. This is where beforeEach and afterEach functions can be very handy.

The beforeEach function runs code before each spec execution that is in the current suite, and afterEach runs code after each spec execution. You can put beforeEach and afterEach inside a suite to affect all the specs. The code example in Listing 10-8 shows how to do that.

Listing 10-8. Using beforeEach and afterEach

```
describe("A spec", function () {
       var a = 0;
       var b = 1;

       beforeEach(function() {
              a = b + 1; // a equals 2
       });

       afterEach(function() {
              a = 0;
       });

       it("that uses matchers", function() {
              expect(a).not.toBe(b);
              expect(a).not.toBe(null);
              expect(a).toEqual(2);
       });
});
```

You can see that before each spec, a is set to 2. Later on, we check if a meets our expectations.

Nesting Suites

You can define nested specs using a nested suite, by nesting the describe function. That behavior helps to create a group of specs inside another suite and to create meaningful groups of tests.

Before a spec is run by the Jasmine runtime, Jasmine will take care and run all the beforeEach functions that are related to the spec. Jasmine will also take care to run the afterEach functions that are related to the spec, after the test has been executed.

For example, Listing 10-9 shows how to nest a suite.

Listing 10-9. Nesting a Suite

```
describe("A spec", function() {
  var num = 0;

  beforeEach(function() {
    num += 5;
  });

  afterEach(function() {
    num = 0;
  });

  it("checks for equality between num and 5", function() {
    expect(num).toEqual(5);
  });

  describe("nested", function() {
    var innerNum;
```

```
  beforeEach(function() {
    innerNum = 5;
  });

  it("checks that num equals innerNum ", function() {
    expect(num).toEqual(innerNum);
  });
 });
});
```

In the preceding code example, you can see how a describe function is nested inside another describe function. Before the nested describe function is run, the beforeEach of the parent describe is run, and then the beforeEach of the nested describe. This is why the test will pass.

Using Spies

Now that you know the basics for creating your tests, it is time to learn about spies. A spy is a test double object that replaces the real implementation. Spies help to fake behaviors that we would like to mock and spy on.

There are two options for creating a spy: creating a spy on an existing object and creating a bare spy. In the first case, you use the spyOn function, which receives an object to spy on and a function name. The following (Listing 10-10) is a simple example of using a spy:

Listing 10-10. Creating a Spy Using the spyOn Function

```
describe("A spy", function() {
        var obj = null;

        beforeEach(function() {
                obj = {
                        doSomething: function() {
                                return "Doing something";
                        }
                };
                spyOn(obj, "doSomething");
                obj.doSomething();
        });

        it("tracks that we called doSomething", function() {
                expect(obj.doSomething).toHaveBeenCalled();
                expect(obj.doSomething).toHaveBeenCalledWith();
        });
});
```

In the code, you can see that we created a spy on the obj object. Later on, we called the doSomething function. The spy tracks that call, and you can later use functions such as toHaveBeenCalled or toHaveBeenCalledWith to see if the function was called or called with the relevant arguments.

The spy also adds to the doSomething function a calls array that includes all the calls for the spied function. For example, obj.doSomething.calls.length will output 1, because there was only one call to doSomething.

The second option to create a spy is to use jasmine.createSpy or jasmine.createSpyObj functions. The **createSpy** function creates a bare spy function to spy on. The createSpyObj function creates a spy object and receives an array of strings that represent the object property names. Listing 10-11 shows how to use the createSpyObj function.

Listing 10-11. Creating a Spy Using the createSpyObj Function

```
describe("Creating a spy object", function() {
        var obj;

        beforeEach(function() {
                obj = jasmine.createSpyObj('obj', ['doSomething']);

                obj.doSomething();
        });

        it("for each requested function", function() {
                expect(obj.doSomething).toBeDefined();
        });

        it("tracks that we called doSomething", function() {
                expect(obj.doSomething).toHaveBeenCalled();
                expect(obj.doSomething).toHaveBeenCalledWith();
        });
});
```

The code is very simple. We create a spy object and set it to the obj variable. Later on, we call the doSomething function, and we expect that it will be defined and called.

There are other functions that you can use with spies. For example, you can use the andReturn function after calling the spyOn function, to fake the returning of a value when calling a spied function. You can also use the andCallFake function to delegate the real spied function call to another function. That can be very handy when you want to fake asynchronous calls. The following example in Listing 10-12 fakes an Ajax call with jQuery:

Listing 10-12. Faking a jQuery Ajax Call

```
it('the success callback is executed', function () {
        spyOn($, 'ajax').andCallFake(function(options) {
                options.success();
        });

        var callback = jasmine.createSpy();
        var error = jasmine.createSpy();
        getAgentDetails(1, callback, error);

        expect(callback).toHaveBeenCalled();
});

function getAgentDetails(id, callback, error) {
    $.ajax({
        type: 'GET',
        url: '/details/' + id,
        dataType: 'json',
        success: callback,
        error: error
    });
}
```

In the preceding example, we spy on the $.ajax function. Once the function is called, we call a fake function. The fake function will run the success function, which was passed as an argument.This is to mimic the behavior we would see if the call was successful. We also create spy functions for the callback and error handlers, and then we call the getAgentDetails with some arguments.

■ **Note**   You can obtain more details about Jasmine spies from the following site:

https://github.com/pivotal/jasmine/wiki/Spies.

Using spies can help to fake integration points, and this is why it is valuable to have them. Jasmine spies are very easy to work with, but they are limited. There are libraries, such as SinonJS, that have more mocking features, and you are encouraged to check them, if you require more mocking functionality.

Testing Asynchronous Code

One of the biggest problems when testing JavaScript, or any other platform, is testing an asynchronous code. Because you can't be sure when a callback for an asynchronous function will return, that might make your testing much more complicated.

In Jasmine, there are a set of functions that help to test asynchronous code:

- runs: the function receives a callback function. The runs function is used to wrap code that you want to run directly. Using runs alone, without one of the other functions, is pointless. If you have multiple runs function calls in a spec, they will run serially.

- waits: the function receives a time-out and pauses the spec for the time-out period. This behavior gives an opportunity for the asynchronous code to finish running. If you don't know the period of time it takes for the asynchronous code to finish, use waitsFor instead.

- waitsFor: receives a function and two optional arguments: a message and a time-out. The waitsFor pauses the spec until the function argument finishes and returns true. This behavior can cause the spec to block forever, and therefore, you can pass a time-out to stop the wait, after a period of time.

■ **Note**   Time-outs in both waits and waitsFor are measured in milliseconds.

Listing 10-13 is a usage example of waitFor and runs.

Listing 10-13. Using waitsFor and runs in a Spec

```
it('making an actual Ajax request', function () {
        var callback = jasmine.createSpy();
        var error = jasmine.createSpy();
        getAgentDetails(1, callback, error);

        waitsFor(function() {
                return callback.callCount > 0 || error.callCount > 0;
        }, "the get agent details call complete", 2000);
```

```
        runs(function () {
                expect(callback).toHaveBeenCalled();
        });
});

function getAgentDetails(id, callback, error) {
    $.ajax({
        type: 'GET',
        url: '/details/' + id,
        dataType: 'json',
        success: callback,
        error: error
    });
}
```

In the spec, we create spies for both the success and error callbacks and then run the getAgentDetails function. We set the waitsFor function to pause the spec execution up until the callback or the error has been called at least once. If the request to the server doesn't return for at least two seconds, the waitsFor terminates. At the end of the spec, we make sure that the success callback has run.

In the example, you saw that we used an asynchronous spec to check for server interaction. In real-world scenarios, you should avoid doing that, because waiting for a response from a server can slow the testing process. Also, you don't want to create a dependency on an external resource. Use spies instead of creating external dependencies.

Writing Tests for TheAgency Project Using Jasmine

Now that you know how to use Jasmine to test an application, it is time to test our application. Because TheAgency uses RequireJS, we will have to adapt the testing accordingly.

■ **Note** We decided to create tests only for one object kind in Backbone.js, in order to show the concept of writing tests. That doesn't mean that you shouldn't test all of your application. Also, we test the version of TheAgency (from the end of Chapter 6) that doesn't include the back-end implementation.

■ **Caution** When you write your tests, pay attention not to test the libraries you use but, rather, your own functionality.

Creating and Setting Up the Environment

Once you opt to start testing your code, you can add all the specs into your project or create a different testing project. We prefer the second choice, as it isolates the tests into their own environments.

In order to test TheAgency code, you start by creating the testing environment, as follows:

- Create a new testing project. Name the project `TheAgencyUnitTests` or your preferred name.

- Download the Jasmine library and all its files.

    - Put the `SpecRunner.html` file in the project root.

    - Create a `jasmine` folder in the project root and put all Jasmine files inside it.

- Create a `scripts` folder in the project root.

- Copy all the folders under the `scripts` folder in TheAgency project into the `scripts` folders. You can use source control to share the files in both of the `scripts` folders.

- Copy the `lib` folder that exists in TheAgency project under the `scripts` folder. We will use jQuery, Underscore.js, and Backbone.js in our tests.

- Create a `specs` folder in the `scripts` folder. The `specs` folder will include all the specs that you are going to run.

- In the `specs` folder, create a folder for each kind of object that you want to test.

- At the root of the `scripts` folder, add a `testsBootstrapper.js` file, which is going to be used as the bootstrapper for the tests.

Figure 10-2 shows how the folders should be organized.

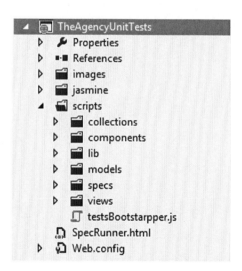

Figure 10-2. *Unit-testing project folders structure*

Now that the folders are organized, we can start working on setting the environment.

■ **Note**　You can choose your own folders structure, as long as you understand where everything is located.

Because TheAgency is working with RequireJS, and we want to use RequireJS to create our suites and to load them, we changed the implementation of the spec runner and a little of its scripts. Listing 10-14 shows how the SpecRunner.html is implemented.

Listing 10-14. SpecRunner.html File

```
<!DOCTYPE HTML>
<html>
<head>
    <title>Jasmine Spec Runner</title>

    <link rel="stylesheet" type="text/css" href="jasmine/jasmine.css">
    <script data-main="scripts/testsBootstrapper.js" src="scripts/lib/require.js"></script>
</head>
<body>
</body>
</html>
```

As you can see, the HTML was shortened, as opposed to Listing 10-1. All the scripts were replaced with a call to RequireJS, and we set the data-main attribute to the testsBootstrapper.js file.

The code in Listing 10-15 is the testsBootstrapper.js file implementation.

Listing 10-15. testBootstrapper.js File

```
require.config({
    baseUrl: "scripts/lib",
    paths: {
        jquery: 'jquery',
        underscore: 'underscore',
        backbone: 'backbone',
        jasmine: '../../jasmine/jasmine',
        'jasmine-html': '../../jasmine/jasmine-html',
        spec: '../test/jasmine/spec/',
        models: '../models',
        collections: '../collections',
        views: '../views',
        components: '../components'
    },
    shim: {
        underscore: {
            exports: "_"
        },
        backbone: {
            deps: ['underscore', 'jquery'],
            exports: 'Backbone'
        },
        jasmine: {
            exports: 'jasmine'
        },
        'jasmine-html': {
```

```
            deps: ['jasmine'],
            exports: 'jasmine'
        }
    }
});

require(['underscore', 'jquery', 'jasmine-html'], function (_, $, jasmine) {
    var jasmineEnv = jasmine.getEnv();
    jasmineEnv.updateInterval = 1000;

    var htmlReporter = new jasmine.HtmlReporter();
    jasmineEnv.addReporter(htmlReporter);
    jasmineEnv.specFilter = function (spec) {
        return htmlReporter.specFilter(spec);
    };

    var specs = [];
    specs.push('../specs/models/agentSpec');
    specs.push('../specs/collections/agentsSpec');
    specs.push('../specs/views/taskViewSpec');

    $(function () {
        require(specs, function () {
            jasmineEnv.execute();
        });
    });
});
```

In the preceding code, you can see that we configured RequireJS to use `jasmine.js` and `jasmine-html.js`. We also set the Jasmine runtime, as was done in the original `SpecRunner.html`, but with a little change. We created a `specs` array, which will include all the spec files that will be loaded and then executed in Jasmine runtime.

Now that the environment is set, we can start writing our specs.

■ **Note**   We implemented only one example spec for a model, a collection, and a view. Those examples can help you understand what is needed to test the whole project.

Models

In the models example, we are going to test the agent model. The agent model is very simple and includes default values and a `validate` function. Models can be very complex and include behavior and functionality that should be checked.

In the `models` folder, which exists under the `scripts/specs` folder, create a new spec file called `agentSpec.js`. Listing 10-16 provides the code you should include in this file.

Listing 10-16. agentSpec.js Implementation

```javascript
define(['models/agent'], function (Agent) {
    return describe('Tests for agent model', function () {
        var agent;

        beforeEach(function () {
            agent = new Agent();
        })

        it('is initialize with default values.', function () {
            expect(agent.get('codeName')).toBe('');
            expect(agent.get('firstName')).toBe('');
            expect(agent.get('lastName')).toBe('');
            expect(agent.get('imagePath')).toBe('');
            expect(agent.get('description')).toBe('');
            expect(agent.get('tasks')).toBeDefined();
        });

        it('is initialize with idAttribute', function () {
            expect(agent.idAttribute).toBe('agentID');
        });

        it('will trigger an invalid event on failed validation.', function () {
            var errorCallback = jasmine.createSpy('errorCallback');

            agent.on('invalid', errorCallback);

            agent.set({ firstName: '' }, { validate: true });

            var errorArgs = errorCallback.mostRecentCall.args;

            expect(errorArgs[0]).toBe(agent);
            expect(errorArgs[1]).toBe('Name must include first name and last name!');
        });
    });
});
```

In the implementation, we define the agentSpec module that will test the agent model. We include all the dependencies of the module, which is only the agent model in the agentSpec. From the defined RequireJS module, we return the suite definition that is going to be executed by Jasmine runtime. This convention will be repeated in all the other specs, and it is taking advantage of RequireJS asynchronous loading functionality and asynchronous dependencies loading.

Once we declare the suite, we use the beforeEach function to initialize a new agent model for each test. We create the first test, to see that all the default values are generated when an agent is created. This is to check that the values of a new agent are set to empty strings or that the task collection is defined.

The second test validates that the idAttribute is set to agentID, as expected. The test uses the toBe matcher and checks if the agent's idAttribute is the string agentID.

The third test is to ensure that the custom validation we created is working. The validation makes sure that first name and last name are not empty. We create a spy object to spy on a callback function that we set to the invalid event. Then we set the first name to an empty string and trigger validation using the validate option in the set function. Then we make sure that we received, as arguments to the invalid event handler, the agent and the validation error message.

Collections

Having verified the model, we move on to verifying that our agent collection is working as expected. In the agent collection, we set the collection model to be Agent; we set the idAttribute to be the agentID; and we have a create function. We will make sure that all the settings we made are verified and that the create function adds a new agent to the agent collection.

In the collections folder that exists under the scripts/specs folder, create a new spec file called agentsSpec.js. In this file, you should include the code in Listing 10-17.

Listing 10-17. agentsSpec.js Implementation

```
define(['models/agent', 'collections/agents'], function (Agent, Agents) {
    return describe('Tests for agent collection', function () {
        var agents;

        beforeEach(function () {
            agents = new Agents();
        });

        it('is initialize for agent model.', function () {
            expect(agents.model).toBe(Agent);
        });

        it('Can create a new agent when provided an options object.', function () {
            expect(agents.length).toBe(0);
            agents.create(new Agent());
            expect(agents.length).toBe(1);
        });
    });
});
```

In the preceding code example, you can see the same definition of model as in agentSpec. The only difference is that we load the agent model and agent collection as dependencies to the agentsSpec module.

In the beforeEach function, we create a new collection for each test. Then we verify that when the collection is initialized, it is empty by default, and when we use the create function and add a new agent, the collection has a length of 1.

Views

As opposed to testing models and collections, views are much more difficult to test. Views include registration to event handlers, rendering, and working with template engines.

Once you decide to test a view, you will have to set up the environment. Because views depend on template engines for rendering, the first thing you will have to do is decide how you are going to handle the templates. One solution is to host template scripts inside the SpecRunner.html. Another solution is to load the templates using the text.js plug-in. In our examples, we chose the first option.

In this section, we are going to check the taskView view. In order to do that, in the SpecRunner.html, add the script for the view template. Now the SpecRunner.html will look like Listing 10-18.

Listing 10-18. SpecRunner.html New Implementation

```html
<!DOCTYPE HTML>
<html>
<head>
    <title>Jasmine Spec Runner</title>

    <link rel="stylesheet" type="text/css" href="jasmine/jasmine.css">
    <script data-main="scripts/testsBootstrapper.js" src="scripts/lib/require.js"></script>
</head>
<body>
    <script type="text/template" id="task-template">
        <td><%- description %></td>
        <td><% if (isComplete) {%>
            <img src="images/Completed.png" alt="completed" />
            <% } else { %>
            <img src="images/NotCompleted.png" alt="in progress" />
            <% } %>
        </td>
    </script>
</body>
</html>
```

Once you set the templates, in the views folder, which is located in the scripts/specs folder, add the taskViewSpec.js file. The taskViewSpec.js should include the code shown in Listing 10-19.

Listing 10-19. taskViewSpec.js Implementation

```javascript
define(['models/task', 'views/taskView'], function (Task, TaskView) {
    return describe('Tests for task view', function () {
        beforeEach(function () {
            this.table = document.createElement('table');
            this.table.id = 'taskTable';
            document.querySelector('body').appendChild(this.table);

            this.model = new Task();
            this.view = new TaskView({ model: this.model });
        });

        afterEach(function () {
            this.view.remove();
            document.querySelector('body').removeChild(this.table);
        });

        it('is initialize with tr as tag name.', function () {
            expect(this.view.tagName).toBe('tr');
        });

        describe('Rendering', function () {
            beforeEach(function () {
                window.app = {
```

```
                agents: jasmine.createSpyObj("agents", ["toJSON"])
            };
        });

        afterEach(function () {
            window.app = undefined;
        });

        it('returns the view object', function () {
            expect(this.view.render()).toEqual(this.view);
        });

        it('is rendering the template with not complete when the task is not complete', function () {
            this.view.render();
            expect(this.view.$el.html()).toContain('<img src="images/NotCompleted.png"
alt="in progress">');
        });

        it('is rendering the template with complete when the task is complete', function () {
            this.model.set('isComplete', true);
            this.view.render();
          expect(this.view.$el.html()).toContain('<img src="images/Completed.png" alt="completed">');
        });

        it('is toggling a task', function () {
            var isComplete = this.model.get('isComplete');
            this.view.render();
            this.table.appendChild(this.view.el);

            var event = new MouseEvent('click', {
                'view': window,
                'bubbles': true,
                'cancelable': true
            });
            this.view.el.querySelector('td').dispatchEvent(event);

            expect(isComplete).toNotEqual(this.model.get('isComplete'));
            expect(window.app.agents.toJSON).toHaveBeenCalled();
            expect(this.model.get('isComplete')).toBe(true);
        })
    });
  });
});
```

In the spec definition, we have dependencies on the task model and on the taskView view that is going to be tested. Because taskView is creating a new table row inside taskTable for each task, we will use the beforeEach function to create the taskTable table and append it to the spec runner's body element. We will also set a task model and a new taskView to be a part of the suite scope. We should also clean up the SpecRunner.html after we finish the tests. We will use the afterEach function to remove the view and the table.

After we set up the testing initialization and cleanup of the entire suite, we can start writing our tests. The first test is to check if the tagName of the view was set to tr, as expected. After the first test, we create an inner suite for all the rendering tests. We do that in order to separate the rendering tests, or tests that depend on rendering from all other tests.

In the rendering suite, you can see that we set beforeEach and afterEach functions, which are used to fake and clean up the window.app object. In the taskView's toggleTask function, we use the dataService function and save the whole agent collection. Inside the save function, we use the app.agents.toJSON function, which should be defined. This is why we fake the toJSON call using a spy; otherwise, we will get an error. That shows that we have a dependency on dataService that we need to re-factor.

Once we set the beforeEach and afterEach functions, we test to ensure the following behaviors:

- After rendering, the view returns itself.

- When render is called and the view holds an incomplete task, the NotCompleted.png image is rendered as part of the table row. We verify that by checking that the $el HTML includes the image after render is called.

- When render is called and the view holds a complete task, the render Completed.png image is rendered as part of the table row. We verify that by checking that the $el HTML includes the image after render was called.

- When clicking a task, its state should toggle.

The first three tests are simple to write. The last test is checking what happens when a DOM event occurs. In order to do that, you will have to fake the mouse-click event. This is why we create a MouseEvent object and later on use the dispatchEvent function on the table cell. After the click event is triggered, we can verify that the state of the model was changed as expected.

There are Jasmine plug-ins that can help you to fake events, for example, the Jasmine-jQuery plug-in, or you can do it in the way that we showed in the code, using the dispatchEvent function. Either way is applicable, as long as you test that the event handlers work as expected.

Now that we have all the tests in place, we can run the SpecRunner.html page and see the result of our tests (see Figure 10-3).

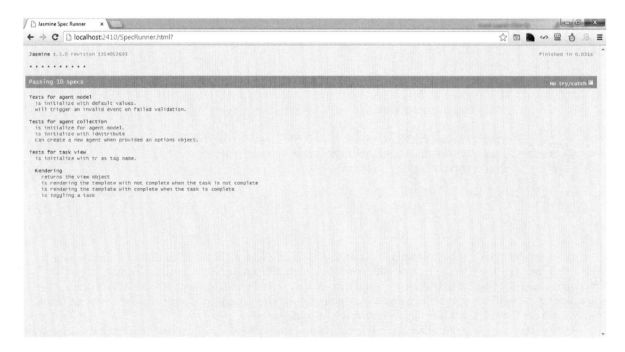

Figure 10-3. *Jasmine Spec Runner after running all the tests*

Summary

Unit testing is a must in any application that you are building. Because an SPA's development weight is in the front end, you must make sure that your code is working as expected. Failing to do so will result in application breakage and in various bugs that might be very difficult to find.

In this chapter, you learned how to test your front-end logic using unit tests. You also learned about one of the popular JavaScript unit-testing libraries—Jasmine. You learned the basics of Jasmine and how to use it to test simple functionality. You also learned how to use Jasmine to test asynchronous code and how to create an automatic environment to run your tests. At the end of the chapter, we explored some unit tests that were written in TheAgency SPA.

CHAPTER 11

SPA Performance Tuning

Performance tuning is a process that should be applied during the development life cycle. It includes a lot of optimizations that you can take advantage of to make your application fast and fluid. A lack of performance will make your application sluggish and slow and result in fewer users.

SPAs are no different from other web applications and, therefore, should be created with performance in mind. Because the weight of development is mostly in the front end, we will have to create high-performing JavaScript code. On the other hand, that doesn't mean that you shouldn't tune your back end as well.

In this chapter, you will be presented with tools to measure performance and learn how to optimize your front end and back end. The first stop in your application optimization is the front end.

Optimizing the Front End

Front-end optimization is one of the major features you must pay attention to when you create your application. In order to understand what you can optimize, it is crucial that you understand how the browser rendering process works. Later on, we will explain Chrome DevTools and how they can assist you in finding performance bottlenecks. At the end of this section, we will provide some tips about optimizations that you can apply to your code.

Browser Rendering Process

Today's modern browsers include very fast, optimized render engines that run HTML, CSS, and JavaScript very efficiently. Modern browsers use just-in-time (JIT) compilers for JavaScript and hardware acceleration for images, videos, and audio. While the new JavaScript compilers are responsible for numerous optimizations in JavaScript, performance is still a concern that you should be aware of.

The first requirement before you begin any optimization process is to understand how the environment works. Knowing what the browser is doing during the rendering process will help you to determine what parts in your implementation can diminish application performance. It will also enable you to determine where you may have created problems or bottlenecks.

Rendering starts when a response with a requested document arrives from the network layer. The flow of the rendering is constructed from four parts, which are shown in Figure 11-1.

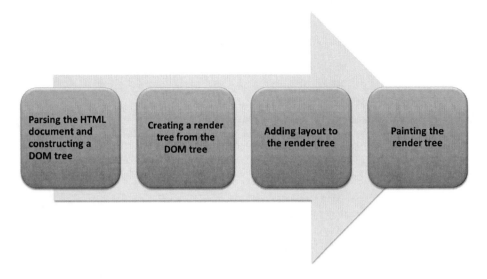

Figure 11-1. Browser rendering process

Every change to the DOM will trigger the same process in the browser. This is why changes to the DOM tree are very costly in terms of performance. The last two steps in the rendering process influence much of the performance of a web page.

■ **Note**　We recommend that you read an article by Tali Garsiel and Paul Irish about the internals of how browsers work. You can find the article on the HTML5Rocks web site at www.html5rocks.com/en/tutorials/internals/howbrowserswork.

The layout process, or reflow, occurs whenever a visual change requires a change in the layout of the page. There can be many causes of reflow. For example, browser resize can trigger a reflow, because the layout has to be changed to the new browser window size. Another example is DOM manipulation that causes a structure change in the DOM. Changes in the layout style or retrieval of layout information, such as `offsetTop` or `scrollTop`, can also trigger a reflow.

Reflows are very expensive, and you can't control when they are occurring. Browsers have optimization on reflows, and they won't trigger them every time there is a visual change. On the other hand, it is vital that web developers understand that reflows can slow down the execution of a web page.

The repaint process occurs when a visual change doesn't require recalculation of the whole layout. Repaint can be triggered by visibility changes of elements, changes in text color or background colors, and changes in background images. They are less expensive than reflows, but whenever there are a lot of repaints, you have to start thinking about your implementation.

Profiling the Front End Using Chrome DevTools

Profiling your implementation can help you to find a lot of problems. Chrome DevTools is one of the top profiling tools for web pages. DevTools are part of the browser, and you can press F12 to start them.

Once you have opened DevTools, there are two main tabs that can help you determine your front-end performance: the Timeline tab and Profiles tab.

Timeline Tab

You use the Timeline tab to monitor the web page execution. The Timeline tab is divided into the following three panes:

- *Timeline*: Includes three inner panes for Events, Frames, and Memory. You use the Events pane to analyze the duration of events and the number of events that were triggered. You use the Frames pane to analyze the amount of frames per second that the application used. If frames per second (FPS) is higher than 60, animations will be sluggish. The Memory pane is used to analyze the amount of memory consumption that the web page uses.

- *Records*: Includes all the browser events that took place during the execution time. This pane can help you determine the execution time for each event and when it has occurred.

- *Counters*: Includes the count of documents, DOM nodes, and event listeners during execution time. It will only appear when the Memory inner tab is selected.

Figure 11-2 shows a time line recording of `www.google.com`.

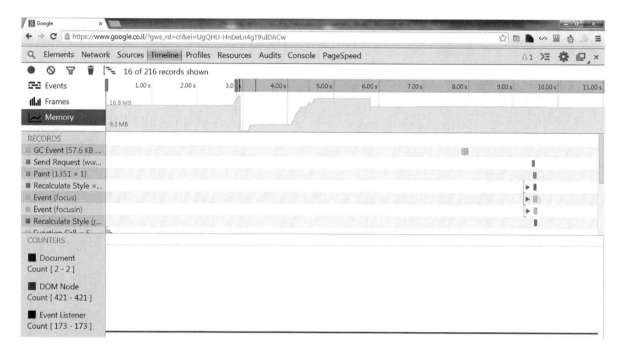

Figure 11-2. *Timeline tab*

Once you want to read the time line, you will use the colors of each event to see what happened. Loading time is marked with blue. Scripting is marked with yellow. If you have a lot of yellow squares, that means you are running a lot of scripts, which might indicate that you are performing a lot of work. The purple color marks the rendering process. A lot of purple squares indicates that you are using a lot of reflows and rendering. The green color marks painting. A lot of green squares indicates that you repaint frequently.

Every time you see too many squares of one color in the time line, you should ask yourself whether you have a performance problem. Too many reflows and too much rendering might indicate that you are making a lot of DOM changes, which might decrease your overall page performance. Too many repaints, which are less expensive than reflows, can also diminish the overall performance of your page. You should find the places where you have too much rendering or painting and figure out whether they can be improved.

Profiles Tab

The Profiles tab is used to profile your web page execution. You choose one of three options and press the Start button to begin the profiling. Then you execute something on your web page and press the Stop button. The following are the three profiling options:

- *Collect JavaScript CPU Profile*: Running this profiler will disclose JavaScript CPU usage. In the report of the profile, you will find the total execution time of JavaScript, and you will be able to drill down to scripts that are executing slowly and consuming a lot of time. You can also find functions that were executed numerous times.

- *Take Heap Snapshot*: You can take heap snapshots and then compare them before and after some function execution. This option can help you see memory distribution.

- *Record Heap Allocation*: You can use the heap allocation profile to find memory leaks in your implementation.

Figure 11-3 shows a Profiles tab, and Figure 11-4 shows an opened profile.

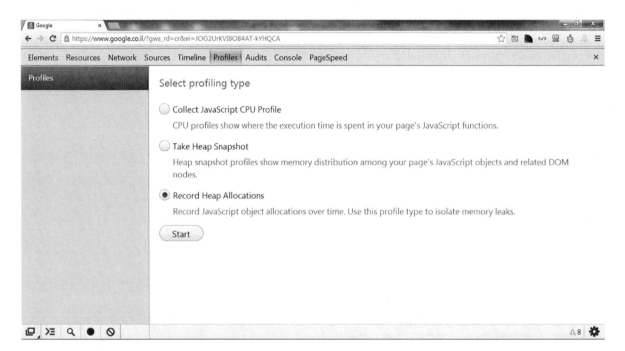

Figure 11-3. Profiles tab

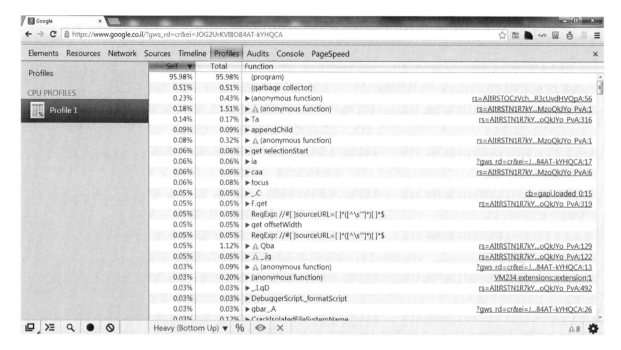

Figure 11-4. *An opened profile*

Once you decide to profile a problem, you will have to take the following steps:

1. Establish a baseline. You will have to record the time line and check if the time it took to execute something was too long. If you suspect that something works slowly, you should take a JavaScript CPU profile. In the profile, you should locate where that function runs slow or where there are too many function executions.

2. Isolate the problem. Once you find a potential slow function, you should try to isolate it in a clean environment and check it again to see if it really runs slowly.

3. Re-factor the implementation and make it faster. When you know that you have a slow function or too many function executions, you can start re-factoring your solution and try to make it run faster.

Repeating this analysis can help you to write faster code.

Static Page Analysis

Apart from the live profiling that is being done using Chrome DevTools, there are also static page-analysis tools, such as PageSpeed and YSlow. The role of static analysis tools is to run the web page and offer suggestions to improve the whole web page performance according to a known set of rules.

Static analysis tools run a set of checks to ensure that the web page follows certain rules. These include:

- Minimize the number of HTTP requests;
- Minimize the number of DOM elements in the web page;
- Use Content Delivery Networks (CDN) for static resources;
- Use compression, such as GZip or Deflate;

- Include style sheet links at the top of the web page;

- Include JavaScript links at the bottom of the web page;

- Include minified JavaScript and CSS files;

- Don't scale images in the HTML;

and many other rules.

All the performed checks are based on good practice, which when used, can decrease the load time of a web page.

There are Chrome extensions for PageSpeed and YSlow that add their support to Chrome. You can download both of the extensions from the Chrome Web Store at `https://chrome.google.com/webstore/category/extensions?hl=en-US`. Once installed, PageSpeed is added as a new tab in Chrome DevTools, and YSlow is added as another dialog.

Once you've installed the extensions, all you have to do is to run when your web page is opened. The static analysis tools will inspect your page and output a list of performance problems that it might include. In Figures 11-5 and 11-6, you can see outputs of running both YSlow and PageSpeed on a web page.

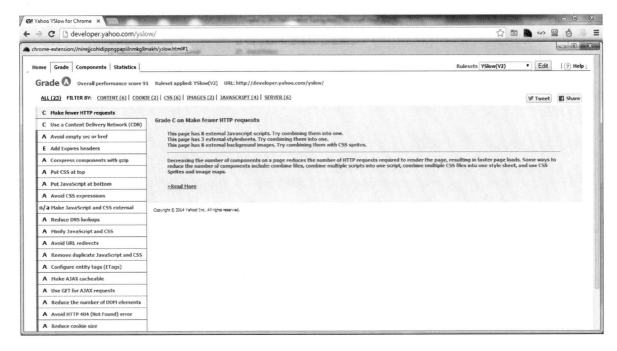

Figure 11-5. *YSlow analysis output*

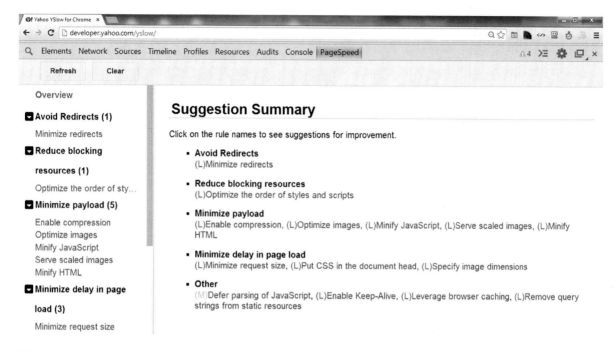

Figure 11-6. *PageSpeed analysis output*

Once you have the output of the static analysis tools, you can start working on improving your web page performance according to the results. After you've fixed the problems, you should run the analysis tools again and check for additional problems.

JavaScript Optimization Tips

A variety of optimizations are available for you to use to increase the efficiency of your JavaScript code and improve your web page performance. The following tips can help you to re-factor and optimize your web pages.

Minimize DOM Changes

DOM changes are the main cause of browser reflows. Making a lot of changes is a classic performance issue that most junior web developers experience. The classic example of a lot of DOM changes can be seen in Listing 11-1.

Listing 11-1. Classic DOM Manipulation Mistake

```
function addElements(element) {
    var div, i;
    for (i = 0; i < 5; i++) {
        div = document.createElement('div');
        div.textContent = 'added';
        element.appendChild(div);
    }
}
```

In the preceding example, you can see that we are creating five divs and appending them to a given element that is part of the DOM. Each iteration of the loop can trigger a reflow, which can negatively impact performance. In order to avoid this problem, you can apply one of the following options:

- *Remove-change-insert*: This optimization allows you to remove an element from the DOM, make changes to that element, and then reinsert the element into the DOM. You use this optimization when you have to make a lot of changes to a DOM element. If you don't have a lot of changes to make to the element, you shouldn't apply this method, and you should use one of the other methods that are explained later. This optimization can help you avoid the triggering of reflows when you make changes. In Listing 11-2, we use the removeAndSave function to remove the element from the DOM and save its parent and next sibling, in order to reattach it to the DOM after all the changes run.

Listing 11-2. Remove-Change-Insert Example

```
function removeAndSave(element) {
        var parentNode = element.parentNode;
        var nextSibling = element.nextSibling;
        parentNode.removeChild(element);
        return function() {
                if (nextSibling) {
                        parentNode.insertBefore(element, nextSibling);
                } else {
                        parentNode.appendChild(element);
                }
        };
}

function addElements(element) {
        var insertElementBack = removeAndSave(element);
        for (i = 0; i < 5; i++) {
                div = document.createElement('div');
                div.textContent = 'added';
                element.appendChild(div);
        }
        insertElementBack();
}
```

- *Hide and show*: This optimization allows you to set a DOM element's display to "none", make changes on that element, and set the element's display back to default. What you gain by using this optimization is repaints instead of reflows. When an element isn't displayed, it is removed from the live DOM by the browser, and changes to it will not cause a reflow. A reflow process is much more costly than a repaint process. Listing 11-3 provides an example of how to use the hide-and-show optimization.

Listing 11-3. Hide-and-Show Example

```
function addElements(element) {
        var div, i, display = element.style.display;
        element.style.display = 'none';
        for (i = 0; i < 5; i++) {
                div = document.createElement('div');
```

```
                    div.textContent = 'added';
                    element.appendChild(div);
            }
            element.style.display = display;
    }
```

- DocumentFragment: You can create a DocumentFragment object, which is an in-memory DOM, and then build the entire DOM that you need to add. Later on, you attach the fragment to the real DOM, and all the changes are applied at once. This optimization can help you to avoid a lot of DOM changes when you insert new DOM elements to your DOM. Listing 11-4 shows how to implement addElements using a DocumentFragment object.

Listing 11-4. Using DocumentFragment Example

```
function addElementsBetter(element) {
        var div,
            fragment = document.createDocumentFragment();

        for (var i = 0; i < 5; i++) {
                div = document.createElement('div');
                div.textContent = 'added';
                fragment.appendChild(div);
        }
        element.appendChild(fragment);
}
```

Use CSS Classes

Another optimization that you can apply is to use CSS classes instead of the element's style property to change styles. Changes in style should be applied using pre-built classes instead of separated styles. Many developers change styles instead of using classes that include a premade style. Using classes instead of adding separate styles can decrease the amount of reflows that you can trigger. For example, you should avoid writing style changes, such as in Listing 11-5.

Listing 11-5. Bad Style Change Example

```
element.style.color = '#fff';
element.style.backgroundColor = '#000';
element.style.width = "100px";
```

Instead of the preceding, create a CSS class, such as in Listing 11-6, and use it as shown in Listing 11-7.

Listing 11-6. CSS Class

```
.myClass {
    color: #fff;
    background-color: #000;
    width: 100px;
}
```

Listing 11-7. Using the Premade CSS Class

```
element.className = 'myClass';
```

Group Changes Together

Another optimization that you can apply is to make changes to the DOM together, instead of one at a time. Browsers include a lot of optimizations in their JavaScript runtime. When you have to make a lot of DOM changes, choose to group them. When a modern browser discovers a group of changes, it might delay the triggering of reflows, and that can help you a great deal in improving your performance.

Other Optimizations That Can Be Used

- *Use HTML5 Web Workers*: You learned about Web Workers in depth in Chapter 4. Web Workers can help you run intensive calculations and algorithms in the background, instead of using the UI thread. Knowing when and how to use Web Workers can affect the performance of your application.

- *Accessing object properties and array items is slower than using variables*: When we program, we tend to use object properties and array items. If you do that frequently, create a variable that will hold the value, instead of accessing the value from the property or array every time.

- *Avoid using unnecessary* try/catch *blocks*: Don't use unnecessary try/catch blocks, because they slow the execution of your JavaScript. This is true of most programming languages.

- *Avoid using* for..in *loops*: for..in loops require more effort from the JavaScript runtime. This is why you should favor for or while loops, which consume fewer runtime resources.

■ **Note**   There are many other ways in which to optimize your JavaScript code, and we could have written a whole book about optimizing code in the front end. We offer here, however, only those options that we consider to be the most effective for improving performance.

Optimizing the Server (Back End and Network)

Optimizing the back-end and network parts of SPA is not an easy task. A web service back end is made up of several components, such as the ASP.NET Web API framework, the IIS hosting environment, and the underlying network connection. Each of those components has its own optimization techniques and a way to monitor and gather performance-related information.

When it comes to performance improvements, we tend to look at two distinct aspects of improvements:

- *Latency*: There are many techniques we can implement to reduce latency, such as improving our code's efficiency, compressing responses, and caching frequently used data. Reducing the latency of the server is twofold: the client-side will receive the response quicker, and the server-side will free up resources faster, making them available to other requests.

- *Load*: Badly performing code, such as code that is not parallelized, or code that does not utilize asynchronous operations (for example, asynchronous database calls), can block running threads, queue up requests, and make your server unavailable, even though your resource consumption, such as CPU, disk, and memory, is low. With proper usage of parallelization and asynchronous work, you can handle more load on the server, increasing and optimizing your resource usage, such as CPU, disk, and memory.

■ **Note**   The two aspects mentioned previously are correlated. For example, you might try to increase the ability of your server to handle load by using more asynchronous processing. This approach will enable your server to handle more requests concurrently but will increase thread context switches and can potentially increase the latency of your requests. The hard part—and beauty—of performance improvement is finding the golden mean between the two.

Tools of the Trade

Before we suggest ways to improve the back end and network performance, we should discuss how to check the performance of your server to determine the parts that need improving.

But how do we define performance improvement? Are we measuring latency—the overall time it takes from sending the request until we receive the response? Throughput—number of requests per second being processed by the server? CPU usage? Memory consumption? Response payload size? There are many parameters we have to take into account, and we must examine how they affect the overall performance of our server.

For example, many server developers in enterprises are accustomed to having their clients and servers connect through a 1GB Ethernet connection, so they pay less attention to the size of the requests and responses and more attention to processing latency, CPU usage, and memory consumption. It is not uncommon to find, in such instances, responses that are over 1MB, something that is usually unacceptable when creating back ends for the Internet.

Next, we will get to know some of the tools commonly used by server developers and provide several tips on how to improve the performance of our server.

Windows Performance Monitor

The Windows Performance Monitor, or perfmon for short (named after its executable), is a built-in tool in Windows that provides live information about the status of components, such as running applications, background services, and installed drivers and hardware, in your Windows operating system.

Perfmon provides counters, which are divided into categories. Each category deals with a specific hardware or software aspect. For hardware, you can find various categories, such as disk operations, memory, CPU, and network. For software, there are categories for specific applications, such as IIS and SQL Server, as well as categories for the .NET Framework itself, the CLR, ASP.NET, and WCF.

When we wish to measure the overall performance of our back end, we often view counters from several categories, for both software and hardware. The following is a list of important categories for web developers and information on their more relevant counters:

- *.NET CLR LocksAndThreads*: With counters such as *# of current logical threads, Contention Rate / sec,* and *Current Queue Length*, you can identify performance issues related to high-thread-context switching, inter-thread locking, and more.

- *.NET CLR Memory*: This category contains counters such as *# Gen 0/1/2 Collections, % Time in GC, Finalization Survivors,* and *Large Object Heap size,* which can help identify performance issues caused by frequent GC collections, high memory consumption, and possible memory leaks.

- *ASP.NET*: This category contains global counters—aggregated counters for all ASP.NET applications running on the server—that show the overall state of ASP.NET. In this category, you will find counters such as *Requests Current, Requests in Native Queue,* and *Requests Rejected.* Request-related counters can assist in verifying that the server is not handling too many requests. In Figure 11-7, we can see request-related performance counters for an IIS web server. By checking the counters, we are able to notice that even when there is a peak in the *Requests Current* counter (number of requests currently executing code), the *Requests in Native Queue* counter (requests being queued by IIS due to excessive load) is very low, meaning there are no queued requests. This is a sign that our server is able to handle the load of requests.

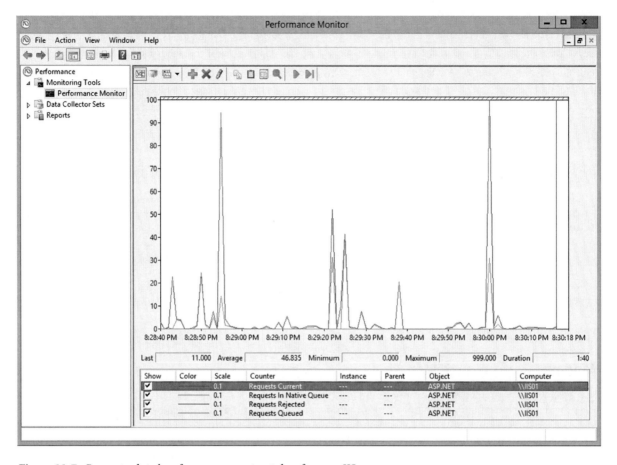

Figure 11-7. *Request-related performance counters taken from an IIS server*

- *ASP.NET Applications*: This category contains counters that are application-specific (you can view the same counter separately for each ASP.NET application). In this category, you will find counters such as *Requests Executing, Requests/sec,* and *Sessions Active,* which provides additional information to the user load and request load in each web application.

- *Process*: Use the *% Processor Time* to measure how CPU-intensive your web application is. If your web application runs unmanaged (native) code, use the *Thread Count* and *Private Bytes* counters, along with the counters from the *.NET CLR Memory* and *.NET CLR LocksAndThreads* categories. This will provide more details on which part, managed or unmanaged, contributes the most to the high number of threads and large memory consumption.

■ **Note**   The counters listed above are often checked when using perfmon to monitor an ASP.NET application. In addition to those counters, you might want to check other counters that may affect your server performance, such as disk operations, virtual memory usage, and database-related counters.

Network Traffic Monitors

Monitoring the HTTP traffic between the browser and the server can help us identify issues at different levels of the communication stack, from frequent closing and reopening of TCP connections to not using HTTP caching headers.

▮ **Note** You will usually run traffic-monitoring tools on the client side, to easily diagnose each request and response. Monitoring traffic on the server is quite difficult, due to the amount of incoming and outgoing data.

There are many tools that can assist us in monitoring traffic. Some, such as Microsoft's Network Monitor and Wireshark, provide in-depth monitoring all the way down to the TCP packet level, as shown in Figure 11-8.

Figure 11-8. *Viewing an image response message in Wireshark*

Other tools, such as Telerik's Fiddler, provide a more HTTP-oriented traffic monitoring. For example, Fiddler provides a breakdown of HTTP headers, such as caching and authentication, and explains the meaning of their content. Fiddler also provides inspectors (viewers) that display the content of the HTTP message body according to its MIME type, so you can view a JSON request as a hierarchical object graph or even see the image that was returned from the server, as shown in Figure 11-9.

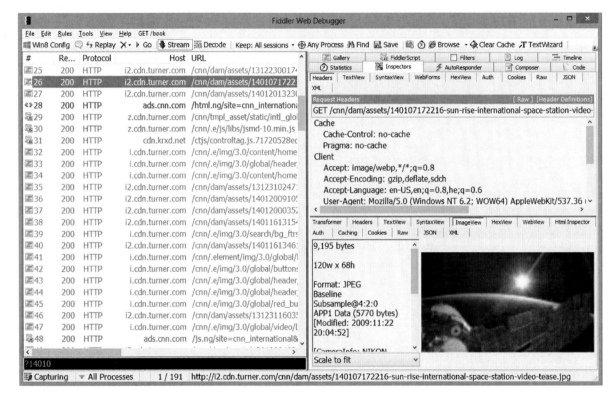

Figure 11-9. *Viewing a response containing an image in Fiddler*

By using network monitoring tools, we can detect issues in the browser, such as latencies when sending requests to the server; issues in the server, such as server responses missing their caching headers; and issues in the underlying network, such as faulty networks causing high-latency due to TCP connections being closed frequently.

IIS Failed Request Tracing

IIS's Failed Request Tracing feature provides developers and IT pros with a way to diagnose faulty requests and responses.

Every module and handler in the IIS pipeline is capable of writing trace information, such as an indication when the component—module or handler—started and exited, status of work, such as succeeded or failed, and any other debug message. For example, the URL Rewrite module writes trace messages for every rewrite rule, indicating if the rule matched the request or not.

However, those trace messages are not written to disk by default, unless you turn on Failed Request Tracing, as shown in Figure 11-10, and configure which requests you want to trace and which trace messages—based on origin and severity—you wish to log, as shown in Figure 11-11.

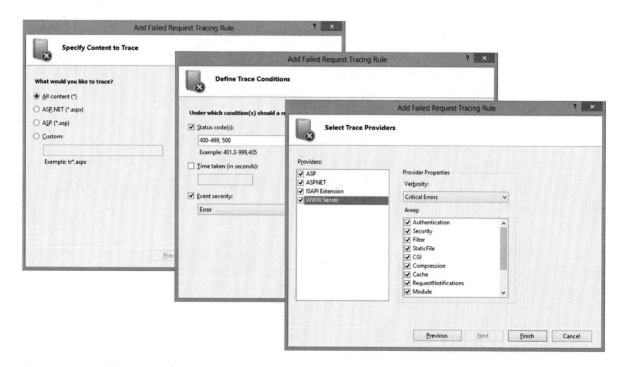

Figure 11-10. *Turning on Failed Request Tracing for an IIS web site*

Figure 11-11. *Adding a Failed Request Tracing rule*

■ **Note**   A better name for this feature would have been *Faulty Request Tracing*, as it also traces requests that completed with a successful status code, but behaved suspiciously. For example, we can configure a rule to store all requests that take more than ten seconds to process, whether they end successfully or fail. Such requests are not necessarily failed requests; however, they do indicate an issue with our code, because this long execution time is irregular.

After you configure the tracing rules for your web application, a trace file will be created whenever a request matches a trace rule. The trace files are stored separately for each web site, in the directory you have set when you turned on the Failed Request Tracing feature, as shown previously in Figure 11-10.

The trace files are XML-based and are best viewed by being opened in Internet Explorer, as it uses a local XSL (XML style sheet) file to format the XML into a human-readable (or at the least, "someone who knows a thing or two about IIS and ASP.NET"-readable), as shown in Figure 11-12.

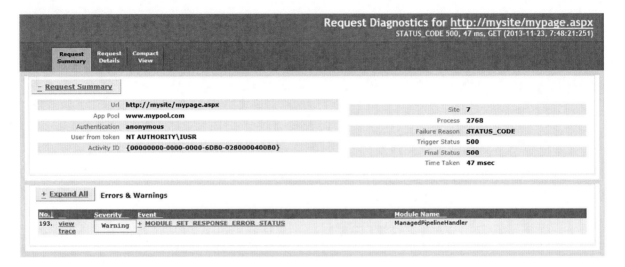

Figure 11-12. A trace file's request summary, viewed in Internet Explorer

You can switch between the tabs to get different views of the processing pipeline. The **Request Summary** tab will only show basic information about the request and response, as well as any warning or error messages that were traced. The other two tabs, **Request Details** and **Compact View**, will show the entire list of invoked modules and handlers and the trace message each of them outputted.

■ **Note**   The *freb.xsl* style sheet file that is used to display the XML in a readable form is located in the trace directory. If you are not careful, you might end up deleting that file while cleaning up the trace directory. If you accidentally delete the file, you can copy it from any computer running IIS 7 and later.

By inspecting trace files, you can collect valuable information that can assist you in pinpointing the cause of faulty requests. Here are some examples of information you can find in trace files:

- Request headers and content of responses
- Time it took for each component to execute (inclusive and exclusive)
- Detailed sub-status codes for general HTTP status, such as for 400 (Bad Request), 401 (Unauthorized), and 403 (Forbidden)
- Exception and debug messages outputted by the various modules and handlers

You can also write your own messages to the trace file, either informative, errors, or debug messages, to assist you in diagnosing your code. To write trace messages from C#, create a new `TraceSource` object and use its `TraceEvent` method, as shown in Listing 11-8.

Listing 11-8. Writing a Trace Message

```
var traceSource = new System.Diagnostics.TraceSource("myTrace");
traceSource.TraceEvent(System.Diagnostics.TraceEventType.Information, 0, "You've reached my code");
```

To get the trace message written to the trace file, you have to connect your trace source to the IIS trace listener. To do that, add the following configuration (Listing 11-9) to your Web.config file:

Listing 11-9. Outputting Custom Traces to the IIS Trace File

```
<system.diagnostics>
    <sharedListeners>
      <add name="IisTraceListener" type="System.Web.IisTraceListener, System.Web, Version=4.0.0.0,
Culture=neutral, PublicKeyToken=b03f5f7f11d50a3a" />
    </sharedListeners>
    <switches>
      <add name="DefaultSwitch" value="All" />
    </switches>
    <sources>
      <source name="myTrace" switchName="DefaultSwitch">
        <listeners>
          <add name="IisTraceListener" />
        </listeners>
      </source>
    </sources>
</system.diagnostics>
```

Figure 11-13 depicts how custom trace messages are shown when viewing the trace file. In the trace shown in the following screenshot, the code that generated the messages belongs to a custom module named TraceRequests. SampleModule. Messages 16 and 19 were outputted by ASP.NET, when activating the custom module, and messages 17 and 18 are custom messages written from the module's code, using the TraceSource.TraceEvent method. If you check the Time column, you will notice that several seconds have passed from when the custom module emitted message 17 to when message 18 was emitted, which could indicate that the code is blocked for some reason.

	Request Summary	Request Details	Compact View

No.	EventName	Details	Time
1.	NOTIFY_MODULE_END	ModuleName="FailedRequestsTracingModule", Notification="BEGIN_REQUEST", fIsPostNotificationEvent="false", NotificationStatus="NOTIFICATION_CONTINUE"	09:11:51.239
2.	NOTIFY_MODULE_START	ModuleName="ConfigurationValidationModule", Notification="BEGIN_REQUEST", fIsPostNotification="false"	09:11:51.239
3.	NOTIFY_MODULE_END	ModuleName="ConfigurationValidationModule", Notification="BEGIN_REQUEST", fIsPostNotificationEvent="false", NotificationStatus="NOTIFICATION_CONTINUE"	09:11:51.239
4.	NOTIFY_MODULE_START	ModuleName="ApplicationInitializationModule", Notification="BEGIN_REQUEST", fIsPostNotification="false"	09:11:51.239
5.	NOTIFY_MODULE_END	ModuleName="ApplicationInitializationModule", Notification="BEGIN_REQUEST", fIsPostNotificationEvent="false", NotificationStatus="NOTIFICATION_CONTINUE"	09:11:51.239
6.	NOTIFY_MODULE_START	ModuleName="WebSocketModule", Notification="BEGIN_REQUEST", fIsPostNotification="false"	09:11:51.239
7.	NOTIFY_MODULE_END	ModuleName="WebSocketModule", Notification="BEGIN_REQUEST", fIsPostNotificationEvent="false", NotificationStatus="NOTIFICATION_CONTINUE"	09:11:51.239
8.	NOTIFY_MODULE_START	ModuleName="RewriteModule", Notification="BEGIN_REQUEST", fIsPostNotification="false"	09:11:51.239
9.	NOTIFY_MODULE_END	ModuleName="RewriteModule", Notification="BEGIN_REQUEST", fIsPostNotificationEvent="false", NotificationStatus="NOTIFICATION_CONTINUE"	09:11:51.239
10.	NOTIFY_MODULE_START	ModuleName="SampleModule", Notification="BEGIN_REQUEST", fIsPostNotification="false"	09:11:51.239
11.	AspNetStart	Data1="GET", Data2="/TraceRequests/default.aspx", Data3=""	09:11:51.239
12.	AspNetAppDomainEnter	Data1="/LM/W3SVC/1/ROOT/TraceRequests-1-130343371059976930"	09:11:51.239
13.	NOTIFY_MODULE_START	ModuleName="IsapiFilterModule", Notification="MAP_PATH", fIsPostNotification="false"	09:11:51.239
14.	NOTIFY_MODULE_END	ModuleName="IsapiFilterModule", Notification="MAP_PATH", fIsPostNotificationEvent="false", NotificationStatus="NOTIFICATION_CONTINUE"	09:11:51.239
15.	AspNetStartHandler	Data1="ASP.global_asax", Data2="Start"	09:11:51.239
16.	AspNetPipelineEnter	Data1="TraceRequests.SampleModule"	09:11:51.254
17.	AspNetModuleDiagStartEvent	Uri="/TraceRequests/default.aspx", eventData="Sample module is handling BeginRequest, starting sleep"	09:11:51.254
18.	AspNetModuleDiagStartEvent	Uri="/TraceRequests/default.aspx", eventData="Sample module is handling BeginRequest, ending sleep"	09:11:55.217
19.	AspNetPipelineLeave	Data1="TraceRequests.SampleModule"	09:11:55.217
20.	NOTIFY_MODULE_END	ModuleName="SampleModule", Notification="BEGIN_REQUEST", fIsPostNotificationEvent="false", NotificationStatus="NOTIFICATION_CONTINUE"	09:11:55.217
21.	NOTIFY_MODULE_START	ModuleName="__DynamicModule_Microsoft.VisualStudio.Web.PageInspector.Runtime.Tracing.SelectionMappingExecutionListenerModule, Microsoft.VisualStudio.Web.PageInspector.Runtime, Version=1.3.0.0, Culture=neutral, PublicKeyToken=b03f5f7f11d50a3a_d5b9cc73-6598-43b2-bf05-440a248c3432", Notification="BEGIN_REQUEST", fIsPostNotification="false"	09:11:55.217
22.	AspNetPipelineEnter	Data1="Microsoft.VisualStudio.Web.PageInspector.Runtime.Tracing.SelectionMappingExecutionListenerModule"	09:11:55.217
23.	AspNetPipelineLeave	Data1="Microsoft.VisualStudio.Web.PageInspector.Runtime.Tracing.SelectionMappingExecutionListenerModule"	09:11:55.217
24.	NOTIFY_MODULE_END	ModuleName="__DynamicModule_Microsoft.VisualStudio.Web.PageInspector.Runtime.Tracing.SelectionMappingExecutionListenerModule, Microsoft.VisualStudio.Web.PageInspector.Runtime, Version=1.3.0.0, Culture=neutral, PublicKeyToken=b03f5f7f11d50a3a_d5b9cc73-6598-43b2-bf05-440a248c3432", Notification="BEGI...	09:11:55.217

Figure 11-13. *Trace file content using Compact View*

■ **Note** For a complete sample of adding IIS trace support to your code, refer to the following link:

www.iis.net/learn/develop/runtime-extensibility/how-to-add-tracing-to-iis-managed-modules.

Failed Request Tracing is a useful tool for diagnosing faulty requests and responses. However, creating many large trace files has its toll on the overall performance of your server. Therefore, you should use it only when needed and refrain from turning it on by default, especially in production environments.

Code Profilers

If execution time is an issue in your application, IIS Failed Request Tracing will tell you which part of the pipeline is to blame. But let's face it, in 99.99% of cases, the blame will be on us, since it will be our code that causes the latency, not IIS or ASP.NET.

If you have to check a specific part of your code—to find the root cause of the latency—you can simply add a Stopwatch check before and after each line of code. Outputting the elapsed time for each line of code will enable you to pinpoint the origin of the latency.

But what would you do if you had to diagnose more than one method? What if your method calls several other methods? And each of them calls another set of methods? And what if the latency is in more than one type of request? Adding Stopwatch measurements to your entire code and gathering all the execution information is time-consuming, not to mention that you must remove it after you finish debugging the code. (Managing your code with source-control tools can be helpful for this part, as you can easily undo your changes.)

This is where code profilers come in. *Code profilers* is a general term for any tool that measures the metrics of your system and your code for the purpose of improving the overall performance of your application. There are various types of code profiles, each with its own profiling technique and type of conclusions.

Time Profilers

The purpose of time profilers is to measure the execution time of your code and to provide you with a list of the most costly methods, with regard to execution time. There are various ways to measure execution time, some more intrusive than others.

For example, line-by-line profiles, also referred to as instrumentation profilers, will add checkpoints between each line in your original code, allowing the profiler to gather an accurate execution time of your methods and information on how many times each method was invoked, as shown in Figure 11-14. Instrumentation profilers will recompile your code and will have a negative effect on your application's performance. However, the information you will gain from them will be very accurate.

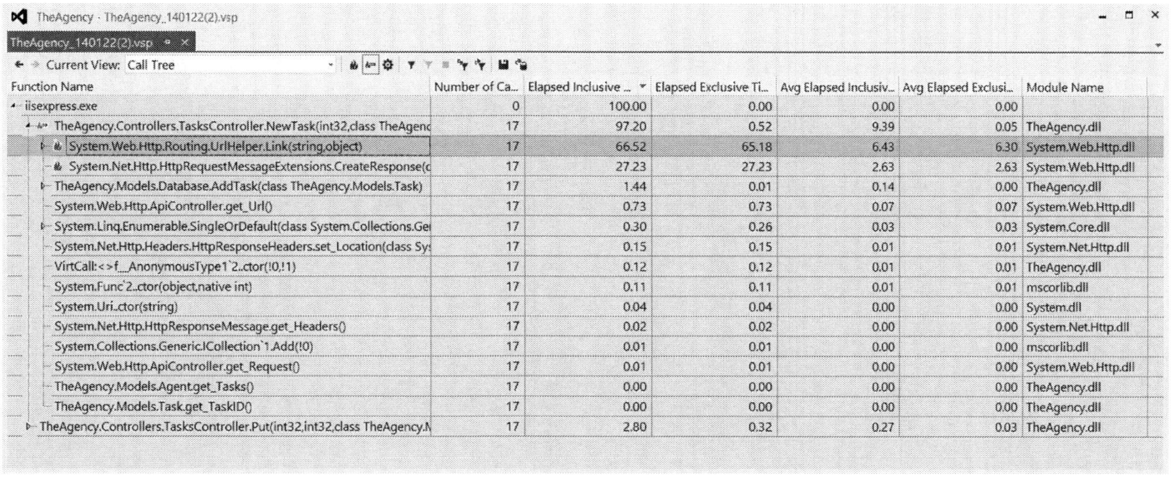

Function Name	Number of Ca...	Elapsed Inclusive ...	Elapsed Exclusive Ti...	Avg Elapsed Inclusiv...	Avg Elapsed Exclusi...	Module Name
iisexpress.exe	0	100.00	0.00	0.00	0.00	
TheAgency.Controllers.TasksController.NewTask(int32,class TheAgenc	17	97.20	0.52	9.39	0.05	TheAgency.dll
System.Web.Http.Routing.UrlHelper.Link(string,object)	17	66.52	65.18	6.43	6.30	System.Web.Http.dll
System.Net.Http.HttpRequestMessageExtensions.CreateResponse(c	17	27.23	27.23	2.63	2.63	System.Web.Http.dll
TheAgency.Models.Database.AddTask(class TheAgency.Models.Task)	17	1.44	0.01	0.14	0.00	TheAgency.dll
System.Web.Http.ApiController.get_Url()	17	0.73	0.73	0.07	0.07	System.Web.Http.dll
System.Linq.Enumerable.SingleOrDefault(class System.Collections.Ge	17	0.30	0.26	0.03	0.03	System.Core.dll
System.Net.Http.Headers.HttpResponseHeaders.set_Location(class Sy	17	0.15	0.15	0.01	0.01	System.Net.Http.dll
VirtCall:<>f__AnonymousType1`2..ctor(!0,!1)	17	0.12	0.12	0.01	0.01	TheAgency.dll
System.Func`2..ctor(object,native int)	17	0.11	0.11	0.01	0.01	mscorlib.dll
System.Uri..ctor(string)	17	0.04	0.04	0.00	0.00	System.dll
System.Net.Http.HttpResponseMessage.get_Headers()	17	0.02	0.02	0.00	0.00	System.Net.Http.dll
System.Collections.Generic.ICollection`1.Add(!0)	17	0.01	0.01	0.00	0.00	mscorlib.dll
System.Web.Http.ApiController.get_Request()	17	0.01	0.01	0.00	0.00	System.Web.Http.dll
TheAgency.Models.Agent.get_Tasks()	17	0.00	0.00	0.00	0.00	TheAgency.dll
TheAgency.Models.Task.get_TaskID()	17	0.00	0.00	0.00	0.00	TheAgency.dll
TheAgency.Controllers.TasksController.Put(int32,int32,class TheAgency.N	17	2.80	0.32	0.27	0.03	TheAgency.dll

Figure 11-14. *Expensive calls shown in Visual Studio's instrumentation profiler*

You can also switch to the code where the profiler detected the expensive (time-consuming) call, as shown in Figure 11-15.

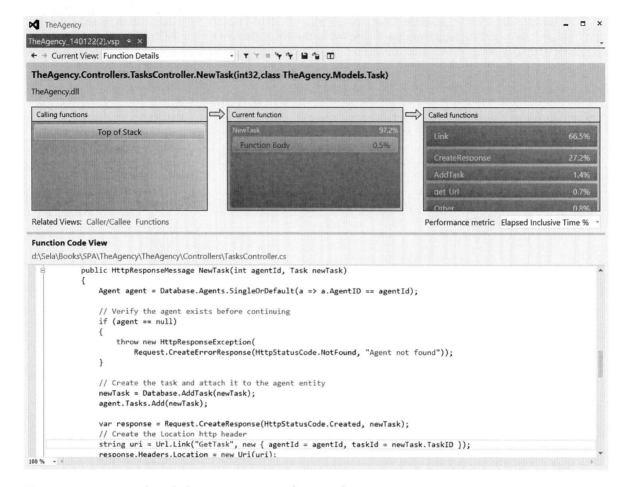

Figure 11-15. *Viewing the code that is most expensive (time-wise)*

Other, less intrusive profilers can, instead, sample your code a couple of times a second, take a snapshot of the call stack in each of your application's running threads, and provide you with a list of methods that were sampled most often. Such profilers, commonly named sampling profilers, are considered nonintrusive, because they do not change your code—you can grab the call stack from a .NET application without adding special code to it—and usually have less effect on execution time than instrumentation profilers.

■ **Note**   As a best practice, you should start by running a sampling profiler, and after understanding which parts of the applications are at fault, use a more intrusive profiler to get a detailed list of which method is doing most of the work.

Memory Profilers

Methods that take a lot of time to execute make up one issue that affects performance; however, this is not the only issue. Another is excessive memory use. For example, after your code handles a request, the objects allocated within that code are eligible for collection—as long as they are no longer referenced. If your code allocates a large set of objects and is called frequently owing to high server load, the Garbage Collector (GC) will run frequently, consume more CPU, and freeze up your executing requests, which will lower your application's overall performance.

■ **Note** In ASP.NET, the GC uses the GC Server flavor. When using this GC flavor, the GC runs on multiple threads, one for each core. When a collection occurs, all the GC threads run at once and suspend all other managed threads. From the outside, this often appears to be an unpredictable, brief latency in server response time. You can read more about server GC on MSDN at `http://msdn.microsoft.com/library/ee787088.aspx`.

Memory profilers, sometimes referred to as allocation profilers, are specialized profilers directed at monitoring memory allocations in your application. Using memory profilers, you can get information on how many objects and how much memory a method allocates, how frequently the GC runs, and which objects are not getting released and why.

Figures 11-16 to 11-20 depict a profiling session in which we used a memory profiler (in this case, RedGate's ANTS memory profiler) to profile our SPA back end. After starting the profiler and loading the application, we performed several actions in the application and took a memory snapshot every couple of seconds.

Figure 11-16 shows the difference between the memory snapshot taken when we started the application and the snapshot taken after several minutes of work. You can see an increase in the number of allocated objects and in the total memory size of the application.

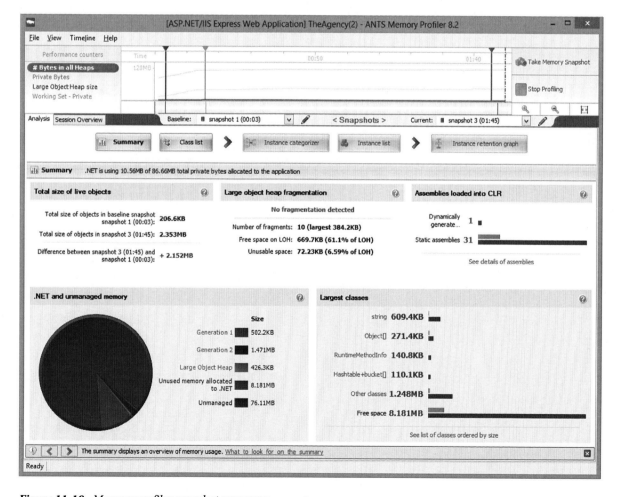

***Figure 11-16.** Memory profiler snapshot summary*

We will start to investigate by switching to the class list, as shown in Figure 11-17. We can see that the objects that take the most memory are `string` objects.

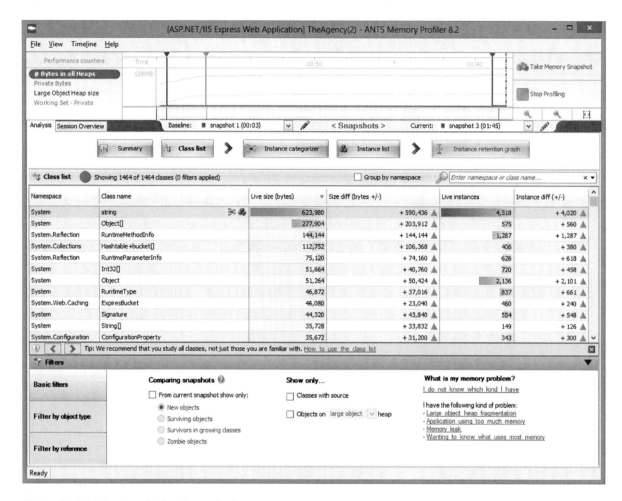

Figure 11-17. *Viewing which objects take the most memory*

This is not surprising, as strings are referenced by many other objects in our application. For example, an Agent object holds the agent's code name first name, surname, description, and image path. If we open the list of string objects, we can see their values, as shown in Figure 11-18. Many of those strings are referenced by the CLR and ASP.NET, so tracking their origin would probably lead us nowhere.

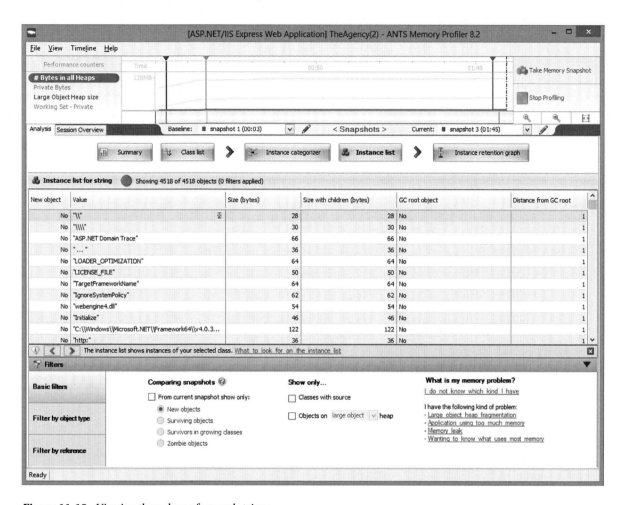

Figure 11-18. *Viewing the values of several strings*

Instead, we'll return to the class list, and look for class types that we know are used in our code. Those types could be cache entries, datasets, and even our domain entities. Figure 11-19 shows the same class list, only this time, the focus is on our domain objects.

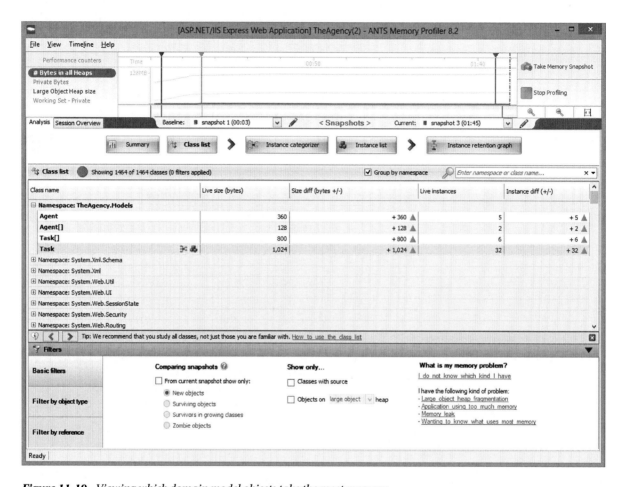

Figure 11-19. *Viewing which domain model objects take the most memory*

We can see now that 32 Task objects were created from the time the application started and are still residing in memory. Opening the Task object's list and picking one of them will show the reference graph for the selected object. All we need now is to follow the references back to the rooted objects that hold a reference to that specific task, as shown in Figure 11-20.

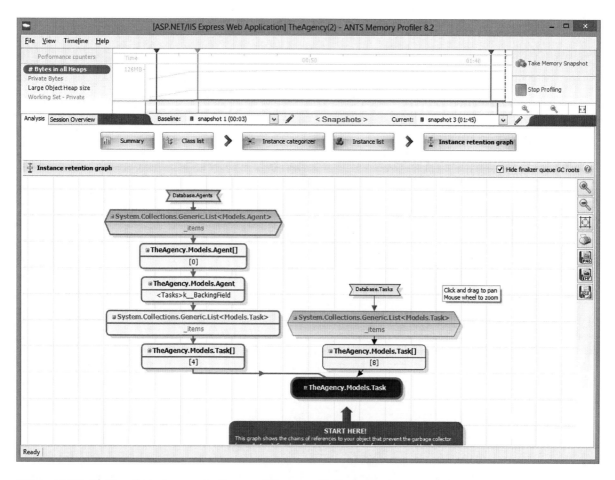

Figure 11-20. *Plotting the instance-retention graph for a specific Task object*

■ **Note** The number and size of the Task objects shown in the screenshot are quite small and usually won't be the target of our attention when analyzing a memory snapshot. When profiling real-world applications, it is not that rare to find tens of thousands of objects created in a code, either directly or indirectly, with total sizes that accumulate to hundreds of megabytes.

We can now track the reference to the Task object back to a list of tasks, which is referenced by an Agent object (the agent's tasks). The Agent object itself is referenced from a list of agents, and that list is referenced by a rooted object, which is the static field Database.Agents. Inspecting the code reveals that the static field stores all of our agents in-memory, instead of in a database. It makes perfect sense, then, that we will see so many Agent and Task objects. This is an example of a common mistake with developers, who tend to store a lot of entities in-memory, such as in the ASP.NET cache, or in privately held static members.

By using memory profilers, we can optimize our code to release references when needed, prevent memory leaks, reduce the number of generation 1 and 2 collections by the GC, and lower our application's memory footprint.

In addition to the timing and memory profilers, which are the most common code profilers that developers use, there are additional profilers, aimed at collecting and analyzing other aspects of our application, such as I/O, database, and thread-context switching.

■ **Note**   If you want to learn more about code profilers and how to optimize your .NET code for better performance, consider reading the book *Pro .NET Performance*, by Sasha Goldshtein, Dima Zurbalev, and Ido Flatow (Apress, 2012).

There are many code-profiling tools on the market, and most of them offer more than one type of profiler. Among the well-known profilers are Microsoft's Visual Studio profilers, RedGate's ANTS profilers, JetBrains's' dotTRACE profilers, and Telerik's JustTrace.

By properly utilizing the tools of the trade, you can learn a lot about the way your server works and apply best practices to improve the overall performance of your SPA back end.

Optimization Tips

Reducing the Number of Requests

When a page loads, additional requests are sent over the network to fetch additional resources, such as CSS, JavaScript, and image files. The more requests your browser sends, the longer it will take for the page to load completely. The waiting time involves two main factors: the time it takes for a request to reach the server, and the limit browsers have on the number of concurrently executing requests (usually about 8–12 concurrent requests per server address, depending on the browser, its version, and whether you are using a proxy server). Therefore, the more links you have on your page, the longer it will take for the browser to load it.

■ **Note**   The maximum number of concurrent requests is per hostname. For example, if all your linked resources (scripts, CSS, images, etc.) are fetched from a single hostname, you will be limited to X concurrent requests. However, if you split the files between two different hostnames, for example, by using two different DNS addresses for your CDN, you will be able to send $2*X$ requests concurrently. This trick should be considered as a workaround, because it does not solve the latency involved in server round-trips.

With the help of traffic-monitoring tools, and IIS logs and performance counters, you can identify the number of requests generated by your page, check how many concurrent requests your web browser can run, and apply best practices to reduce the number of requests.

Bundling

If we have to fetch several CSS files for our page, why not simply bundle all the CSS definitions in the same file? This way, we can reduce the round-trips by having only one request, instead of multiple requests. The concept of bundling works for both CSS and JavaScript files and is supported by ASP.NET 4.5.

To bundle a set of script files in ASP.NET, add the **Microsoft ASP.NET Web Optimization Framework** NuGet package to your web application project, in addition to the code shown in Listing 11-10, to the Application_Start method in your global.asax file.

Listing 11-10. Creating a Script Bundle

```
using System.Web.Optimization;

protected void Application_Start()
{
    Bundle myScriptsBundle = new ScriptBundle("~/bundles/MyScripts").Include(
        "~/Scripts/myCustomJsFunctions.js",
        "~/Scripts/thirdPartyFunctions.js",
        "~/Scripts/myNewJsTypes.js");

    BundleTable.Bundles.Add(myScriptsBundle);
    BundleTable.EnableOptimizations = true;
}
```

■ **Note**   By default, ASP.NET will bundle the files only when the web application's compilation mode is set to release. To enable bundling even when in debug mode, we set the EnableOptimizations property to true.

To use the bundle in your web page, add the code shown in Listing 11-11 to your page, where you want to create the <script> tag.

Listing 11-11. Adding a <script> Tag to a Bundle (Razor Syntax)

```
@Scripts.Render("~/bundles/MyScripts")
```

Just as you would use the ScriptBundle class to bundle script files, you can use the StyleBundle class to bundle CSS files. On the web page, use the Styles.Render static method to generate a <link> tag for the bundled CSS.

■ **Note**   The total size of the bundled response will be roughly the same as the combined size of all the individual responses, minus the size of the HTTP headers (a reduction that can be significant on its own). Shortly, we'll present some tips on handling large responses.

CSS Image Sprites

CSS sprites refer to the technique of bundling several images into a single image file, as shown in Figure 11-21. Just as with bundling, the purpose of CSS sprites is to reduce the number of round-trips that are needed to retrieve all of the site's images.

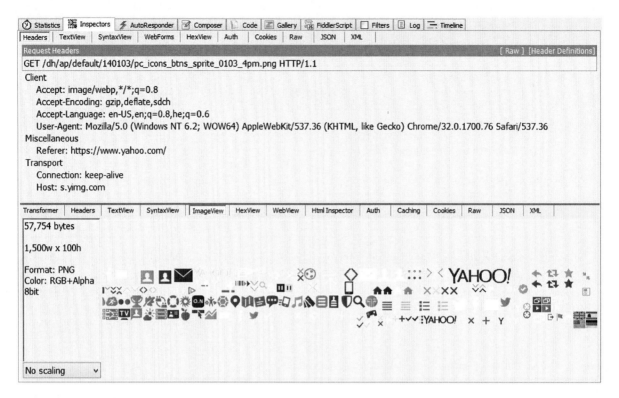

Figure 11-21. CSS sprite response containing all of Yahoo!'s icons

However, unlike with CSS and JavaScript, you cannot just combine all of your images to a single, large image without changing your HTML. Without sprites, each tag that shows an image is set to its specific image file, using the `background-image` CSS property. With sprites, it is not enough to point all the tags to the same file, because then all the tags will show the same image. We need each tag to show a specific area from the sprite. To achieve this, we use the `background-position` CSS property and specify the X and Y offsets in the sprite, as shown in Listing 11-12. The result can be seen in Figure 11-22.

Listing 11-12. Pointing to a Specific Icon in a CSS Sprite

```
.img-sprite {
background-image: url(https://s.yimg.com/dh/ap/default/140103/pc_icons_btns_sprite_0103_4pm.png);
}
#nav-mail {
background-position: -43px -66px;
}
```

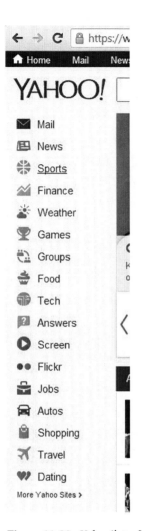

Figure 11-22. Yahoo!'s toolbar. Each icon was taken from a specific position in the sprite

---

■ **Note**   There are many web sites that create CSS sprites from a given set of images, for example, http://spritegen.website-performance.org. In addition to the generated image, most sprite generators will provide a matching CSS file containing the X and Y positions of each icon in the sprite.

Embedding Images in CSS

Although CSS sprites is a useful technique to reduce the number of requests, the maintenance of sprites, such as replacing an image, or changing the size of images, can be quite tedious.

Image embedding is a different technique for reducing the number of image requests. To embed an image in the CSS, we transform its image to a base64 string, and then place the string, using the Data URI syntax, directly in the CSS file. The result is shown in Listing 11-13.

Listing 11-13. Embedding an Image in the CSS File as a Data URI (The base64 String Was Shortened for Brevity)

```
.navIcon {
  background-repeat: no-repeat;
  background-image: url(data:image/png;base64,iVBORwOK..........8yY5cn1HLV9/d3yQv//oB/hKBKe/GD4VPySL5RJkmY5
//7JHZK1/4vgVFVTDcbu+0AAAAASUVORK5CYII=);
}
```

■ **Note**   As for CSS sprites, you can find many web sites that convert images to base64 strings, such as
`www.base64-image.de`. You can also use Fiddler to create Data URI strings from images: locate the image you want to
convert in the session list, switch to the "ImageView" inspector, right-click the image, and then click "Copy as DataURI."

There is, however, a downside to using Data URIs, as the base64 format usually generates a string that is larger
in size than the original image size. You will have to verify the cost-benefit of reducing the number of requests, in
comparison to increasing the size of the response.

Reducing the Size of Responses

The bigger your response is, the longer it will take to reach the client. By checking the size of responses, you can
identify problematic requests and responses and apply best practices to reduce the size of the response body.

Minification

When we create content, such as HTML, JavaScript, and CSS, we tend to indent the content and add line breaks to
make it more readable. With JavaScript code, we also tend to give meaningful, long names to variables and functions,
so it will be easier for us to maintain the code later on.

Minification is the process of changing the contents of HTML, JavaScript, and CSS files for the purpose of reducing
the size of the file, without changing the ability of the browser to use the file just as before. For HTML, JavaScript, and
CSS, minification mostly removes whitespaces and comments, as demonstrated in Listing 11-14 and Listing 11-15.

Listing 11-14. CSS Content Before Minification

```
html {
    background-color: #e2e2e2;
    margin: 0;
    padding: 0;
}

body {
    background-color: #fff;
    border-top: solid 10px #000;
    color: #333;
    font-size: .85em;
    font-family: "Segoe UI", Verdana, Helvetica, Sans-Serif;
    margin: 0;
    padding: 0;
}
```

Listing 11-15. CSS Content After Minification

```
html{background-color:#e2e2e2;margin:0;padding:0}body{background-color:#fff;border-top:
solid 10px #000;color:#333;font-size:.85em;font-family:"Segoe UI",Verdana,Helvetica,
Sans-Serif;margin:0;padding:0}
```

For JavaScript files, the minification process also shortens the names of variables and functions, as demonstrated in Listing 11-16.

Listing 11-16. Example of Minified Content from the jQuery Library

```
(function(a,b){function G(a){var b=F[a]={};return p.each(a.split(s),function(a,c){b[c]=!0}),b}
function J(a,c,d){if(d===b&&a.nodeType===1)...
```

If you are wondering how much smaller the response can get by being minified, following are some examples to give you a ballpark estimate:

- The jQuery library v1.8.2 is 262KB in size. Its minified version is only 93KB in size, reducing the size of the response by 65%.

- The eBay homepage HTML is 174KB, of which 19.3% is whitespace.

- jQuery UI's CSS file is 31KB. The minified version of the CSS is only 25KB, 20% less than the non-minified file.

■ **Note** The jQuery library, as are many other libraries, ships with both a minified version of the script and a non-minified script. The non-minified version is mostly intended for debugging and educational purposes.

If you are using ASP.NET Web Forms or MVC to build your SPA web pages, you can add the minified versions of your CSS and JavaScript files to your project and use the bundling feature. The bundling feature, which was introduced earlier, supports the bundling of normal versions of files when in debug mode and the minified version of files when running in release mode. For more information on controlling the minification and bundling in ASP.NET, refer to the ASP.NET web site at `www.asp.net/mvc/tutorials/mvc-4/bundling-and-minification`.

In addition to ASP.NET minification and bundling, you can find other tools that provide the same base functionality, with additional capabilities. For example, **Grunt** (`http://gruntjs.com`) and **Gulp** (`http://gulpjs.com`) are automation tools capable of performing many optimization tasks, such as minification, bundling, linting (checking JavaScript code for bad practices), and CSS sprite creation. You can use those tools in your build process, to perform the various optimization tasks, after successfully compiling your back end, or call them manually, whenever you have new content you want to optimize.

■ **Note** Both Grunt and Gulp are written in Node.js and require installing the Node.js framework prior to using them.

There are many web sites that offer minification services for HTML, CSS, and JavaScript, such as `http://cssminifier.com`, `http://jscompress.com`, and `www.willpeavy.com/minifier` (for minifying HTML pages).

HTTP Response Compression

If minification hasn't convinced you that you can easily reduce the size of responses, perhaps the following figures will. As mentioned, the size of the minified jQuery library v1.8.2 is 93KB. If we apply HTTP compression to our web server, that same minified file will now be only 34KB. By minifying and compressing the script file, we've managed to reduce its size by 87 percent.

If you are hosting your back end on IIS, there are two types of compressions that you can use.

- *Static compression*: Static compression is applied to static files, such as CSS, HTML, and JavaScript files. With static compression, files are compressed when requested for the first time, and the compressed content is then stored locally in the disk. Subsequent requests to the same resources will return the compressed content instead of recompressing it.

- *Dynamic compression*: When turned on, dynamically created content, such as the result of rendering an HTML page in ASP.NET MVC, or a JSON response from ASP.NET Web API, will be compressed before being sent to the client. Dynamically compressed content is not stored on disk, because it may change frequently.

To use static and dynamic compression, make sure you install the *Static Compression* and *Dynamic Compression* modules in IIS. After you install both modules, verify that your content types (MIME types) are registered in the appropriate compression module. The process of installing the compression modules and adding MIME type is well-documented at the IIS learning web site at `www.iis.net/configreference/system.webserver/httpcompression`.

■ **Note**   IIS does not support dynamic compression of JSON responses by default. With SPA, we usually create JSON-based back ends, so it is advisable that you add support for JSON compression, by adding the `application/json` MIME type to the dynamic types list.

Optimizing Images

Web servers do not compress images, as most image formats, such as JPEG and PNG, are already compressed. There are, however, several other ways to make your images smaller in size.

- *Scale down images files to their viewable size*: If you show an image in a 50 × 50 area, make sure your downloaded image isn't bigger than those dimensions. For example, if a 200 × 200 image is 39KB, scaling it down to 50 × 50 can reduce its size to 8KB—an 80 percent reduction in size.

- *Remove excessive metadata*: Some photo-editing software tends to add large metadata blocks to the image file. That metadata is usually less relevant in the context of a web site, and removing it will reduce the size of the image. Figure 11-23 shows the same image, before and after removing its metadata. Removing the metadata reduced the payload by 25 percent—from 115KB to 87KB.

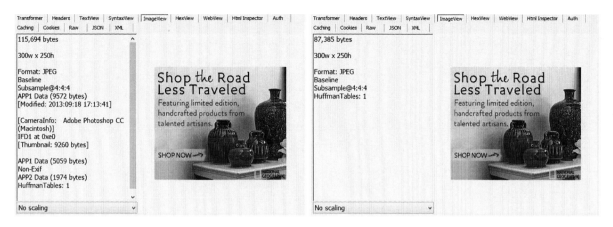

Figure 11-23. *Image with and without metadata (original image taken from the National Geographic web site)*

■ **Note** Some network monitoring tools, such as Fiddler and Wireshark, are capable of showing information about image responses. Fiddler, for example, can show the image's dimensions, as well as its metadata content.

- *Do not use expensive image formats*: There are image formats that are great for publishing and printing, but not for web sites. Opt not to use BMP or TIF image formats in browsers, and instead use JPG, PNG, and GIF. GIF images are best for small images and simple graphics, while JPG and PNG are great for larger graphics. You can also try using JPG and PNG lossless compression to reduce the size of an image, while still preserving its quality.

Caching Content in the Client

Caching HTTP content in the browser enables browsers to use the cached content, such as scripts and images, instead of sending a request for the same content again and again. Using cached content reduces the number of requests sent to the server, which helps to speed page loads. You can use network monitoring tools to verify that responses contain caching headers, such as Expires and Cache-Control.

Another option is to use the ETag HTTP header. ETag, short for *Entity Tag*, is a header whose value represents the version of the returned resource.

■ **Note** A version can be any string value, such as the last modification date of the resource, a version number, or a unique identifier (GUID) that changes whenever the resource changes. For example, for static content, IIS will return a response with an ETag header set to the last modification date of the file.

If the browser caches the response—depending on its caching headers—that response will be cached, along with its ETag value. When the cache expires, and the browser sends a request to retrieve the resource, it will send the request with its cached ETag value, using the If-none-match HTTP header. In the server, you compare the ETag value to the current version of the resource and act according to the result.

- If the version has changed, return the new content—with an updated ETag value.

- If the version hasn't changed, return a 304 (Not Modified) response with the existing ETag.

Optionally, you can add an updated cache header—Expires or Cache-Control—to extend the caching period of the resource.

■ **Note** For static files, IIS compares the browser's ETag to the last modification date of the requested file.

The technique for adding caching and ETag headers to your ASP.NET Web API responses was discussed in Chapter 8.

Increasing Server Availability

As explained previously in this chapter, performance improvements deal with both latency and load. We've already discussed some tips for obviating latency—reducing the size and number of responses. To improve the ability of our server to handle more load, we must learn how to increase our server's availability.

■ **Note** Reducing the number of requests for static files consequently reduces the load on the server, enabling it to handle more requests, for dynamic content. On the other hand, some forms of size reduction, such as dynamic compression, increase CPU usage and might cause performance to drop.

By *server availability*, we mean the ability of our back end—IIS and our code—to handle incoming requests. There are many factors that can lower server availability, such as not having available threads to handle new requests, or under-utilizing the server resources we have (for example, by not parallelizing our code, or running in a 32-bit process in a 64-bit machine). It is also possible that our web application will not be running when IIS receives a request for it. In this case, IIS will start the process that hosts the web application, and then send the request to it, thus increasing the request's latency.

To increase the server's availability, we strive to optimize our code, so it will work faster and be able to handle more concurrent requests. In addition, we try to increase our server's availability, by making sure our web application will always be available to handle new requests.

IIS Application Pool Configuration

The IIS application pool controls the life cycle of the IIS worker process—the process hosting our code. The application pool controls various activation parameters, such as which .NET framework the worker process will use, whether the process will be 32-bit or 64-bit, and under which user identity the process will run. In addition to activation parameters, the application pool controls when the worker process will start and when it will be shut down or get recycled.

■ **Note** Recycle is the process of shutting down the worker process gracefully, exiting the process, and then starting it again. Application pools also support overlapped recycle, in which the new process starts before the old process shuts down, to lower the recycle time to a minimum. The default behavior of the application pool is to enable overlapped recycle.

You can improve the performance of your web application by applying some best practices to configuring your application pools, as in the following list. You can control most of the application pool's settings in the IIS Manager window, by opening the pool's **Advanced Settings** popup.

- *Start mode*: By default, the worker process will start on demand—when IIS receives the first request for the web application. During the time it takes to load the process, new requests are queued in IIS and are not handled. By changing the start mode to **AlwaysOn**, you can have the worker process load automatically, even before the first request arrives.

- *Idle time-out*: By default, the application pool will shut down the worker process, if it is idle for a period of 20 minutes. If you find that the worker process shuts down many times during the day only to start a couple of minutes afterward, consider increasing the time-out value.

■ **Note** IIS writes an entry to the event log whenever a worker process is shut down due to inactivity. To view those entries, open the Event Viewer, select the System Log, and filter the events to only show the WAS event source.

- *Recycling on regular time intervals*: By default, the application pool recycles the worker process every 1740 minutes, which is 29 hours—a prime number guaranteeing that the recycle will occur on a different hour each day. The time interval recycle was meant to help reduce memory pressure caused by memory leaks. However, in practice, due to the default setting, the recycle may occur during work hours, which causes more problems than it solves. If you do not require recycle intervals, you can change this setting to 0 (zero). If you do require recycle intervals, try setting the recycle to specific times when users are least likely to use the application.

■ **Note** For instructions on how to set the recycle interval to specific times, refer to the following article on the TechNet web site at http://technet.microsoft.com/library/cc754494.aspx.

Tweaking the Managed Thread Pool

Let us begin with a brief explanation on how ASP.NET and the .NET-managed thread pool work when a new request arrives from IIS. After the request reaches ASP.NET, it is queued in the thread pool and waits for an available worker thread to handle it. The thread pool then handles the queued request in any of the following ways:

- If there is an available, idle thread, the thread pool will assign the thread to the function and execute it.

- If there is no available thread, and the number of running threads is lower than the thread pool's MinWorkerThreads, the thread pool will create a new thread, assign it to the request, and start handling it. The default value for MinWorkerThreads is set according to the number of cores in the computer.

- If there is no available thread, and the number of running threads is higher than the thread pool's MinWorkerThreads, the thread pool will not create a new thread and, instead, will wait for a fixed time of 500ms. After waiting for 500ms, the thread pool will again check if there are available threads. If still there are no threads available, the thread pool will create a new thread and assign it the request.

If you have read to this point, you now understand that with a burst of requests, new requests may wait for 500ms before being served by the thread pool. If the burst comes after a long period of idle time, or immediately after the application starts, requests will get queued for a long time, and may even time out without being processed.

■ **Note**   The thread pool disposes of threads that are idle for too long. If a web application handles a burst of requests and then becomes idle for more than a minute, most of the threads that were created will be destroyed. When the next burst starts, the thread pool will again have to create many threads.

If you expect bursts of requests, consider increasing the minimum number of worker threads. To set this new minimum, call the `ThreadPool.SetMinThreads` static method. Take into consideration that this technique is useful for handling bursts that involve both CPU and I/O work. If your code is CPU-intensive, then having many CPU-intensive threads running concurrently will lead to context switches. Having too many context switches will lower the performance of your back end. You can check your application's context switches using Performance Monitor, as explained previously in this chapter.

ASP.NET Web API Asynchronous Actions

Instead of having the thread pool create many threads on demand, which may lead to high context switching, we can try to optimize our code, so that we can have our running threads become available as soon as possible.

If our thread is performing CPU-bound operations, we will probably have to run code profilers and determine how we can speed up the processing, for example, by parallelizing some of our code.

If our thread is also performing I/O operations, such as a call to the database, to the disk, or to an external service, we might be able to increase the availability of our thread pool threads by using asynchronous I/O calls and asynchronous ASP.NET web API actions.

When calling an I/O operation, such as reading from the disk or writing to a network channel, you can use asynchronous calls, which do not block the managed thread. When calling asynchronous I/O methods, the managed thread is returned to the thread pool, making it available to handle new requests. When the I/O operation completes, a callback is invoked in the thread pool; a worker thread is pulled from the pool—assuming there is an available thread; and the method code continues executing.

To use asynchronous I/O calls in ASP.NET web API, you have to adhere to the following rules:

- When handling I/O, always use asynchronous methods, such as `Stream.WriteAsync`, `SqlCommand.ExecuteReaderAsyc`, and `HttpClient.GetAsync`.

- Apply the `await` operator to the result of the asynchronous method.

- Mark the calling method with the `async` modifier.

Listing 11-17 demonstrates how to write an asynchronous ASP.NET web API action that calls another service asynchronously.

Listing 11-17. Creating an Asynchronous ASP.NET Web API Action

```
public class CountriesController : ApiController
{
    private async Task<IEnumerable<Country>>GetCountries()
    {
        var client = new HttpClient();
        var response = await client.GetAsync("http://someserver/api/countries");
        var result = await response.Content.ReadAsAsync<IEnumerable<Country>>();
        return result;
    }
}
```

There are many other tips for improving the performance of SPA and web applications that you can find online, such as Google's web performance best practices (`https://developers.google.com/speed/docs/best-practices/rules_intro`) and Yahoo!'s best practices for speeding up your web site (`http://developer.yahoo.com/performance`). Both Google and Yahoo! also offer analysis tools—PageSpeed and YSlow, respectively—that scan your web application and provide you with specific tips on the parts requiring fixing.

Summary

In this chapter, you learned how to monitor and profile your front end, your back end, and the network that connects both ends. You also encountered various techniques and tips you can implement in each part to improve the overall performance of your SPA and back-end services.

Performance tuning is not a one-time process. It is a continuous process that involves load tests, continuous monitoring of your application, and deciding which performance pitfalls you want to address at each step.

On a final note, it is a good idea to monitor your application's performance as you develop it and to improve parts of it that are not performing well. (You might also want to save the test results for future reference.) But, if you stop and fix every performance issue, you will never deliver your product. Remember that your main goal is to provide a working, bug-free, well-performing—not necessarily super-performing—application.

CHAPTER 12

■ ■ ■

Search Engine Optimization for SPAs

Search engine optimization (SEO) is a means of optimizing your web site or application for search engines' crawlers. Using SEO techniques might help your web site/application to obtain a higher rank in the search engine ranking algorithms and affect the position of your web site/application on the search engine's search-result page. The position and frequency of appearance in search-result pages affect the visibility of the web site/application and, therefore, the number of visitors it will receive.

SEO can target different search factors, such as images searches, video/audio searches, news searches, or any other content factor. For example, a site like Instagram may prefer to optimize for image searches, and a site like YouTube may prefer to optimize for video searches. Each web site/application is responsible for implementing its own SEO, according to its content.

In order to understand what SEO is and how it relates to SPAs, we will first explore what search engines are, how search engines work, and the problem that SPA development imposes on SEO. Later, we will present a few techniques that can help to solve the problem. But first things first: what is a search engine crawler?

The Search Engine Crawler

A search engine crawler crawls over web sites in order to index them. Crawlers use the natural structure of web pages, which includes hyperlinks for resources the web page uses for navigation. When a crawler finds a web site, it starts from the web site root page and begins to crawl on the web site, using the links it has found in the root. There are crawlers that can also crawl on forms. When the crawler finishes, the web site is added to the search engine's index. Later on, the indexed content is added to the search engine's search-result algorithms. The end result of this process is search-result pages ordered by page rank.

Not every crawled web page is indexed by crawlers. A lot of logic goes on inside the crawler to decide whether or not to index a web page. For example, there are crawlers that check the distance of the web page from the root and don't index web pages that are far from the root. This is why crawlers are sometimes considered to be artificially intelligent.

Using a White List: XML Sitemap

You can help crawlers to crawl your web site by using an XML sitemap feed. You can put an XML sitemap in your web site root. The sitemap should include all the links for your web site web pages. Once a crawler finds a sitemap, it might use it to index your web site. Listing 12-1 shows how an XML sitemap might look:

Listing 12-1. XML Sitemap

```
<?xml version="1.0" encoding="UTF-8"?>
<urlset xmlns="http://www.sitemaps.org/schemas/sitemap/0.9">
  <url>
    <loc>http://www.mysite.com/</loc>
  </url>
  <url>
    <loc>http://www.mysite.com/about</loc>
  </url>
  <url>
    <loc>http://www.mysite.com/contact</loc>
  </url>
</urlset>
```

As you can see, the XML sitemap starts with a `urlset` element and includes all the links in the web site. Every link exists in the `url` element, and the link itself is added in the `loc` (location) element. For example, in TheAgency, we could have created an XML sitemap that points to the home page and to the details page. All the other web pages shouldn't be indexed, because they are forms that help to manipulate the data that is stored in the application.

▪ **Note**   You can learn more about XML sitemap and the protocol from the following web site: `www.sitemaps.org`.

Using a Blacklist: robots.txt File

Another option is to prevent crawlers from crawling your web site, using a `robots.txt` file, which is a crawler's blacklist standard. You should put a `robots.txt` file in the web site root folder, if you want to use the standard. In the `robots.txt`, you put all the links you want to prevent crawlers from crawling. In the file, you can indicate the crawler user agent and the links it is not allowed to crawl. The code in Listing 12-2 is an example of a `robots.txt`.

Listing 12-2. robots.txt File Example

```
User-agent: googlebot
Disallow: /private

User-agent: BadBot
Disallow: /
```

In Listing 12-2, we disallow Google crawler to index the `/private` link. We also disallow a BadBot crawler from indexing our entire web site, using the /, which indicates the web site root. Another example, which is related to TheAgency, is to disallow the indexing of the Create Agent page, which is a page that you shouldn't index, because it is a form that collects data. You can provide any number of links after the `User-agent` label. You can also use the * character with the `User-agent` label, to indicate that you are disallowing all crawlers from crawling on the specified links.

▪ **Note**   You can learn more about the `robots.txt` standard on the following web site: `www.robotstxt.org`.

Now that you understand how crawlers work, let's investigate the problem we face.

The Problem with SPAs and SEO

In the past, web pages were static and were rendered on the server side. Today, web sites/applications heavily use Ajax to dynamically create web pages, and rendering also can be done on the client side. While using Ajax doesn't affect users, it presents a big problem to search engine crawlers.

As opposed to browsers, which can execute scripts and create dynamic web pages, search engine crawlers can't execute JavaScript. Figure 12-1 shows an example.

- list item 0
- list item 1
- list item 2

Figure 12-1. *A simple web page*

As a user, you can see that the web page includes an unordered list with three list items. That web page was created by the HTML (Listing 12-3) and JavaScript (Listing 12-4) codes. Listing 12-5 shows the web page after running the JavaScript code.

Listing 12-3. The Simple Web Page with HTML

```
<!DOCTYPE html>
<html>
  <head>
    <title>MovieInfo</title>
    <script language='javascript' src='script.js'></script>
  </head>
  <body>
     <div id="container"></div>
  </body>
</html>
```

Listing 12-4. The Simple Web Page with JavaScript

```
(function() {
   function loaded() {
       var container = document.getElementById('container'),
           ul = document.createElement('ul'),
           li;
       for (var i = 0; i < 3; i++) {
             li = document.createElement('li');
             li.textContent = 'list item ' + i;
             ul.appendChild(li);
       }
       container.appendChild(ul);
   }

   window.addEventListener("DOMContentLoaded", loaded);
}());
```

269

Listing 12-5. The Web Page After Running the JavaScript Code

```
<!DOCTYPE html>
<html>
<head>
    <title>MovieInfo</title>
    <script language="javascript" src="script.js"></script>
  </head>
  <body>
    <div id="container">
       <ul>
              <li>list item 0</li>
              <li>list item 1</li>
              <li>list item 2</li>
       </ul>
    </div>
</body>
</html>
```

The unordered list is created dynamically, using JavaScript, and, therefore, the browser renders it correctly, and we see an unordered list. On the other hand, a search engine crawler can't execute JavaScript, and, therefore, it will only see the code in Listing 12-3. That means that if the unordered list is the web page's main content, the crawler won't index it, resulting in its not being searchable.

Does that mean that SPAs can't be searchable? The answer is of course not. But you will have to solve this problem first.

Options to Optimize Your SPA for SEO

There are a few ways to optimize an SPA for SEO.

- Create a static web page, then start to enhance it with Ajax. This option is called Hijax, and it is used in a lot of web sites.

- Use an Ajax crawler scheme and escaped fragments. This option derives from Google's guidelines for making Ajax-enabled web sites/applications crawlable.

- Create a static representation of your web site/application and direct crawlers to use it.

Let's look at each of these in turn.

Hijax

Hijax is a term that was proposed by Jeremy Keith to explain how to build Ajax-enabled applications that are progressively enhanced with Ajax. That means that you start to write your web pages, without JavaScript and Ajax, and later add the behavior layer with Ajax. The result of using this technique is that you plan for Ajax from the beginning of application writing, but you add Ajax at the end of the development process.

Let's review how it works. You first begin writing your web site/application using the traditional page refresh. That means all data is sent to the server, using links and form submissions. Later on, the server returns an updated web page, which results in a refreshed page in the browser. If the client has JavaScript enabled, you will intercept the links and form submissions using JavaScript and use Ajax instead. Once you have added Ajax, the server will respond only with the relevant data to render, and you can partially render the web page.

Let's take a look at an example (Listing 12-6) of how Hijax works. At first, we write the traditional web application with page refresh. We start with the view, which includes a simple login form that is rendered by the ASP.NET server-side render engine, **Razor**.

Listing 12-6. The Login View

```
@model Hijax.Models.User
@{
    ViewBag.Title = "Index";
}
@section scripts
{
    <script src="~/Scripts/globalFunctions.js"></script>
}

Index</h2>
<form id="userDetails" action="/" method="post">
    <p>
        <label for="username">Username:</label>
        <input type="text" id="username" name="username">
    </p>
    <p>
        <label for="password">Password:</label>
        <input type="password" id="password" name="password">
    </p>
    <p>
        <input type="submit">
    </p>
</form>
<div id="response">
@if (Model != null)
{
    <div>
        You inserted user name: @Model.Username and password: @Model.Password
    </div>
}
</div>
```

The web page is using a `User` model, which will be shown in the next listing. As you can see, we have a simple form that is used to post data to a controller. The controller will echo that data, and we will have full refresh. Once the response of the posted data is returned, we will have a model to use, and the `if` statement will show the data that the user inserted.

■ **Note**   This book does not cover ASP.NET MVC, which is a server-side framework used to create web applications according to the Model/View/Controller design pattern. Our example uses the framework only to explain the Hijax concept. If you are interested in ASP.NET MVC, you are encouraged to learn more about the framework from its official web site: www.asp.net/mvc.

The following code (Listing 12-7) shows the User model class, which is a simple class that is used as the view model:

Listing 12-7. The User Class

```
namespace Hijax.Models
{
  public class User
  {
    public string Username { get; set; }
    public string Password { get; set; }

    public static User CreateUser(string username, string password)
    {
      return new User
      {
        Username = username,
        Password = password
      };
    }
  }
}
```

There is nothing unusual in the User class. Listing 12-8 shows the HomeController that interacts with the login page.

Listing 12-8. The HomeController Class

```
namespace Hijax.Controllers
{
  public class HomeController : Controller
  {
    //
    // GET: /Home/
    public ActionResult Index()
    {
      return View();
    }

    //
    // POST: /Home/
    [HttpPost]
    public ActionResult Index(FormCollection collection)
    {
      return View(Hijax.Models.User.CreateUser(collection["username"],
        collection["password"]));
    }
  }
}
```

Once the HomeController receives an HTTP GET request, it will return the view in the preceding Listing 12-6. Once the HomeController receives an HTTP POST request, it will return the view with the User model.

We also added to the solution an `ApiController`, which will act as the controller for the Hijax part. Listing 12-9 shows how the controller should look.

Listing 12-9. The HijaxController Class

```
namespace Hijax.Controllers
{
    public class HijaxController : ApiController
    {
        // POST api/hijax
        public User Post(FormDataCollection collection)
        {
          return Hijax.Models.User.CreateUser(collection.Get("username"),
            collection.Get("password"));
        }
    }
}
```

The controller reuses the `CreateUser` function to return the `User` response to the client. As in the case of the `HomeController`, there is nothing remarkable in the `HijaxController`.

The only noteworthy aspect of the example is the code in the `globalFunctions.js` file. Listing 12-10 shows the code.

Listing 12-10. The globalFunctions.js File

```
(function () {
    $(document).ready(function () {
        $('#userDetails').submit(function (evt) {
            evt.preventDefault();

            $.ajax({
                url: 'api/hijax',
                data: $(this).serialize(),
                type: 'JSON',
                method: 'POST',
                success: function (data) {
                    $('<div>').text("You inserted user name: " + data.Username + ' and password: '
+ data.Password).appendTo('#response');
                }
            });
        });
    });
}());
```

When the view is loaded, we add an event listener to the form submit event. In the handler, the first line of code will prevent the form from submitting the content to the server. Instead, we will use jQuery to perform a HTTP POST request to the server, with the relevant form data. Once the Ajax request completes successfully, we will render a similar result, as we did in the `if` statement in the view.

The same method can also be used with links. You set the `href` attribute to the relevant server-side URL and Hijax it; this prevents it from navigating to different things, if JavaScript is enabled.

Using Hijax results in a modular and reusable server side, because web pages are created by joining different modules, if JavaScript isn't supported. If JavaScript is supported, the modules should also be exposed as an API, to enable the Ajax functionality.

On the other hand, Hijax forces us to write more code and, sometimes, to create duplications between server-side rendering and client-side rendering. Hijax is less recommended today, even though it is used in a lot of web sites/applications.

Escaped Fragments

In 2009, Google released a specification that describes how to use escaped fragments to enable their crawler to crawl a JavaScript-oriented web site. Most of the major browsers have aligned to this method in recent years.

At its core, the escaped fragments idea is just an agreement between a crawler and a web site. The web site will supply an Ajax crawling scheme that works as follows:

1. A crawler tries to crawl on the web site.

2. The web site indicates to the crawler that it supports the crawling scheme, by using a #! sign instead of only # in the URL. That means that if you have a URL that looks like www.mywebsite.com/#details, it will become www.mywebsite.com/#!details. In the specifications, the part that includes the # sign and the rest of the URL is called a hash fragment, and the URL itself is called a 'pretty' URL.

3. The crawler will replace the #! sign in the URL with ?_escaped_fragment_= and create a request to the server with the new URL. That means that if we had the URL from step 2, the crawler would send the server the following URL: www.mywebsite.com/?_escaped_fragment_=details. In the specifications, a URL that uses _escaped_fragment_ is called an 'ugly' URL.

4. The web site receives the ugly URL, transforms it back to the pretty URL representation, and invokes a headless browser (a browser that has no graphic user interface).

5. The headless browser executes the page and its JavaScript part and produces an HTML fragment for the pretty URL.

6. The generated HTML fragment is returned by the server to the crawler, which indexes it as if it were the web page it crawled.

Figure 12-2, which is taken from the Google web site, shows the process.

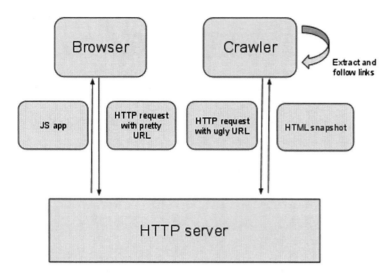

Figure 12-2. *Escaped fragments process*

Sometimes, you can't use # or #! in your URLs, because of the nature of your application. In these situations, you can use a Meta tag to indicate that the current page uses the escaped fragments scheme. The following Meta tag (Listing 12-11) should be used in the head section of the web page:

Listing 12-11. Escaped Fragments Meta Tag

```
<meta name="fragment" content="!">
```

■ **Note**　This Meta tag must appear in the head section, in pages that don't have hash fragments in their URL, and must include a content attribute that is set to !.

When the crawler sees the Meta tag, it will replace the URLs with ugly URLs, as if they had a hash fragment. For example, if you have a URL www.mywebsite.com, it will become www.mywebsite.com?_escaped_fragment_=.

You will have to set the server environment to handle the ugly URLs. There are open-source projects that can help you to implement these features.

■ **Tip**　One open-source solution that we used in a project is called AJAX Crawling for .NET, which is used with the ASP.NET MVC framework.

You can use headless browsers such as Phantom.js to create the HTML fragments and pass them to the crawler. Phantom.js is a headless WebKit browser. You can run Phantom.js in Node.js, a server-side JavaScript environment. Once you run Phantom.js, you can pass it a URL, and you will get the processed HTML fragment. Later on, you can pass the HTML fragment to the crawler, as a response to the crawler's request.

■ **Note** Phantom.js can be downloaded from: http://phantomjs.org. A useful tutorial that explains how to set up Phantom.js to enable an escaped fragments scheme is available via the following link: http://backbonetutorials.com/seo-for-single-page-apps.

If you don't want to set up a server environment to handle an escaped fragments scheme, you can use products that set it up for you, such as BromBone, for example.

Static Web Site/Application Representation

■ **Caution** This technique is the worst of all the options. Nonetheless, we have seen it implemented, so it is mentioned here for your information.

In the static web site representation, you have two representations of your web site/application. The first representation is the real SPA application, which uses JavaScript heavily in the client side. The second representation is a static representation of your web site/application.

The static representation is just your web site, created without Ajax and JavaScript. Once you identify that a search engine crawler is trying to get into your web site, you can direct it to crawl the static representation.

■ **Note** You can identify a crawler by its user agent or use the server configuration options to configure the redirect.

This option should be avoided, because you will have to maintain two different web sites/applications. Also, some search engines will lower the web site/application rank because you have content duplication and are serving different content.

Summary

In this chapter, you learned what SEO and how a search engine crawler operates. You also learned that SPAs are more difficult to optimize for SEO, owing to their asynchronous nature and because a lot of an SPA's rendering is done on the fly on the client side.

We also explained a few options that can help you optimize your SPA for SEO. You can use Hijax techniques to progressively enhance your web site/application with Ajax. You can use HTML snapshots in accordance with Google guidelines. You can use the robots.txt file to direct search engines to index only static parts of your web site/application.

In the end, a lot of web applications don't have to be indexed by search engines, because not all of their content should be searchable. It is the decision maker's responsibility to decide what should be indexed and what shouldn't. It is your responsibility to implement SEO in your SPA according to those decisions. Now that you have the tools to confront the SEO and SPA problem, you can continue to this book's last chapter—on SPA deployment.

CHAPTER 13

SPA Deployment

By some weird coincidence (or not), the last chapter in most web development books deals with deployment. Although deployment is a step you take after you have finished developing your SPA, it is still an important part of the application's life cycle.

Deployment is not the last step in an application life cycle. The life cycle of an SPA, as with any other type of web application, is iterative. As the time frame for iterations has shrunk over the years (today there are methodologies that advocate two-week iterations), the importance of choosing an efficient deployment technique and set of tools has become greater than ever. Choosing the proper technique to deploy will save you time, money, and headaches, as well as increase your ability to deliver new content in shorter periods of time.

In this chapter, we will go over several well-known deployment techniques and take a quick look at the concept of continuous deployment and how to implement it. We will finish with an explanation of ways to host and deploy your SPA to public clouds.

Deployment Techniques

There are many ways to deploy your SPA to the server. Some deployment techniques are straightforward and based on copying the SPA files from your local computer to the server. Other deployment techniques rely on servers and services that manage code versions and are delegated with the responsibility of pushing new versions of your SPA to the server.

■ **Note** Although this chapter refers to the server in the singular, you can use all of the following techniques if you have to deploy your SPA to multiple servers. You may be required to run the tool repeatedly, for each of your servers, or to run it once and provide the tool with a list of destination servers.

Some of the following techniques have been around for decades (literally), while others are relatively new and have been in use only within the past couple of years.

Xcopy

Xcopy deployment is a general term referring to a deployment process in which you copy the application files directly from your computer to the server, overriding the previously deployed files. The term *xcopy* derives from a command-line utility of that name, which has been part of the Microsoft operating system ever since the early days of DOS 3.2 in 1986.

Xcopy is the simplest deployment technique, as it does not require installing any tools on the target server. Xcopy is used mostly on an intranet, such as enterprise networks, as it requires opening specific ports on the remote server to enable remote authentication and file system access.

Although the term *xcopy* derives from a command-line utility of the same name, it also refers to copy-and-paste and drag-and-drop actions, such as copying a folder to a server's network share using Windows Explorer.

If you are planning to use command-line tools for direct copy, consider using the Robocopy command-line tool instead of xcopy. Robocopy is included in Windows from Vista and on, and it is capable of copying files faster than xcopy.

FTP

Today, FTP is one of the most common ways to deploy web applications to servers on the Internet. With FTP, very much as with xcopy, you upload your SPA content to the target server, overriding the existing content.

■ **Note**   Among the forces that drove the use of FTP are web hosting providers, who tend to block xcopy and other deployment techniques to their servers. This restriction left FTP as one of the common ways to push deployments to servers. Today, FTP is an option supported by most web hosting providers, including cloud providers.

To use FTP for deployment, you must first install an FTP server application in your server. If you are using IIS to host your SPA, you can install the FTP feature, which is part of IIS. If you are not using IIS, or if you cannot install the FTP feature of IIS, you can try installing other FTP server tools, such as the FileZilla server.

For your computer, you will require an FTP client. If you are using Windows, you can use both Internet Explorer and Windows Explorer to open an FTP connection to a server. If you prefer using an FTP client utility, there are many free FTP clients, such as FileZilla and FireFTP (Firefox add-on).

To secure FTP deployments, you are usually required to provide credentials in the form of a username and a password. However, FTP does not provide a secured (encrypted) channel. If you wish to secure the communication channel between the client and the server, consider using FTPS, which is an SSL-based connection, much like HTTPS.

■ **Note**   Another means of securing an FTP connection is to use SFTP. Unlike FTPS, which uses public key certificates, SFTP (SSH FTP) passes FTP messages over an SSH (secured shell) connection. IIS does not support hosting an SFTP server, but there are many SFTP server applications for Windows—free and commercial—which you can use. You can find a list of SFTP servers for Windows on Wikipedia at `http://en.wikipedia.org/wiki/List_of_SFTP_server_software`.

Version Control

Xcopy and FTP have the following disadvantages:

- You need direct network access to the destination server.

- You have to open the relevant ports in the server's firewall.

- You have to manually maintain old versions in case you need to roll back the deployed version.

- FTP/xcopy only deploys the software. Any additional step, such as notifying stakeholders about the new version, is done separately.

Version control systems (VCSs) are used for managing versions of your code, not for deployment. However, it does not mean you cannot use them to assist with deploying your SPA.

> ■ **Note** The term *source control management* (SCM) is identical to the term *version control*. Source control tools are version control tools. Both terms are used throughout this chapter and are interchangeable.

Deploying with version control means that after you commit your changes (or check them in, depending on your source control's lingo), you connect to your remote server and pull the committed version (or take the latest version, again, depending on lingo).

For example, if you use GitHub, you use `git push` to upload the recent version to the remote GitHub repository and then use `git pull` from the server to retrieve the updated code from the repository.

> ■ **Note** The ability to pull the latest version of the code to your server is not unique to Git. You can achieve the same result with many other VCSs, such as TFS, SVN, and Mercurial. Each of those VCSs has its own client tools, either CLI or GUI, which you can use to get the latest version of your code.

Pulling your content from your source control also provides you with the ability to roll back your deployment. If you need to roll back your deployed version, for example, in case you suddenly find a no-go bug in the new version, you can always pull the previous version from the repository.

Manually pulling the new version from the source control is still, well, manual. If you want to automate this process, there are other techniques that you can apply in your server.

- *Periodic pull*: You can create a scheduled task in your server, which will trigger the pull command every couple of minutes, or at specific times. For example, you can set the job to run late at night, after working hours, to reduce the chance of disconnecting users, making them lose some of their work.

- *Server notifications*: Several VCSs, such as GitHub and BitBucket, support sending a POST request after a repository update. You can create an HTTP listener on your server, receive the request, and perform the pull according to the information you receive.

- *Third-party deployment tools*: If you don't want to manage the deployment process yourself, or spend time on creating and maintaining custom notification listeners, you have the option of using online deployment services. Online deployment services can receive notification from your VCS and push the updated content to your server, using techniques such as FTP, SSH, and HTTP. You can even find deployment services that will host your Git and SVN repositories for you, provide deployment notification to stakeholders through e-mails, and manage multiple environments, such as testing, staging, and production.

Another option you have is to create the remote repository directly in your server and have your local repository push its content to the server. For example, project Kudu (`https://github.com/projectkudu/kudu`) provides a Git engine that enables you to create Git repositories on Windows servers. You can then point to the remote repository from your local Git repository and use `git push` to push the content to the server, using HTTP. With remote repositories, you can also implement Git hooks, to execute scripts locally on the server after the push operation completes.

Web Deploy Tool

The problem with deploying content to the server is that deployment on its own is often one of a long list of steps. Version deployment often requires additional steps, such as registry updates, changing database schemas, and updating local certificates.

Instead of using FTP or Git to update your server files and then doing the rest manually, or with scripts, you can try doing both with Microsoft's Web Deploy tool.

The Web Deploy tool is intended to simplify the process of web application deployment, which usually involves more than just file copy. Following is a partial list of Web Deploy features, in addition to file copy:

- Configure IIS settings

- Changing text in files, based on input parameters

- Setting file system permissions (ACLS)

- Write keys and values in the registry

- Execute database scripts

- Install certificates

You can also create custom Web Deploy providers to perform your own specific tasks, such as sending e-mail notifications, executing batch files on the server, or purging content from CDN servers.

Web Deploy is part of Visual Studio and is one of the deployment options you can select when you publish a web application, as shown in Figure 13-1.

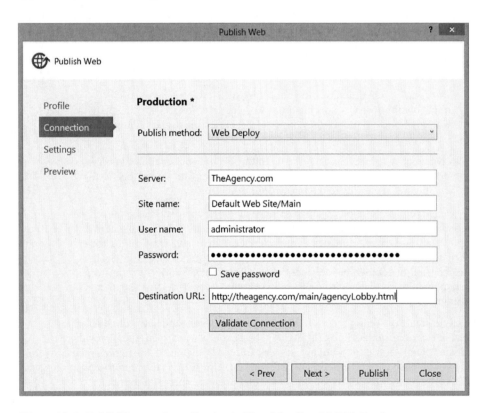

Figure 13-1. *Publishing a web application in Visual Studio with Web Deploy*

When you publish a web application with Web Deploy, it will compare the local files and the remote files on the server and will only copy newer files to the destination. Having Web Deploy identify new content relieves you of the need to manually select the files to deploy and reduces the deployment time, as it copies less files.

Web Deploy is also available outside of Visual Studio, by installing the Web Deployment Framework. After you install the framework, you can run Web Deploy from the following:

- Command line, using the `MSDeploy.exe` utility

- PowerShell, using the cmdlets in the `WDeploySnapin3.0` snapin

- IIS, using the Export Application and Import Application options

---

■ **Note**   You can download the latest version of Web Deploy from `www.iis.net/downloads/microsoft/web-deploy`. After you install Web Deploy, you can run `MSDeploy.exe` from the `%ProgramFiles%\IIS\Microsoft Web Deploy V3` folder.

For example, the command in Listing 13-1 will deploy a web application running locally in IIS to a remote IIS server.

Listing 13-1. Deploy a Web Application with MSDeploy.exe

```
msdeploy -verb:sync -source:iisApp="Default Web Site/TheAgency" -dest:iisApp="Default Web Site/
TheAgency",computerName=Server1
```

In addition to live server-to-server deployment, you can also create deployment packages and deploy them at a later time. For example, if you do not have permission to deploy the web application to the server, you can create the deployment package and send it to the administrator. The administrator will use any of the Web Deploy tools—command-line, PowerShell, or IIS—to deploy the package to the server.

Listing 13-2 shows how to create a package from a locally deployed web application and then deploy the package to a remote server.

Listing 13-2. Create a Web Deploy Package and Deploy It to a Remote Server

```
msdeploy -verb:sync -source:iisApp="Default Web Site/TheAgency" -dest:package=c:\MyApp.zip
```

```
msdeploy -verb:sync -source:package=c:\MyApp.zip -dest:iisApp="Default Web Site/
TheAgency",computerName=Server1
```

■ **Note**   If you open the Publish Method drop-down shown in Figure 13-1, you will see another option named Web Deploy Package. You can use the package created by Visual Studio with any of the Web Deploy tools mentioned before, to publish the package to the server.

Web Deploy also provides you with an option to test your deployment instructions. Running Web Deploy with the `-WhatIf` flag will only print what each provider is going to do, without actually having the provider perform the task. Listing 13-3 shows how to test a deployment with the PowerShell Web Deploy cmdlets.

Listing 13-3. Use PowerShell's Web Deploy Cmdlets with WhatIf

```
$cred = Get-Credential
New-WDPublishSettings -ComputerName Server2 -Credentials $cred -AgentType MSDepSvc -FileName:"C:\
Server2.publishsettings"
Sync-WDApp -SourceApp "Default Web Site/TheAgency" -DestinationApp "Default Web Site/TheAgency"
-DestinationPublishSettings "C:\Server2.publishsettings" -WhatIf
```

■ **Note** To run PowerShell cmdlets, you have to open a PowerShell window. You cannot call cmdlets from a command (cmd) window.

The above script first uses the New-WDPublishSettings cmdlet to set the credentials the deployment will use. Running the Sync-WDApp cmdlet with the -WhatIf switch will result in a list of files to be copied, without actually having them deployed to the server.

■ **Note** The "What if" feature is supported in PowerShell, MsDeploy.exe, IIS, and Visual Studio. In Visual Studio, you can activate this option by clicking the Start Preview button on the Preview tab in the Publish Web dialog.

As mentioned previously, in addition to packaging a web application and deploying it to a remote server, you can also use Web Deploy to apply other changes to a remote server, such as editing the server's registry, setting files and folder permissions, and updating database content and schemas. Each of those features is handled by a provider, and each provider has its own set of configuration that you will be required to use. For a complete list of built-in providers in Web Deploy, refer to the documentation at http://technet.microsoft.com/en-us/library/dd569040.aspx.

Continuous Deployment

Whether you use manual or automatic deployment, there are some questions you will probably want to answer before you start using any of the deployment techniques mentioned in the beginning of this chapter. For example, when are you going to deploy your web application? Will you deploy after each check-in or on-demand? Will you deploy only after the code passes unit tests? Will you deploy every couple of days or deploy nightly, to have an up-to-date testing environment the following day? And will you manually build, test, and deploy the application every time, or use automated, scheduled tasks?

Some of these questions, if not all, are answered by a process called continuous deployment. If used correctly, it can help you increase the quality of your application.

Continuous deployment is a development approach whereby you release every good version of your application to the production environment; that is, as soon as you are confident that your product is of sufficient quality and that you can put it in front of your end users. You must determine how frequently this happens: once a month, twice a week, or even multiple times during a single day.

When you apply continuous deployment, you set up a pipeline that applies to all code changes that you make to the application. This pipeline usually includes the following:

1. Building the web application

2. Running unit and integration tests

3. Deploying the web application to a staging environment and running functional tests

4. (Optional) Deploying the web application to the production environment

■ **Note**   When the web application is developed by a team of developers, the continuous deployment process begins with an integration and merge of all the code pieces. This process is often referred to as Continuous Integration (CI) and is the first step in the continuous deployment pipeline.

It would be impractical to have a human perform all the previous steps for every code change. Therefore, continuous deployment implies the use of the following automation:

- Every new code that is checked to the repository triggers an automated build.

- After the application successfully compiles, it must pass all unit and integration tests.

- If all the tests pass, the application will be deployed to the server.

- If a test fails, the application will not be deployed, and you will receive a notification.

Some products, such as Microsoft's TFS (Team Foundation Server), provide an end-to-end system that has both the version control system and a build server application. Having both features in a single tool eases the use of implementing continuous deployment.

■ **Note**   You can read more about the TFS build server and continuous deployment support on the MSDN web site at `http://msdn.microsoft.com/en-us/library/ee308011.aspx`. In addition to the on-premises TFS, there is also an online version of TFS, called Visual Studio Online `www.visualstudio.com`). With Visual Studio Online, you also get a source control and a build server, with the added ability of deploying to the Microsoft Azure cloud, as explained later on in this chapter.

Other VCSs, such as Git and Mercurial, depend on external services to perform the build, test, and deployment steps. Jenkins, TeamCity, and CruiseControl.NET are some of the products that support those VCSs for building and deploying .NET web applications.

■ **Note**   You can find a detailed list of products, including a list of supported SCM (source control management) systems on Wikipedia at `http://en.wikipedia.org/wiki/Comparison_of_continuous_integration_software`.

Deploying to the Cloud

The purpose of this section is not to compare hosting your web application with web hosting companies to hosting in the public cloud but to explain the additional deployment techniques and tools that are used with public cloud hosting.

Hosting your web applications in a public cloud might be more expensive than using web hosting companies—assuming they are not overcharging you; however, public clouds have a lot to offer to the hostee in regard to scalability, availability, and reliability, which just might make it worth your while. Most public clouds also offer services, such as file storage, CDN, cache, and database (SQL and no-SQL), in addition to web hosting. Having such services available on-demand, and not having to worry about maintenance, increases public clouds' value-for-money.

Web Hosting and Platform as a Service

You are probably familiar with the concept of web hosting. Your web application is hosted on a remote web server, which may be a dedicated server or a shared server, and you may have full administrator access to it, or only FTP access.

One of the evolutions of web hosting in the era of cloud computing is the Platform as a Service (PaaS) model. With PaaS, it is up to you to provide the application, and it is up to the cloud provider to provide the servers, the storage, the load-balancer, and any other service you may require to host and run your web application. The promise of PaaS is scalability and availability, while requiring minimum maintenance on your end.

Most cloud providers have a PaaS solution for web hosting. You have only to deploy your web application, and the provider will take care of the rest—create the servers; deploy the application to them; configure the load balancing, firewall, storage; etc. Following are some of the well-known cloud providers and their solutions for web hosting with PaaS:

- *Amazon*: AWS Elastic Beanstalk manually deploys .NET web applications to an IIS server with Web Deploy packages. Automatic deployment with continuous deployment environments, such as TFS and Jenkins, is also supported but requires some custom configuration.

- *Microsoft Azure*: Cloud Services and Web Sites offer two PaaS models, the first with more control over the server instances and the second as a closed web hosting PaaS solution. Web Sites support manual deployment via Web Deploy and Git, and continuous deployment with various tools, such as GitHub, Dropbox, and Visual Studio Online. Cloud Services support manual deployment, using a proprietary form of deployment packages, and automatic deployment with continuous deployment, using Visual Studio Online.

- *Rackspace*: Cloud Sites manually deploys .NET web applications to hosted IIS servers with FTP. Because Cloud Sites uses FTP to deploy updated content, you can use any continuous deployment tools that support pushing content through FTP.

- *AppHarbor*: AppHarbor offers PaaS solutions for hosting .NET applications. Both manual and continuous deployment is supported. You can use Git and Mercurial for manual deployments or integrate with continuous deployment services, such as GitHub, CodePlex, and BitBucket.

Static-File Hosting

SPA development usually requires the use of back-end services for retrieving and manipulating data. However, the SPA itself does not necessarily require a server-side framework, as it can be built using static HTML pages.

If you choose not to use any server-side framework to build your SPA, and instead use only static files, you can host your SPA in static file hosting.

Many of the public cloud providers offer static files web hosting, which is basically file storage that is accessible through HTTP. For example, Rackspace has Cloud Files, Amazon has S3 (Simple Storage Service), and Microsoft Azure offers Blob storage as a web hosting for static files.

To get started with static web sites, you first have to upload your content to the remote storage. Each cloud provider has its own way of doing so, but most use either S/FTP or HTTP.

After you upload your content to the remote storage, you can access it from the browser, using HTTP GET, just as if you had hosted your static files on an IIS server. In addition to simple file hosting, most of the cloud providers also support the following:

- Setting common HTTP headers, such as caching and content-type

- Secured access through HTTPS

- Assigning custom domain names to the storage DNS

- Connecting the storage to a CDN

- Automatic file replication for disaster recovery

- Hiding private files so they can only be accessed by authorized parties

- Real-time monitoring and operation logs

Figure 13-2 shows how to configure an Amazon S3 bucket for static web site hosting.

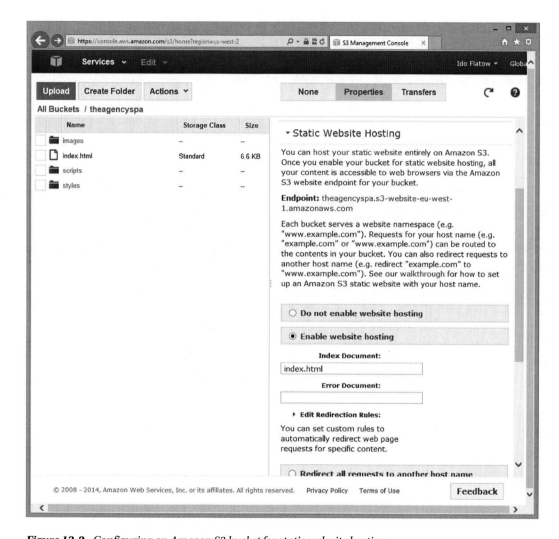

Figure 13-2. *Configuring an Amazon S3 bucket for static web site hosting*

■ **Note** If you want the static web application in Amazon S3 to be publicly available, open the bucket permissions and add view permissions for everyone.

The result of browsing the web site are shown in Figure 13-3.

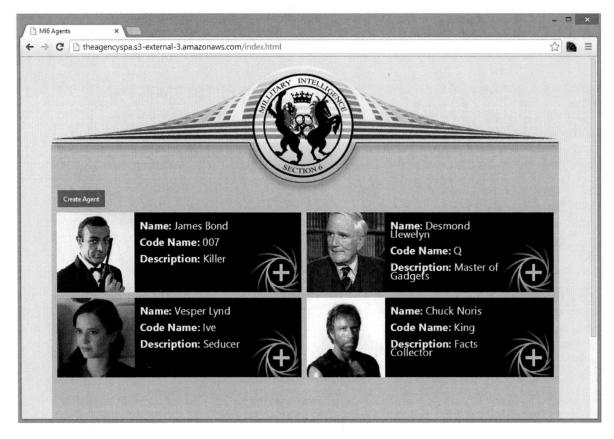

Figure 13-3. *Running an SPA from a static web site hosted in Amazon S3*

The services the SPA consumes are located on a different server—one that supports running .NET applications and had to be configured to support CORS (cross-origin resource sharing). Without enabling CORS, the browser would have prevented the SPA from contacting the service, which is in a different domain.

Deploying new content to static web hosting can be done either manually or automatically.

- *Manually*: Copy the files to the remote storage. Depending on the storage provider, you might have to use an FTP client or a provider-specific tool. For example, Rackspace Cloud Files supports S/FTP access, while Azure Blob storage has a specific HTTP API you must use. You can upload single files to Blob storage from Visual Studio—after installing the Azure SDK. If you have to copy entire sets of folders, consider using third-party tools, such as the free CloudBerry Explorer tool.

- *Automatically*: If you are using continuous deployment services, check if your deployment service supports your cloud provider. For example, if you use Jenkins for continuous integration and deployment, you can configure it to push the new content to cloud providers, such as Amazon S3 and Azure Blob storage.

Summary

In this chapter, you have learned how to use various techniques to deploy your SPA to the server. Each technique has its advantages and disadvantages, so when you get to the point of choosing which one to use, consider which techniques are supported by your web hosting provider and the amount of investment you will be required to put in—and the return on investment of—using continuous deployment tools.

You also learned how you can use continuous deployment to automate the process of deploying new versions of your application. Finally, you learned how to host dynamic and static web applications in public clouds, such as Microsoft Azure, Rackspace, and Amazon.

In the book, we covered a lot of SPA topics that you can use to create a successful SPA. We started by providing essential JavaScript background that can help you understand how to write the SPA parts, and we explained the building blocks of a successful SPA, which is created mainly with JavaScript, HTML, and CSS. Knowing how to write professional JavaScript can help you both in SPAs but also in emerging platforms such as Node.js, writing apps for operation systems that run JavaScript, and more. You can also use the concepts you learned in non-SPA web applications, which can benefit from your knowledge of writing better front ends.

You then continued to learn how to use the Backbone.js library in order to add MV* to your front end and to structure it. After we finished discussing the front end, we covered ASP.NET Web API, the framework we choose to use to create the back end, and how to use the services we created from the front end, using both Backbone.js API and other communication APIs. You can take the set of tools you learned and use them separately in web applications or you can combine both Backbone.js and ASP.NET Web API to create SPAs such as TheAgency. The knowledge is in your hands now.

In the last part of the book, we explained different SPA advanced topics, such as unit testing, SEO, performance, and deployment. Most of what you learned is very relevant to SPAs, but you can also use this valuable information to improve your current web applications.

We hope that you learned a lot during your reading and that you enjoyed the overall experience.

Gil and Ido.

If you have any questions or comments about the book, please contact us.

Gil: @gilfink, www.gilfink.net

Ido: @idoflatow

Index

Get the eBook for only $10!

Now you can take the weightless companion with you anywhere, anytime. Your purchase of this book entitles you to 3 electronic versions for only $10.

This Apress title will prove so indispensible that you'll want to carry it with you everywhere, which is why we are offering the eBook in 3 formats for only $10 if you have already purchased the print book.

Convenient and fully searchable, the PDF version enables you to easily find and copy code—or perform examples by quickly toggling between instructions and applications. The MOBI format is ideal for your Kindle, while the ePUB can be utilized on a variety of mobile devices.

Go to www.apress.com/promo/tendollars to purchase your companion eBook.

Printed by Publishers' Graphics LLC